UNIVERSITY OF NORTH CAROLINA AT CHAPEL HILL
DEPARTMENT OF ROMANCE LANGUAGES

NORTH CAROLINA STUDIES
IN THE ROMANCE LANGUAGES AND LITERATURES

ESSAYS; TEXTS, TEXTUAL STUDIES AND TRANSLATIONS; SYMPOSIA

Founder: URBAN TIGNER HOLMES

Distributed by:

UNIVERSITY OF NORTH CAROLINA PRESS
CHAPEL HILL
North Carolina 27514
U.S.A.

NORTH CAROLINA STUDIES IN THE
ROMANCE LANGUAGES AND LITERATURES
Essays
Number 7

STYLE AND STRUCTURE IN GRACIÁN'S
EL CRITICÓN

STYLE AND STRUCTURE IN GRACIÁN'S *EL CRITICÓN*

BY

MARCIA L. WELLES

CHAPEL HILL

NORTH CAROLINA STUDIES IN THE ROMANCE
LANGUAGES AND LITERATURES
U.N.C. DEPARTMENT OF ROMANCE LANGUAGES
1976

Library of Congress Cataloging in Publication Data

Welles, Marcia L.
  Style and structure in Gracián's El Criticón.

  (North Carolina studies in the Romance languages and literatures: Essays; no. 7)
  Bibliography: p. 203.
  1. Gracián y Morales, Baltasar, 1601-1658. El Criticón. 2. Gracián y Morales, Baltasar, 1601-1658 — Technique. 3. Gracián y Morales, Baltasar, 1601-1658 — Style. I. Title. II. Series.

PQ6398.G3C98   863'.3   75-2127

ISBN 9780807891667

DEPÓSITO LEGAL: V. 4.195 - 1975

ARTES GRÁFICAS SOLER, S. A. - JÁVEA, 28 - VALENCIA (8) - 1976

ACKNOWLEDGMENT

My deepest thanks to my colleagues, friends, and family who helped me complete this work.

TABLE OF CONTENTS

	Page
ACKNOWLEDGMENT	7
CRITICAL PREFACE	11

CHAPTER

I. EL DISCRETO—PRELUDE TO EL CRITICÓN 19
    Relationship Between Form and Content in El Discreto ... 20
        Content of El Discreto 25
        Form of El Discreto and Its Relationship to the Esthetic as Expressed in the Agudeza 27
    Uses of Rhetoric in El Discreto 35
        The Didactic Nature of El Discreto—Rhetoric as an Animating Factor 35
        The Static Nature of El Discreto—Rhetoric as a Compensating Factor 41

II. EL CRITICÓN AS A NOVEL 53
    Theme of El Criticón 55
    Structural Principle of El Criticón 59
    Spatial and Temporal Structure of El Criticón 63
        Spatial Structure 64
        Temporal Structure 67
    Novelistic Devices 79

III. ALLEGORY IN EL CRITICÓN 91
    Symbol-Allegory in El Criticón 93
        Characterization in El Criticón and the Quijote 93
        The Protagonists as Symbol-Allegories 97
        The Protagonists and Perspectivism 113

    Personification-Allegory in El Criticón 117
        Allegory as Dynamic Direction 117
        Secondary Personification-Allegories: "Generalization" and "Spectator" Allegories in El Criticón 119

	Primary Personification-Allegory: "Participation" Allegory in *El Criticón*	133
	Structure of Allegorical Imagery in *El Criticón*	140
	Apocalyptic and Demonic Symbols	141
	Antithetical Patterns of Apocalyptic and Demonic Imagery	143
	Presentation of Allegorical Personifications	148
IV.	SATIRE IN *EL CRITICÓN*	153
	Presentation of Satire in *El Criticón*	156
	Content of Satire in *El Criticón*	159
	The Patterns of Satire	163
	The Rhetoric of Satire	169

CONCLUSION	195
LIST OF RHETORICAL FIGURES	198
INDEX OF ABBREVIATIONS	202
BIBLIOGRAPHY	203

CRITICAL PREFACE

The scholarship devoted to the works of Baltasar Gracián has concentrated primarily on the author's esthetic and literary theory as presented in the *Agudeza y arte de ingenio*, his ideology, and his style of writing.[1] Before the discussion of the intent of this study, a brief survey is given of the main contributions in each of these areas of critical interest.

Discussion of Gracián's literary esthetic begins in the late nineteenth century with Marcelino Menéndez y Pelayo,[2] who classifies the *Agudeza* as a rhetoric of the metaphysical or *conceptista* style. Benedetto Croce[3] denies originality to the esthetic

---

[1] Bibliographic information is included in the edition of the *Obras completas* edited by Arturo del Hoyo (Madrid: Aguilar, 1960), pp. cclv-cclxxi, as well as in the appendix of Evaristo Correa Calderón's study, *Baltasar Gracián. Su vida y su obra* (Madrid: Gredos, 1961). Correa Calderón's edition of the *Agudeza y arte de ingenio* (Madrid: Castalia, 1969), I, 30-32, also has a select bibliography. Miguel Batllori and Ceferino Peralta include much information in the carefully footnoted "Estudio preliminar" of their edition of the *Obras completas* (in B.A.E., Vol. CCXXIX [Madrid: Ediciones Atlas, 1969]), I, 1-77. This edition also has a bibliographic appendix listing Batllori's studies on Gracián, pp. 225-229. Miguel Batllori, in "Un lustro de estudios gracianos: 1959-1963," *AHSI*, XXXIV (1965), 162-171, reviews the studies on Gracián appearing between 1959 and 1963, concentrating on the works of Correa Calderón, Arturo del Hoyo, Klaus Heger, and Karl-Ludwig Selig's edition of the inventory of Lastanosa's library. For an annotated bibliography surveying criticisms up to 1966 of Gracián's literary theory, see Virginia Ramos Foster, "The Status of Gracián Criticism: A Bibliographic Essay," *RJ*, XVIII (1967), 296-307.

[2] *Historia de las ideas estéticas en España*, III (Madrid: Hernando, 1930).

[3] "I trattatisti italiani del 'concettismo' e Baltasar Gracián," *Atti della Accademia Pontaniana*, XXIX, Series II, Vol. IV, memoria no. 7 (Naples, 1899), pp. 1-32, included in *Problemi di estetica* (4th ed.; Bari, 1949), pp. 313-348.

theory expressed in the *Agudeza,* and, in spite of Gracián's statements to the contrary, considers the conceit a metaphor. This opinion has subsequently been denied. Edward Sarmiento,[4] in his reply to what he considers to be the limited views of Croce as well as of Adolphe Coster,[5] rejects the idea that the conceit is merely a decorative trope. T. E. May continues Sarmiento's groundwork of classification and logical analysis of the conceit,[6] and in a later article[7] raises the problem of truth in wit, or whether the conceit, interpreted by Gracián as an essentially subjective act, can represent any objective, permanent order of reality.

Studies on the antecedents of Gracián's theory of wit vary in their designation of sources. Classical origins are pointed out by Ernst Robert Curtius,[8] who, disagreeing with Ludwig Pfandl's[9] psychological interpretation of *conceptismo* as an exaggeration of Spanish individualism, considers the *Agudeza* a descendant of Latin Mannerism. This opinion is reiterated by S. L. Bethell in his statement that the whole European movement of metaphysical wit stems from the Jesuit revival of patristic wit.[10] M. J. Woods,[11] on the other hand, relates the seventeenth-century treatises of wit to the classical theory of topics, used as

---

[4] "Gracián's *Agudeza y arte de ingenio,*" *MLR,* XXVII (1932), 280-292, 420-429. Further articles are "Clasificación de algunos pasajes capitales para la estética de Baltasar Gracián," *BH,* XXXVII (1935), 27-56, and "On Two Criticisms of Gracián's *Agudeza,*" *HR,* III (1935), 23-35.

[5] "Baltasar Gracián," *RH,* XXIX (1913), 347-752, later translated into Spanish by Ricardo del Arco y Garay (Zaragoza: Institución "Fernando el Católico," 1947).

[6] "An Interpretation of Gracián's *Agudeza y arte de ingenio,*" *HR,* XVI (1948), 275-300.

[7] Gracián's Idea of the 'Concepto,'" *HR,* XVIII (1950), 15-41.

[8] *Europäische Literatur und lateinisches Mittelalter* (Bern: Francke, 1948), translated into English by Willard R. Trask as *European Literature and the Latin Middle Ages* (New York: Harper & Row, 1963).

[9] *Geschichte der spanischen Nationalliteratur in ihrer Blütezeit* (Freiburg im Breisgau: Herder & Co., 1929), translated into Spanish by Jorge Rubió Balaguer as *Historia de la literatura nacional española en la Edad de Oro* (Barcelona: Sucesores de Juan Gili, 1933).

[10] "Gracián, Tesauro, and the Nature of Metaphysical Wit," *The Northern Miscellany of Literary Criticism* (Autumn 1953), pp. 19-38.

[11] "Gracián, Peregrini and the Theory of Topics," *MLR,* LXIII (1968), 854-863.

a source of arguments. Other critics, such as J. A. Mazzeo,[12] Miguel Batllori,[13] and Arthur Terry[14] stress the deviation of Gracián, as well as of contemporary Italian theoreticians, from the mimetic tradition of the Renaissance. J. A. Mazzeo specifies the influence of the "doctrine of correspondence" in converting the poet from an imitator to a creator who explored and related the network of analogies in the universe. This view is reiterated by Terry, who studies the transitional function of Herrera in the development of Spanish poetic theory. Batllori stresses Gracián's replacement of the Jesuitic *Ratio Studiorum*, based on Aristotelian principles, by the inventive theory of the conceit. Karl-Ludwig Selig[15] contributes to these studies by analyzing the influence of emblematic literature on significant elements of Gracián's theory.

The study of Gracián's ideology has been the basic concern of the eminent *gracianista* M. Romera-Navarro, both in the introduction to his definitive edition of *El Criticón*[16] and in his *Estudios sobre Gracián,*[17] where the allegory and satire of the novel are analyzed on the basis of their content. The sames is true of Evaristo Correa Calderón,[18] whose biographic-literary study supplies not only a unified view of Gracián's total work but also information on its sources and influence. The conceptual basis of Gracián's ideology is the subject of Hellmut Jansen's[19] descriptive semasiological survey, in which Gracián's key concepts

---

[12] "A Seventeenth-Century Theory of Metaphysical Poetry," *RR*, XLII, (1951), 245-255; "Metaphysical Poetry and the Poetic of Correspondence," *JHI*, XIV (1953), 221-234; "A Critique of Some Modern Theories of Metaphysical Poetry," *MP*, L (1952), 88-96. The first two articles are reprinted in *Renaissance and Seventeenth Century Studies* (New York: Columbia University Press, 1964), pp. 29-43 and 44-59, respectively.

[13] *Gracián y el Barroco* (Roma: Edizioni di Storia e Letteratura, 1958).

[14] "The Continuity of Renaissance Criticism: Poetic Theory in Spain Between 1535 and 1650," *BHS*, XXXI (1954), 27-36; "A Note on Metaphor and Conceit in the Siglo de Oro," *BHS*, XXXI (1954), 91-97.

[15] "Gracián and Alciato's *Emblemata*," *CL*, VIII (Winter 1956), 1-11; "Some Remarks on Gracián's Literary Taste and Judgments," *Homenaje a Gracián* (Zaragoza: Institución "Fernando el Católico," 1958), pp. 155-162.

[16] *El Criticón* (3 vols.; Philadelphia: University of Philadelphia Press, 1938-40).

[17] Hispanic Studies, Vol. II (Austin: University of Texas Press, 1950).

[18] *Op. cit.*

[19] *Die Grundbegriffe des Baltasar Gracián* (Genève: E. Droz, 1958).

are systematized into three groups (normative, tactical, and contemplative), and the principal terms within each are described and classified. The political ideology of the period is the subject of Monroe Hafter's [20] comparative study of Quevedo, Saavedra Fajardo, and Gracián, all of whom faced the problem of maintaining Christian ethics in a period of increasing secularization of society and politics. The author traces the movement from the extreme idealism of Quevedo's *Política de Dios* to the increased realism of Gracián's attempts to reconcile political strategy with Christian precepts.

Syntax and form have been the primary concerns of three German scholars. Werner Krauss [21] notes the dynamic interrelationship between the conceptual and linguistic in Gracián, seeing the themes of strife and artifice reflected in the tension of the carefully wrought language. Klaus Heger, [22] by means of a comparative stylistic analysis between relevant passages in the *Criticón* and the *quissat* considered a common source for the novel and the *risala* of Ibn Tufayl, concludes that the outstanding characteristics of Gracián's writing are the verbs in primary position and the use of a dualistic structure to express different perspectives. Heger stresses the interdependence of style and ideology. Because the *ingenio* is an indispensable attribute of the *discreto*, style is transformed from a compendium of dead rules to an active mode of thought and behavior. The most recent study is that of Gerhart Schröder, [23] who, refining on Romera-Navarro's designation of Greco-Latin sources, emphasizes the importance of the writings of the Stoics and surveys the origins of Gracián's allegorical images. Although Schröder's concern is primarily eth-

---

[20] *Gracián and Perfection. Spanish Moralists of the Seventeenth Century*, Harvard Studies in Romance Languages, Vol. XXX (Cambridge: Harvard University Press, 1966).

[21] *Graciáns Lebenslehre* (Frankfurt am Main: Vittorio Klostermann, 1947), translated into Spanish by Ricardo Estarriol as *La doctrina de la vida según Baltasar Gracián* (Madrid: Rialp, 1962).

[22] Diss. Heidelburg, 1952, translated into Spanish by the author as *Baltasar Gracián; estilo lingüístico y doctrina de valores. Estudio sobre la actitud literaria del conceptismo* (Zaragoza: Institución "Fernando el Católico," 1960).

[23] *Baltasar Graciáns "Criticón." Eine Untersuchung zur Beziehung zwischen Manierismus und Moralistik* (München: W. Fink, 1966).

ical, for the first time Gracián's images and symbols are submitted to an esthetic analysis, and their effectiveness is seen to depend upon an ingenious play of language. Like Heger, Schröder is concerned with the relationship between moralism and mannerism. He notes that Gracián's ideas as an artist, expressed in the *Agudeza*, parallel his ideas expressed as a moralist in his other writings. The artist as well as the statesman must employ strategy and cunning to win his audience. The *agudeza* is seen to have a practical value, for it is this quality of perception which enables the individual to distinguish between appearance and reality.

The earliest stylistic analysis is that of José Manuel Blecua,[24] who finds a Baroque attitude of pessimism and disillusion reflected in Gracián's writing. He emphasizes the means by which the author achieves intensity and brevity of style, and examines the abstract, intellectual quality of his didacticism. Further contributions in this area are found in the *Homenaje a Gracián*. Francisco Ynduraín[25] describes the sentence structure as being primarily binary in its rhythm and organized in such a way as to create suspense. Like Blecua, Ynduraín associates ideology and style, seeing rigidity reflected in Gracián's frequent use of antithesis, and dogmatism in his abstract intellectualism. Helmut Hatzfeld[26] divides the Baroque style into two modes, one tending towards amplification and the other towards condensation, and suggests that the *Criticón* exemplifies the first tendency and the *Oráculo manual* the latter. He proceeds to analyze the intellectual, aristocratic qualities of the *Oráculo manual* which he considers symptomatic of the pre-Rococo, such as the word play, elegant balance, and semantic condensations. Gracián's personal system of semantics also interests Benito Sánchez Alonso,[27] who compiles a useful lexicographical appendix of the author's vocabulary, including words infrequently used as well as words which Gracián imbued with special meaning.

---

[24] "El estilo de *El Criticón* de Gracián," AFA, I (1945), 7-32.

[25] "Gracián, un estilo," *Homenaje a Gracián* (Zaragoza: Institución "Fernando el Católico," 1958), pp. 163-188.

[26] "The Baroquism of Gracián's *El Oráculo manual*," *Homenaje a Gracián* (Zaragoza: "Institución Fernando el Católico," 1958), pp. 103-117.

[27] "Sobre Baltasar Gracián (Notas linguo-estilísticas)," RFE, XLV (1963), 161-225.

El Criticón has not yet, however, been fully analyzed on the basis of its novelistic qualities. It has been treated in general terms as didactic allegory. The result of this has been a fossilization of El Criticón. This is clearly expressed in the comments of impressionistic critics. Unamuno censures the structure and style of the novel:

> Lástima grande que, además de su longitud y su latitud, que quitan mucho a su profundidad, dilatándola y desvaneciéndola, esté la obra maestra del gran conceptista manchada, no con juegos de conceptos, sino con juegos de palabras. [28]

Azorín compares its ideology adversely with that of Cervantes:

> Cervantes es el hombre de los caminos, entregado a las angustias y los azares de una vida precaria. Gracián vive en su biblioteca, entre libros y antigüedades, seguro, placentero. Cervantes es para los infortunados y los opresos; Gracián para los bienhallados y poderosos. [29]

Jorge Luis Borges, in his poem entitled "Baltasar Gracián," condemns the author's intellectual aloofness and lack of imaginative appeal:

> No hubo música en su alma; sólo un vano
> Herbario de metáforas y argucias,
> Y la veneración de las astucias,
> Y el desdén de lo humano y sobrehumano. [30]

This study is an attempt to remove the impression of lack of pertinence and lack of vitality of El Criticón, an impression which is caused by our shift in sensibility. Esthetically, the abstractness of an allegorical novel does not attract a reader accustomed to natural representation. Morally, the didacticism of

---

[28] "Leyendo a Baltasar Gracián," *Nuevo Mundo*, 23 julio 1920, rpt. in *Obras completas* (Madrid: Afrodisio Aguado, 1952), V, 112.
[29] "Baltasar Gracián," *Lecturas españolas* (Buenos Aires: Espasa-Calpe, 1943), p. 58.
[30] *Sur*, No. 252 (1958), pp. 9-10.

the allegory may or may not be appealing to the reader. As a genre, an allegory seems unjustified to us because it is a literary form in which imaginative appeal is subordinated to moral principles.

It can be seen that Gracián himself was aware of all these difficulties inherent in didactic literature, and was intensely sensitive to the needs and reactions of the reader. Because of this realization, he consciously utilized the structural and rhetorical means available to the artist to maintain the reader's interest.

The second section of the *Agudeza y arte de ingenio*, which deals with the compound conceit, contains theoretical statements on the modes of narrative fiction, the possible methods of their organization, and their usefulness for instruction. This theory is put into practice by the author for the first time in *El Discreto*. Previous studies have mentioned only a thematic correspondence between *El Discreto* and *El Criticón*. Therefore, the first chapter of this study will discuss details of the intent, organization, and stylistic characteristics of *El Discreto* which enable it to be considered an exploratory prelude to *El Criticón*.

The second chapter deals with the problem of whether the simple, embryonic forms of *El Discreto* were, in effect, developed into a complex unity in *El Criticón*. In order to see the evolution from a fragmented treatise to a unified novel, the thematic, temporal, and spatial organization of *El Criticón* is considered. Special attention is given to the devices used by the author which may be considered "novelistic," their purpose being to heighten the interest and suspense of the reader.

As the main components of the novel are allegory and satire, these are the subjects of the ensuing chapters. The long and complex tradition in which Gracián's allegory is rooted has been studied previously. The allegory, therefore, is not analyzed here for its doctrinal or ethical significance, but viewed from a structural standpoint. Emphasis is placed on the variety and dynamism with which Gracián infused the mode, as well as on the imagery he employed to make it an effective didactic tool. Gracián's satire is also based on an ethical tradition. Its successful conveyance, however, depends on descriptive elements. The final chapter focuses on the patterns of imagery and rhetorical devices employed in the satirical passages.

It is hoped that it may be seen that Gracián in no way subordinated esthetic considerations to doctrinal concepts. In *El Criticón* idea and image are fused into a significant and dynamic unity.

Chapter I

EL DISCRETO — PRELUDE TO EL CRITICÓN

El Discreto is a unique work because it constitutes the point of transition between Gracián's fragmentary aphoristic treatises and his novel, El Criticón. It consists of twenty-five chapters, which Gracián chose to call realces instead of capítulos. The avoidance of the common term capítulo can be explained by the author's need to condense the maximum amount of meaning in the smallest unit possible,[1] for the word realce much more aptly defines the content of the book. Each section analyzes a quality which Gracián considers indispensable for the "man of the world," with the result that, as stated by Evaristo Correa Calderón, "... cada una de las partes en que el libro se divide vendría a ser el retrato moral de una prenda de perfección, y su conjunto la suma de méritos y virtudes deseables en el hombre de mundo, algo así como la culminación en un modelo de las excelencias de muchos."[2] A variety of expository modes are used to present the heterogeneous material. The modes of praise include the *elogio* (I), the *encomio* (X), the *apología* (XIX), and the *panegiri* (XXIV); the modes of vituperation include the *sátira*

---

[1] Stylistic analyses of Gracián's writing stress intensity and brevity as one of its chief characteristics. See José Manuel Blecua, "El estilo de El Criticón de Gracián," AFA, I (1945), 7-32; Francisco Yndaraín, "Gracián, un estilo," Homenaje a Gracián (Zaragoza: Institución "Feranndo el Católico," 1958), pp. 163-188; and Helmut Hatzfeld, "The Baroquism of Gracián's El Oráculo manual," Homenaje a Gracián (Zaragoza: Institución "Fernando el Católico," 1958), pp. 103-117.

[2] Baltasar Gracián. Su vida y su obra (Madrid: Gredos, 1961), p. 170.

(IX, XI, and XX), the *satiricón* (XVI), the *crisis* (VI), and the *invectiva* (XIV); the modes of explication bear the subtitles of *discurso académico* (II), *memorial* (IV), *razonamiento académico* (V), *carta* (VII, XII, and XXII), and *diálogo* (VIII and XVII); the modes of narrative fiction are named *alegoría* (III), *apólogo* (XIII), *ficción heróica* (XVII), and *fábula* (XXIII). The *problema* (XV) and *emblema* (XXI) combine explication and fiction.

El Discreto was published in 1646, and the First Part of *El Criticón* appeared in 1651. The publication of the *Oráculo manual y arte de prudencia* a year after *El Discreto* does not interrupt the direct line of development between *El Discreto* and *El Criticón*. In spite of a year's lapse in the publication dates of the *Discreto* and the *Oráculo*, there is a strong possibility that these works were simultaneously conceived. The references which Gracián makes in *El Discreto* to his *Avisos al varón atento* suggest that this may well have been the original title of the *Oráculo manual*.[3]

This discussion of *El Discreto* as a transitional work will touch upon the relationship between the content and the form of the work and the doctrine of the *Agudeza y arte de ingenio*. Mention will be made of the didactic, static nature of *El Discreto*, and how Gracián, aware of the difficulties of maintaining a reader's interest, uses rhetoric to animate and vary his text.

Relationship Between Form and Content in El Discreto

Both the content and the form of *El Discreto* have merited attention. The similarity in content between *El Discreto* and *El Criticón* is startling. Adolphe Coster mentions characters such as "Zahorí" and "Momo," and concepts such as the "House of Fortune" or the "reform of proverbs" which are shared by the two works.[4] Correa Calderón comments on the significance of the last *realce*, subtitled "Culta repartición de la vida de un discreto": "Se trata de un proyecto de vida perfecta, que es

---

[3] See Arturo del Hoyo, "Estudio preliminar," *Obras completas*, ed. by Arturo del Hoyo (Madrid: Aguilar, 1960), pp. cli-clii.

[4] *Balta ar Gracián*, trans. by Ricardo del Arco y Garay (Zaragoza: Institución "Fernando el Católico," 1947), pp. 113-124.

germen evidente de *El Criticón,* en el que ha de referirse (II, cr. I) a las tres vidas del hombre, la vida vegetativa, la vida sensitiva, y la vida racional, que han de dar lugar a la estructura de la gran novela." [5]

The difference in form between *El Discreto,* with its *diálogos, fábulas, alegorías, sátiras, discursos,* etc., and *El Héroe, El Político Don Fernando el Católico,* and the *Oráculo manual* is equally surprising. Its organization is considered disjointed. Coster insists that "No hay que buscar trabazón: estos realces se suceden sin que se alcance por qué el uno va detrás del otro; cabe exceptuar el primero, que, naturalmente, debía dirigirse a Baltasar Carlos, y el último, resumen de la vida del Discreto," [6] and attributes this lack of coherence to the possibility that the various sections were read in academic gatherings. This would also explain the eulogies at the end of the various *realces* which were added for the benefit of the illustrious visitors of the day. Alfonso Reyes concurs in this opinion, describing *El Discreto* as "... una colección de ensayos cada uno dedicado a un realce.... Se ha podido fijar la fecha de la mayoría, y se ha visto que *El Discreto* es un libro fragmentario, escrito a través de muchos años." [7] Only Arturo del Hoyo states that the work has an internal cohesion, that the different parts do, in fact, form a whole, [8] but refers to the underlying attitude of the work rather than to its structural organization.

In order to understand the devices which Gracián used in *El Discreto,* and which he subsequently refined and expanded to create *El Criticón,* it is necessary to consider the *Agudeza y arte de ingenio.* This is Gracián's only theoretical work in which he presents his ideas on the nature and function of literature. That the *Agudeza y arte de ingenio* was published two years after *El Discreto* does not invalidate this approach, for a first edition of this work, entitled *Arte de ingenio,* had appeared in 1642, four years before the publication of *El Discreto.* [9]

---

[5] *Op. cit.,* pp. 170-171.
[6] *Op. cit.,* pp. 115-116.
[7] *Cuatro ingenios* (Buenos Aires: Espasa-Calpe, 1950), p. 108.
[8] "Noticia de *El Discreto," Insula,* XIV, No. 147 (1959), 1 and 9.
[9] Alberto Navarro González has studied the differences between the 1642 and 1648 editions of the *Agudeza.* In the later edition, the text is

The *Agudeza* is divided into two parts. The First Part consists of fifty chapters, or *discursos,* which deal with the "agudeza suelta," defined as "... aquélla en la cual, aunque se levantan tres o cuatro y muchos asuntos de un sujeto, ya en encomio, ya en ponderación, pero no se unen unos con otros, sino que libremente se levantan y sin correlación se discurren" (*Ag.,* LI, 457). [10] The author begins by distinguishing the conceit from the simple trope — "Válese la agudeza de los tropos y figuras retóricas, como de instrumentos para exprimir cultamente sus concetos; pero contiénense ellos a la raya de fundamentos materiales de la sutileza, y cuando más, de adornos del pensamiento" (*Ag.,* "Al lector," 233), with the result that, as stated by Marcelino Menéndez y Pelayo, the *Agudeza* "... en el fondo viene a ser una originalísima tentativa para sustituir a la retórica puramente *formal* de las escuelas, a la retórica de los tropos y de las figuras, otra retórica *ideológica,* en que las condiciones del estilo reflejen las cualidades del pensamiento y den cuerpo a los más enmarañados conceptos de la mente, que es lo que él llama, *escribir con alma.*" [11] The conceit is essentially defined as the artistic product of an act of understanding by means of which reality is grasped, as "... un acto de entendimento que exprime la correspondencia que se halla entre los objetos" (*Ag.,* II, 240). As is stated more explicitly later:

---

amplified by the inclusion of more quotes and the translations of Martial by Manuel de Salinas. In addition to this, the material is more logically organized, stylistic corrections are made for the purposes of greater clarity, and new classifications are added. In the First Part, which deals with the "agudeza suelta," sections on the "Agudeza enigmática" (XL), "Observaciones sublimes y de las máximas prudenciales" (XLIII), and "De las suspensiones, dubitaciones y reflexiones conceptuosas" (XLIV) further refine the analysis of the causes of wit. In the Second Part, which deals with the "agudeza compuesta," sections pertaining to the uses of erudition (LVIII and LIX) and the section entitled "Ideas de hablar bien" (LXII) are added. See "Las dos redacciones de la *Agudeza y arte de ingenio,*" *Cuadernos de Literatura,* IV (1948), 201-213.

[10] References to the *Agudeza y arte de ingenio,* and to all Gracián's works other than *El Criticón,* are to the text of the *Obras completas,* ed. by Arturo del Hoyo (Madrid: Aguilar, 1960). Henceforth the *Agudeza y arte de ingenio* will be cited as *Ag., El Discreto* as *D., El Héroe* as *H., Oráculo manual y arte de prudencia* as *O.* Capital Roman numerals indicate the chapter, and Arabic numerals the page.

[11] *Historia de las ideas estéticas en España* (9 vols.; Madrid: Editorial Hernando, 1930), III, 474.

La materia es el fundamento del discurrir; ella da pie a la sutileza. Están ya en los objetos mismos las agudezas objetivas, especialmente los misterios, reparos, crisis, si se obró con ellas; llega, y levanta la caza el ingenio. Hay unas materias tan copiosas como otras estériles, pero ninguna lo es tanto que una buena inventiva no halle en qué hacer presa, o por conformidad o por desconveniencia, echando sus puntas del careo. (Ág., LXIII, 513)

Once Gracián has delved into the nature of wit, he classifies the possible varieties of the conceit, arriving at a division into four modes, which are "de correlación," "de ponderación," "de raciocinación," and "de invención" (Ag., III, 245). Although this division is expanded upon, each of the types is discussed in turn, with examples given of each. Because as many types of the conceit are included as possible, the names assigned to them are valid more for their descriptive value than for purposes of classification.[12]

---

[12] For discussion of the *Agudeza* and the metaphysical conceit, see Edward Sarmiento, "Gracián's *Agudeza y arte de ingenio*," *MLR*, XXVII (1932), 280-292 and 420-429; "Clasificación de algunos pasajes capitales para la estética de Baltasar Gracián," *BH*, XXXVII (1935), 27-56; and "On Two Criticisms of Gracián's *Agudeza*," *HR*, III (1935), 23-35. Also consult T. E. May, "An Interpretation of Gracián's *Agudeza y arte de ingenio*," *HR*, XVI (1948), 275-300; "Gracián's Idea of the *Concepto*," *HR*, XVIII (1950), 15-41; as well as Arthur Terry, "The Continuity of Renaissance Criticism: Poetic Theory in Spain Between 1535 and 1650," *BHS*, XXXI (1954), 27-36; "A Note on Metaphor and Conceit in the Siglo de Oro," *BHS*, XXXI (1954), 91-97; "Quevedo and the Metaphysical Conceit," *BHS*, XXXV (1958), 211-222. For information on Gracián and contemporary theoreticians, see Benedetto Croce, "I trattatisti italiani del 'concettismo' e Baltasar Gracián," *Atti della Accademia Pontaniana*, XXIX, Series II, Vol. IV, memoria no. 7 (Naples, 1899), pp. 1-32, later included in *Problemi di estetica* (4th ed.; Bari, 1949), pp. 313-348. Also consult articles by Joseph Anthony Mazzeo, "A Seventeenth Century Theory of Metaphysical Poetry," *RR*, XLII (1951), 245-255, and "Metaphysical Poetry and the Poetic of Correspondence," *JHI*, XIV (1953), 221-234, both included in *Renaissance and Seventeenth Century Studies* (New York: Columbia University Press, 1964), pp. 29-43 and pp. 44-59, respectively, as well as "A Critique of Some Modern Theories of Metaphysical Poetry," *MP*, L (1952), 88-96. Also useful are S. L. Bethell, "Gracián, Tesauro, and the Nature of Metaphysical Wit," *The Northern Miscellany of Literary Criticism* (Autumn 1953), pp. 19-38; and M. J. Woods, "Gracián, Peregrini and the Theory of Topics," *MLR*, XLIII (1968), 854-863. For a summary of criticism up to 1966 on Gracián's literary doctrine, see Virginia

After Gracián has analyzed the individual conceit in the First Part of the *Agudeza,* he proceeds in the Second Part, which consists of thirteen *discursos,* to describe the compound conceit, or "agudeza compuesta," which is "... aquélla en que los asuntos, así de la panegiri, como de la ponderación suasoria, se unen entre sí como partes, para componer un todo artificioso mental" (*Ag.,* LI, 458). It is subdivided into two forms, the more simple "conceptos incomplejos" composed of "... tres o cuatro reparos, paridades, etcétera, unidos entre sí y que hagan juego de correspondencia" (*Ag.,* LI, 461) and the more complex "... compuesto por ficción, como son las épicas, alegorías continuadas, diálogos, etc." (*Ag.,* LI, 461). As can be seen, the "agudeza compuesta" encompasses all imaginative literature.

In this Second Part of the *Agudeza* Gracián attempts to apply the conceit, as used in narrative fiction, to the moral end of *desengaño.* According to the author, the conceit can serve moral ends because "Son las verdades mercadería vedada, no las dejan pasar los puertos de la noticia y desengaño, y así han menester tanto disfraz para poder hallar entrada a la razón, que tanto la estima" (*Ag.,* LVI, 479). It is in the "agudeza compuesta," therefore, that art and morality meet. Although the appeals of the "agudeza suelta" are obvious, Gracián also praises the advantages of the "agudeza compuesta," for "Siempre un todo, así en la composición física, como en la artificial, es lo más noble, el último objeto, y el fin adecuado de las artes; y si bien su perfección resulta de la de las partes, pero añade él la mayor de la primorosa unión" (*Ag.,* LI, 459).

The "agudeza compuesta" is difficult — "Arduo es el asunto, pero nunca la dificultad fué descrédito, así como ni la facilidad ventaja; mucho cuesta lo que vale, y al contrario" (*Ag.,* LI, 459). I should like to suggest that *El Discreto* is Gracián's early experiment in trying to resolve the pitfalls inherent in the "agudeza compuesta." From the simple, embryonic forms of *El Discreto* would develop the complex, mature unity of *El Criticón.*

Ramos Foster, "The Status of Gracián Criticism: A Bibliographic Essay," *RJ,* XVIII (1967), 296-307. The edition of E. Correa Calderón of the *Agudeza y arte de ingenio* (Madrid: Castalia, 1969) includes a useful introduciton as well as a select bibliography.

Content of El Discreto

If we begin by looking into the influences which may have prompted Gracián to change his style in *El Discreto*, a first consideration must be the modification in his concept of the *persona* at the time of writing *El Discreto* and the *Oráculo*. This has been pointed out by many critics. Werner Krauss comments that in these works "... se deshace el esplendor del *Héroe* ... se construye la imagen ejemplar del hombre. Ya que la vida reviste constantemente un carácter de lucha, toda la moral se reducirá a las reglas tácticas de la autoafirmación en medio de una amenaza general." [13] Monroe Hafter sees a pattern of progression from perfect to possible standards as "Gracián turns away from the imitation of loftly models; instead he bases his moral counsels on the maximum exercise of human reason." [14]

A division is usually made between the "early works" and the *Criticón*. According to Gerhart Schröder, the qualities of cleverness and manipulation of the early *persona* develop, under the influence of Senecan thought, into the judgment and perception embodied in Critilo. [15] Hafter states that in the earlier works the individuals are concerned with excellence, with advancing beyond themselves, while in the *Criticón* it is the return to the self which predominates. [16] Yet there is much in *El Discreto* which differentiates it from *El Héroe* and *El Político* and approximates it to the *Criticón*.

The focus in *El Discreto* becomes more transcendental, less worldly and politically oriented — "Es corona de la discreción el saber filosofar.... La misma Filosofía no es otro que meditación de la muerte" (*D.*, XXV, 145); the relationship with the self rather than with others is accentuated — "Comience por sí

---

[13] *La doctrina de la vida según Baltasar Gracián*, trans. by Ricardo Estarriol (Madrid: Rialp, 1962), p. 32.

[14] *Gracián and Perfection. Spanish Moralists of the Seventeenth Century*, Harvard Studies in Romance Languages, Vol. XXX (Cambridge: Harvard University Press, 1966), p. 8.

[15] *Baltasar Graciáns "Criticón." Eine Untersuchung zur Beziehung zwischen Manierismus und Moralistik* (München: W. Fink, 1966), p. 122.

[16] *Op. cit.*, p. 107.

mismo el Discreto a saber, sabiéndose" (*D.*, I, 79); the *discreto*, like Critilo, seeks to discover truth in a world of deceptive appearances — "Sagaz anotomía, mirar las cosas por dentro. Engaña de ordinario la aparente hermosura, dorando la fea necedad" (*D.*, I, 79). It is no longer sufficient for the *discreto* to *ver* or *mirar*, he must *sondar* and *adivinar:* "Bien es verdad que el varón sabio ha de ir deteniéndose, y más donde no conoce; entra con recato sondando los fondos ..." (*D.*, II, 82).

The theme of *El Discreto* is no longer the hero, but the more ordinary man, such as Critilo would be. This accounts for the inclusion of *sátiras* in the work. In discussing the superior being, only virtues need be mentioned; in teaching the ordinary man, pitfalls must be pointed out so that they may be avoided. Hafter writes that Gracián's posture is usually haughty, but that "In his last work, however, the preceptor and his ideal personality are more closely bound to human nature; Critilo is keenly aware of his own manhood." [17] This same broader view of humanity is evidenced in *El Discreto*. Gracián no longer implores his reader, as he did in *El Héroe*, "¡Qué singular te deseo!" (*H.*, "Al lector," 5). The reader is now placed midpoint between *virtudes* and *defectos*. He has, therefore, the possibility of choice open to him. Gracián has realized the duality of man. He has learned that man is both human and bestial, that, in the words of Sir Thomas Browne, he is ".... that great and true *Amphibium,* whose nature is disposed to live, ... in divided and distinguished worlds." [18]

Gracián's cognizance of man's equal propensity for good and for evil causes him to have a twofold purpose in the writing of *El Discreto*. He must persuade the reader towards virtue and the search for truth, and away from error and defective behavior. The difficulty of the task is evident to Gracián, as expressed in one of the *diálogos* when the "Doctor" laments: "Muy dificultoso es darse por entendido en puntos de censura y desengaño, porque se cree mal aquello que no se desea. No es menester mucha elocuencia persuadirnos lo que nos está bien y toda la de Demóstenes no basta para lo que nos está mal" (*D.*, VIII, 98).

---

[17] *Op. cit.*, p. 110.
[18] *Religio Medici* (New York: E. P. Dutton, 1951), p. 39.

A normal reader's resistance to truth and disillusionment is stressed in the *Agudeza y arte de ingenio:* "Son las verdades mercadería vedada, no las dejan pasar los puertos de la noticia y desengaño, y así han menester tanto disfraz para poder hallar entrada a la razón, que tanto la estima" (*Ag.,* LVI, 479). In an allegorical tale neglected Truth must take "Agudeza" as her ally, with the result that Truth "... dió desde entonces en andar con artificio, usa de las invenciones, introdúcese por rodeos, ... y por ingenioso circunloquio viene siempre a parar en el punto de su intención" (*Ag.,* LV, 473).

Form of El Discreto *and Its Relationship to the Esthetic as Expresesd in the* Agudeza

It is suggested that in *El Discreto* Gracián faced the challenge of trying to convince his readers of difficult truths, and realized that this change of content in his writing required a change of form. It will be objected that the *Oráculo*, a compendium of three hundred aphorisms, each one followed by a succinct analysis of its meaning, [19] has much the same content as the *Discreto*, yet nevertheless maintains its aphoristic form.

One approach, however, does not exclude or denigrate the other. Throughout the *Agudeza* Gracián praises Don Juan

---

[19] The problems relating to the *Oráculo manual y arte de prudencia* involve the extent of Lastanosa's collaboration, the extent to which it is an "anthology" of previous works or an original book, and what its relation is to the *Avisos al varón atento*, a title which appears in *El Discreto* and is mentioned by Lastanosa. Miguel Romera-Navarro, in his edition of the *Oráculo* (Madrid: Jura, 1954), concludes that Lastanosa was responsible only for the publication of the work; that it can be considered an original work, for of the 300 aphorisms, only 72 are from other works, and of these only 21 are transcribed literally without change. He also believes that the unpublished *Avisos al varón atento* was indeed incorporated into the *Oráculo* (see the "Introducción," pp. xx-xxviii). For discussion of these problems, see also Correa Calderón, *op. cit.*, pp. 172-179; Hoyo (ed.), *Obras completas*, pp. cli-clx; Coster, *op. cit.*, pp. 131-142. The following works might also be consulted: Victor Bouillier, "Notes sur *l'Oráculo manual* de Balthasar Gracián," *BH*, XIII (1911), 316-336; Ricardo del Arco y Garay, "Gracián y su colaborador y mecenas," *Baltasar Gracián, escritor aragonés del siglo XVII. Curso monográfico* (Zaragoza: Hospicio provincial, 1926), pp. 133-158; Maurice Lacoste, "Les sources de *l'Oráculo manual* dans l'œuvre de Gracián et quelques aperçus touchant a *l'Atento*," *BH*, XXXI (1929), 93-101. For stylistic analysis of the work, see Hatzfeld, *op. cit.*, pp. 103-117.

Manuel, author of *El Conde Lucanor,* for "Este sabio príncipe puso la moral enseñanza de la prudencia y de la sagacidad en algunas historias, parte verdaderas, parte fingidas, y compuso aquel erudito, magistral y entretenido libro, titulado *El Conde Lucanor,* digno de la librería délfica" (Ag., XXIII, 341). Gracián believes that "Por cuentos y por chistes, han intentado algunos sabios el introducir la moral filosofía y comunicar sus desengaños a la razón, ..." and adds that "Fué único en este género el príncipe Don Manuel, en su nunca debidamente alabado libro del *Conde Lucanor,* entretejido de varias historias, cuentos, ejemplos, chistes y fábulas, que entretenidamente enseñan" (Ag., LVII, 484). It is important to remember that Juan Manuel varied his methods of presentation in *El Conde Lucanor.* The form of *El Discreto* is comparable to the *enxemplos,* where Juan Manuel tries to make truth more palatable "... segúnd la manera que fazen los físicos, que quando quieren fazen alguna melizina que aproveche al fígado ... mezclan, con alguna melezina que quieren melezinar el fígado, açúcar o miel o alguna cosa dulçe"; [20] the form of the *Oráculo* is more akin to the subsequent books of *El Conde Lucanor,* where difficult proverbs present similar material in a manner which is "... más avreviado et más oscuro que en l'otro." [21]

Gracián could interest and instruct his reader by entertaining him, or by titillating him with difficult laconism. In *El Discreto* he chose entertainment as his method of captivating his audience. [22]

It is important to define Gracián's concept of "entertainment," for it does not simply mean the use of narrative fiction. In the

---

[20] Ed. by José Manuel Blecua (Madrid: Castalia, 1969), p. 52.

[21] *Ibid.,* p. 273.

[22] Edward C. Riley, in "Aspectos del concepto de *admiratio* en la teoría literaria del Siglo de Oro," *Studia Philológica (Homenaje a Dámaso Alonso),* III (1963), 173-183, points out the difference in attitude towards the reader in Golden Age literary theory as well as practice: "Se trata sobre todo de cautivar el ánimo del lector o espectador. ... Esta concentración sobre el lector refleja, en cierto modo, un cambio profundo en las ideas literarias, que empieza a manifestarse durante la segundo mitad del siglo XVI. Entre escritores — incluso teóricos — se hace notar una preocupación intensificada por las reacciones del lector individual y del pública en general. Se reconoce, de manera explícita o implícita, su intervención en la creación literaria" (p. 183).

Agudeza it is apparent that Gracián considers variety and novelty the chief inducements to a reader's enjoyment. [22] These, however, had to be achieved through style rather than content. Content is exhausted: "Estamos ya a los fines de los siglos. Allá en la Edad de Oro se inventaba, añadióse después, ya todo es repetir. Vense adelantadas todas las cosas, de modo que ya no queda qué hacer sino elegir. Vívese de elección" (*D.*, X, 101). Servile imitation is to be eschewed at all costs, in order to avoid "... el asco de lo rancio y el enfado de lo repetido, que suele ser intolerable y más en imitaciones, que nunca pueden llegar ni a la sublimidad ni a la novedad de primero" (*D.*, XXII, 136).

Therefore, novelty must be introduced either by means of stylistic innovations or through careful selection of the available material. Stylistic novelty can create the impression of newness, for "... aunque sean las cosas muy sabidas, si el modo del decirlas en el retórico y del escribirlas en el historiador fuere nuevo, las hace apetecibles" (*D.*, XXII, 136). This rhetorical imperative is extended even further: "Cuando las cosas son selectas, no cansa el repetirlas hasta siete veces; pero, aunque no enfadan, no admiran, y es menester guisallas de otra manera para que soliciten la atención" (*D.*, XXII, 136). If a choice presents itself in the material to be selected for illustration, the new must be preferred: "Los flamantes hechos y modernos dichos, añadiendo a lo excelente la novedad, recambian el aplauso, porque sentencias rancias, hazañas carcomidas, es tan cansada como propia erudición de pedantes y gramáticos" (*D.*, V, 91). Above all, any material chosen must be suitable to the public and not just pleasing to the author or speaker, for "¿Qué importa que sean muy al gusto del orador las cosas si no lo son del auditorio? ¿Para quién se sazonan?" (*D.*, X, 102).

Gracián put these theories concerning variety, novelty, and suitability into practice for the first time in *El Discreto*. First and foremost, there is variation in the format, which encompasses fables, allegories, letters, dialogues, etc. Second, there is a restriction in length in the continued use of any one form. It is specified in the *Agudeza* that allegories or parables: "... no han

---

[22] Schröder, *op. cit.*, stresses these qualities as "strategies" of the artist. See Ch. III, "Die Allegorie in der Agudeza-Asthetik."

de ser muy largas ni muy continas; alguna de cuando en cuando, refresca el gusto y sale muy bien" (*Ag.*, LV, 475). Third, there are variations in the structures of the various *realces*, in the methods of attaining internal unity within the chapters. Gracián considered this to be the most demanding task of an author: "Lo más arduo y primoroso destos compuestos de ingenio falta por comprehender, que es la unión entre los asuntos y conceptos parciales. El arte de hallarla sería superlativo primor de la sutileza" (*Ag.*, LIV, 467).

Gracián discusses the possible methods of organization in the *Discurso* LIV of the *Agudeza*, which is entitled "De la acolutia y trabazón de los discursos" (*Ag.*, LIV, 467-472). In order to discuss this point, I shall first cite Gracián's description of the method, and then give an example of its application in one or more of the *realces* of *El Discreto*. The terms used in the *Agudeza* to describe content, such as "discursos morales," "discursos por cuestión," or "discursos sobre una virtud o vicio," are vague, and could all be used to describe each *realce*. Therefore, the structure rather than the content of the *realce* is used as a basis for classification.

(1) *Discursos metafóricos:* "... es aún más facil, pues consiste en ir acomodando las partes, propiedades y circunstancias del término, con las del sujeto translatos, y cuanto más ajustada es la correspondencia campea más el discuro" (*Ag.*, LIV, 468). In *Realce* XIV, "No rendirse al humor," Gracián begins his discusión using a metaphor. The first paragraph is a description of Mt. Olympus, whose outstanding characteristic of immutability is then applied to the superior individual. The metaphor is effective because of its method of presentation. A statement is made — "Rey es de los montes el celebrado Olimpio ..." (*D.*, XIV, 113), various explanations for the superiority are sought and subsequently rejected in a series of sentences beginning "no porque,..." and finally the climactic solution is given: "Sí, empero, porque nunca se sujeta a vulgares peregrinas impresiones, que es el mayor señorío el de sí mismo" (*D.*, XIV, 113). More importantly, however, this paragraph shows the process by which Gracián has arrived at the "ground" for his metaphor. Of the various qualities of the mountain which might be compared, only the final one is accepted as the apt "término de correspondencia"

to the superior man. Such a procedure is described for the "agudeza por semejanza": "En este modo de conceptear, caréase el sujeto, no ya con sus adyacentes propios, sino con un término extraño, como imagen, que le exprime su ser o le representa sus propriedades, efectos, causas, contingencias y demás adjuntos; no todos, sino algunos" (Ag., IX, 275).

Furthermore, because the obvious physical analogy of height is rejected, this comparison is a "difficult" one. This is an added advantage, because "Cuanto más escondida la razón, y que cuesta más, hace más estimado el concepto, despiértase con el reparo la atención, solicítase la curiosidad, luego lo exquisito de la solución desempeña sazonadamente el misterio" (Ag., VI, 264). The metaphor also contains a "moralidad provechosa" (Ag., XII, 287). If a man can attain the immutability of the mountain, he too can be king.

(2) *Discursos por cuestión:* "... consiste la unión en ir discurriendo por las partes y términos entre quienes está la duda" (Ag., LIV, 471). Realce XV, "Tener buenos repentes," is subtitled *problema*, and is basically a discussion of the proposition "¿Qué es mejor, presto o bien?" [23] The first paragraph argues for the superiority of the well done, the remainder of the *realce* for the virtue of rapidity, which Gracián has redefined so as to include both possibilities of the *problema*: "Pero si a todo acierto se le debe estimación, a los repentinos, aplauso" (D., XV, 115). Realce XXIV, "Corona de la Discreción," is organized on the basis of the "... contienda que tuvieron entre sí las más sublimes prendas de un varón consumadamente perfecto ..." (D., XXIV, 140). The contestants present their claims to a tribunal presided over by Truth, who decides among them.

(3) *Unión con palabra equívoca:* "Hasta en una palabra equívoca pueden unirse los cabos del discurso, y se toma ocasión della para levantar las propuestas" (Ag., LIV, 471). The fable of Realce XXIII, "Arte para ser dichoso," depicts a conflict between the complaining ass and Fortune. The solution on behalf of Fortune lies in the question "... si él es un asno, ¿de quién se queja?"

---

[23] See note 2, p. 115, of ed. Arturo del Hoyo, defining *problema* and interpreting this *realce*.

(*D*., XXIV, 139). The wit of the question is based on the play between the literal and figurative meanings of the word "ass." The fable is further enhanced because the solution, the "acertada salida," is at the end. This is praised in the *Agudeza* because "Va con suspensión el auditorio aguardando en qué ha de venir a parar, que es más arte que el declararse luego al principio, y así de más gusto ..." (*Ag*., LIV, 471).

(4) *Propuesta que contiene muchas partes:* "Aquí no es menester más unión que el ir singularizando por partes aquella proposición primera universal" (*Ag*., LIV, 469). In this method of organization a general statement is made which is then proven, if necessary, or analyzed into its component parts. *Realce* XVIII, "De la cultura y aliño," most closely approximates this analytical type of structure. The *realce* begins with the proposition that the personified "Aliño" is "perfección de todo" (*D*., XVIII, 123). This is followed by a description and discussion of the qualities which characterize "Aliño" and which prove its perfection. The personification is maintained throughout: "Fué tu padre el Artificio, Quirón, de la naturaleza ..." (*D*., XVIII, 123); "Tuviste por madre a la Buena Disposición ..." (*D*., XVIII, 124); "Tus hermanos fueron el Despejo, el Buen Gusto y el Decoro ..." (*D*., XVIII, 125); "Hijos son tuyos el Agrado y el Provecho ..." (*D*., XVIII, 126).

(5) *Discursos sobre alguna virtud o vicio:* "Cuando se discurre sobre alguna virtud o vicio, es por sus principales efectos y actos ..." (*Ag*., LIV, 470). In *Realce* III, "Hombre de espera," the virtue personified is "la Espera." The author proceeds by means of an orderly physical description, each detail of which corresponds to a moral attitude. For example, "... la nariz grande, prudente desahogo de los arrebatamientos de la irascible y de las llamaradas de la concupiscible ..." (*D*., III, 84); "... dilatado pecho, donde se maduran y aun podrecen los secretos ..." (*D*., III, 84). This is followed by a description of her dress, also symbolic of spiritual qualities — "Su vestir no era de gala, sino de decencia ..." (*D*., III, 84). The color is green "de la Esperanza," for "la Espera" detesta red "... por lo encendido de su cólera primero y de su empacho después" (*D*., III, 85).

(6) *Discursos morales:* "... es primorosa unión, y aun disposición, proponer dos partes encontradas, comenzar como apoyando

paradojamente algún vicio, discurriendo en favor dél, y luego revolver contra él, y refutarle" (*Ag.*, LIV, 472). *Realce* XIII, "Hombre de ostentación," most closely approximates this method of procedure, although it is not a "vice" which is first defended, but simply a type of behavior.

In this *realce* Gracián composes a modern fable to argue the relative merits of modesty and ostentation. The first step is an argument by the enemies of the peacock against ostentation. The *realce* depends for its effect upon the plausibility of their point of view.

Their argument is, at first glance, convincing:

> "Siempre fué vulgar la ostentación, nace del desvanecimiento. Solicita la aversión, y con los cuerdos está muy desacreditada. El grave retiro, el prudente encogimiento, el discreto recato, viven a lo seguro, contándose con satisfacerse a sí mismos; no se pagan de engañosas apariencias, ni las venden. Bástase a sí misma la realidad, no necesita de extrínsicos engañados aplausos...." (*D.*, XIII, 110)

The choice of words is astute. Their praise of "el prudente encogimiento" and "discreto recato," their condemnation of "engañosas apariencias" and "engañados aplausos" is in keeping with the ideals reiterated by Gracián. Although their position appears conclusive, the seeds of the refutation are already planted in these same words.

From the beginning of the fable, the credibility of the enemies has been undermined by their attitude of resentful envy. The author alludes to this continually, from the beginning words of the *realce* — "Prodigiosos son los ojos de la envidia..." (*D.*, XIII, 108), to the following comment: "Es la envidia pegajosa, siempre halla de qué asir, hasta de lo imaginado. Fiera cruelísima, que con el bien ajeno hace tanto mal a su dueño propio" (*D.*, XIII, 109). The result of this is that the words of the enemies are invalidated because of the strongly ironic overtones which they have.

The peacock's refutation of his enemies is eventually succeeded by the typical resolution, which consists of a synthesis between two extremes. Appearance must always be supported by reality,

"... que sin méritos no es más que un engaño vulgar ..." (*D.,* XIII, 112), and ostentation must be mitigated by humility, "... y criminalmente se le ordene, que todas las veces que desplegue al viento la variedad de su bizarría, haya de recoger la vista a la fealdad de sus pies ..." (*D.,* XIII, 113).

(7) *Trabazón extrínsica:* This method is differentiated from the previous "trabazones intrínsicas" and is disparaged by Gracián for being "... de menos arte, aunque más platicada ..." (*Ag.,* LIV, 472). An author employs it "... trayendo alguna historia primero, o suceso remoto, y aplicándole por la semejanza o paridad al caso presente" (*Ag.,* LIV, 472). There are several examples of this technique in *El Discreto. Realce* XV, "Tener buenos repentes," begins with a mythological tale of Jupiter which is then applied to the problem at hand (*D.,* XV, 115). *Realce* XVI begins with the story of Diogenes which is then made relevant to the satire against *figurería* (*D.,* XVI, 117).

There is yet a fourth means by which variety and novelty are injected into the text. It is apparent that the examples used for illustration have been selected with extreme care.

As might be expected, the examples of erudite sayings and heroic actions are used primarily in the *realces* which have the form of a *discurso,* rather than those in which fiction is employed. These latter forms are considered interesting enough not to require extra means of attraction. Each genre has different and defined requisites: "La historia con su suspensión de los sucesos, entretiene. Las comedias, épicas y otras ficciones, con sus enredados empeños, deleitan. Los discursos, si no se favorecen de la erudición, son secos, estériles y empalagan" (*Ag.,* LVIII, 490).

An overall glance at *El Discreto* bears witness to the variety in the illustrations of word and deed which are cited. Intellectual and military figures; Biblical and mythological personages; figures from the past and present are all included. Martial and Cervantes, Alexander and Caesar, Charles V and "el Gran Capitán," Moses and Jupiter appear, the only criterion for their inclusion being their relevancy to the matter under discussion, for "El ser a propósito, es gran ventaja de la autoridad" (*Ag.,* LVIII, 489). In some instances, as a means of added mental stimulation, names or acts are alluded to rather than stated outright. Antonio Pérez is referred to as "nuestro Anfión aragonés" (*D.,* VIII, 97);

Pompey is simply "el romano" (*D.*, XII, 107); and Martial is mentioned as "el más sabroso de nuestra patria" (*D.*, X, 102). Caesar's outcry "Teneo te, Africa" is admired by Gracián as a "buen repente," and alluded to as "... plausible el de éste al caer, ..." but it is not quoted in the text (*D.*, XV, 116).

Gracián had written that examples should be "... así heroicos como donosos" (*D.*, V, 91). Although heroic actions predominate, there is an example of an amusing anecdote, concerning the lady who reprimanded the soldier who could not dance (*D.*, VII, 96). Further variety is apparent in the use of examples within the text. Some provide a negative contrast. In a *realce* praising equanimity, Demetrius and Nero appear as prototypes of failures in this respect (*D.*, VI, 93). On the other hand, in the satire "No ser malilla" Popea appears as a paragon of moderation, the importance of which is stressed by the exclamatory formulation of the praise — "¡Qué bien conoció este vulgar riesgo, y qué bien supo prevenirlo la celebrada Popea de Nerón, la que mejor supo lograr la mayor belleza!" (*D.*, XI, 105). Two examples may be juxtaposed, one illustrating a virtue and the other its opposing defect. The "Gran Capitán" as an "hombre de todas horas" is thus contrasted to the narrow-minded soldier (*D.*, VII, 95).

Uses of Rhetoric in El Discreto

The Didactic Nature of El Discreto—Rhetoric as an Animating Factor

This stress on variety is successful in distracting the reader's attention from the didactic nature of the content of the *realces*. Gracián is first and foremost a moralist, and as such moves between the extremes of the panegyric and the epideictic. The majority of the *realces* of *El Discreto* are written either in praise of a quality, whether it be *espera* or *galantería* or *erudición plausible,* or in condemnation of a defect, such as *desigualdad* or *figurería* or *hazañería.* Other *realces* are deliberations upon a moral question. These follow a pattern of breaking down a subject into alternatives, which are subsequently synthesized into a "middle way" between extremes. Among the alternatives presented which are later reconciled are the pair "genio-ingenio" ("El uno sin el otro fué en muchos felicidad a medias ..." [*D.*, I,

78]), "hacer presto o bien" ("Pero si a todo acierto se le debe estimación, a los repentinos, aplauso ..." [*D.*, XV, 115]), "diligente-inteligente" ("Tanto necesita la diligencia de la inteligencia como el contrario" [*D.*, XXI, 133]).

In all of the *realces* Gracián is essentially arguing for his point of view. He is trying to exhort the reader to adopt the positive qualities, and to dissuade him from accepting the bad. The author's success will depend on how convincing an argument he presents. Various methods of argumentation may be designated — argument from authority, argument by analogy, and argument from consequences.

Actions and words of approved authorities are frequently employed to substantiate an argument. A reference at the end of a paragraph serves to culminate previous points made, as seen in the sentence "Vale más un sí de un valiente juicio déstos que toda la aclamación de un vulgo; que no sin causa llamaba Platón a Aristóteles toda su escuela, y Antígono a Zenón todo el teatro de su fama" (*D.*, XIX, 129). Other times the reference acts as a "primary statement," forming the core of Gracián's ensuing discussion. The aphorism of "Quilón" — "Conocerse y aplicarse" — is immediately applied to "el Discreto" — "Comience por sí mismo el Discreto a saber, sabiéndose" (*D.*, I, 79). The story of Diogenes' search forms the basis of *Realce* XVI, "Contra la figurería." Usually these sayings are sparsely interspersed. Only one example is found of an accumulation of erudite citations, when Truth praises "la Entereza": "Llamóla Séneca, el único bien del hombre; Aristóteles, su perfección; Salustio, blasón inmortal; Cicerón, causa de la dicha ..." (*D.*, XXIV, 141). The synonymous reiteration is extremely emphatic.

The argument by analogy is seen in the use of similes or metaphors to illustrate and clarify a point under discussion. To animate the distinction between men of good and bad taste, Gracián draws an analogy to the animal world: "Extremada elección la de la abeja y qué mal gusto el de una mosca, pues en un mismo jardín solicita aquélla la fragancia y ésta la hediondez" (*D.*, X, 102-103). To substantiate the warnings against overexposure in the satire "No ser malilla," the author draws an analogy to paintings — "Pensión es de las pinturas muy excelentes, ... que en todas las fiestas hayan de salir, ... presto vienen a ser inútiles, o comunes, que es peor" (*D.*, XI, 104), as well as to food — "El manjar más delicioso, a la segunda vez pierde mucho de aquel primer agrado ..." (*D.*, XI, 105). A more developed metaphor is used in the discussion of "El hombre en su punto" (*Realce* XVII). A parallel is drawn between the maturation of the individual and the aging of wine: "... tiene cuando comienza una ingratísima dulzura, una insuave rigidez, como no está aún hecho; pero, en comenzando a hervir, comienza a defecarse, pierde con el tiempo aquella enfadosa dulzura y cobra una suavísima generosidad ..." (*D.*, XVII, 121). These terms for wine fermentation are transferred to describe human development, from the "enfadosa dulzura" and "insuave crudeza" of youth, until maturation when "... todo él huele a una muy viril generosidad" (*D.*, XVII, 122).

It is interesting to note that the use of the metaphor to illustrate, clarify, and impress a point upon the reader is more in keeping with the Renaissance theory of the metaphor than with the *conceptista* theory. Renaissance theory, based on Aristotle's statements on the subject, stressed the pedagogic use of the metaphor. It was used as "... the best means of impressing the reader with an important subject matter, *doctrina* by means of *eloquentia*, and thereby facilitated the retention of knowledge. ..." [24]

The argument from consequences in *El Discreto* concentrates on the bad effects of inappropriate behavior. The passages describing these consequences act as warnings to the reader. For example, the *hombres de burlas* suffer the following repercussions: "... ganan fama de decidores y pierden el crédito de prudentes; pásase el gusto del chiste y queda la pena del arrepentimiento: lloran por lo que hicieron reír" (*D.*, X, 100). The *malilla* is similarly doomed to failure: "Codícianlo todos por lo excelente, con que se viene a hacer común; y perdiendo aquella primera estimación de raro, consigue el desprecio de vulgar, y es lástima que su misma excelencia le causa su ruina. Truécase aquel aplauso de todos en un enfado de todos" (*D.*, XI, 104).

---

[24] Mazzeo, "Seventeenth-Century Theory of Metaphysical Poetry," in *Renaissance and Seventeenth Century Studies*, p. 31.

Gracián, an extremely successful preacher,[25] was aware of the need to captivate the audience's attention in order to make them more receptive to moral teachings. He mentions in the *Agudeza* that "Los discursos persuasivos, participan tal vez del ingenioso artificio, y es entonces adecuada su perfección, porque se van introduciendo con notable agrado, y es cebo lo gustoso para lo importante" (*Ag.*, LIII, 467). Sacred rhetoric had a long and distinguished history in Spain,[26] and this concept of combining delight with instruction was not a new one. Fray Luis de Granada, in his *Retórica eclesiástica* (published in 1576), praises the merits of adornment:

> ...Realmente es corto el mérito de los que hablan con pureza y claridad, pues esto más es carecer de vicios, que tener alguna gran virtud. Ni contribuye poco á una causa este adorno, porque los que oyen con gusto están más atentos, creen con más facilidad, se prenden ordinariamente con el mismo deleite, y no rara vez se transportan de admiración.
> ... ...
> Mas San Agustín, de este adorno de la oración con que grandemente se recrean los ánimos de los oyentes, dice así: "Al modo que muchas veces deben tomarse amargos saludables, así debe evitarse siempre la dulzura perniciosa. Pero, ¿qué cosa mejor que una medicina dulce? Porque cuanto más allí se aparece la suavidad, tanto más facilmente aprovecha la medicina. ..."[27]

The most famous of the seventeenth-century orators in Spain, Fray Hortensio Felix de Paravicino, is admired by Gracián throughout the *Agudeza*. He is "culto y aliñado" (*Ag.*, XLIV, 436), "... atento siempre a la perfección de estilo, así en el verso

---

[25] Contemporary testimony records that during Gracián's stay in Madrid from 1641-1642, he sometimes preached twice a day, to churches filled to capacity and with crowds thronged outside. See Evaristo Correa Calderón, "Gracián y la oratoria barroca," *Acta Salmanticensia. Filosofía y Letras*, XVI (1962), 132.

[26] For a summary and brief analysis of the development of sacred rhetoric in Spain, see Antonio M. Martí, "La retórica sacra en el Siglo de Oro," *HR*, XXXVIII (1970), 264-298.

[27] *Los siete libros de retórica eclesiástica*, in *B.A.E.*, Vol. XI (Madrid: Rivadeneyra, 1849), p. 571 (Bk. V, ch. iv).

como en la prosa ..." (*Ag.*, L, 453), and can be considered Góngora's equal — "En la prosa fué igual suyo el agradable Hortensio: juntó lo ingenioso del pensar con lo bizarro del decir; es más admirable que imitable" (*Ag.*, LXII, 510). [28] Like Gracián, Paravicino realized that sermons were expected to provide not only doctrinal instruction but also delight and entertainment, for "... por nuestra desgracia han llegado los sermones tan a la necesidad misma de agrado que las comedias." [29] It was impossible to introduce novelty in the content of the sermon, and therefore the orator had to concentrate on the form of expression. As stated by Emilio Alarcos: "Paravicino desea, sin duda, que sus oyentes queden edificados con el sermón; pero, antes que nada, quiere que éste les produzca sorpresa y deleite, maravilla y entretenimiento. Todo en sus oraciones está dispuesto y organizado para conseguirlo." [30] The instrument he employed to accomplish his goal of persuasion was rhetoric. [31]

Gracián uses this same tool in *El Discreto*. The work abounds in examples of the rhetorical use of questions and exclamations. For instance, the author anticipates the objections of an imagined interlocutor and answers the remarks in advance (procatalepsis). [32]

---

[28] Correa Calderón, "Gracián y la oratoria barroca" (above, p. 38, note 25), believes that Gracián, showing more mature judgment, later retracts this earlier enthusiasm for Paravicino. He bases his opinion on a section in the *Criticón* which criticizes preachers who "Dexaron la sustancial ponderación del Sagrado Texto, y dieron en alegorías frías, metáforas cansadas, haciendo soles y águilas los santos, inares las virtudes, teniendo toda una hora ocupado el auditorio, pensando en una ave o una flor. Dexaron esto y dieron en descripciones y pinturillas; ... mezclando lo sagrado con lo profano ... dexando la sólida y sustancial doctrina ..." (III, x, 330-331). It seems to me, however, that here Gracián is not criticizing the metaphysical style of oratory, but rather the lack of novelty and variety of bad preachers, whose allegories are "frías," whose metaphors are "cansadas," and who spend "toda una hora" using only one image. As we have already seen, Gracián stresses the need for variety and novelty in the *Agudeza*.

[29] Emilio Alarcos, "Los sermones de Paravicino," *RFE*, XXIV (1937), 173, note 3. Alarcos quotes from the *Oraciones evangélicas o discursos panegyricos y morales*, I (Madrid: Ibarra, 1766), p. 176.

[30] *Ibid.*, p. 265.

[31] For detailed analysis of Paravicino's style, see article of Alarcos, *op. cit.*, especially pp. 273-319.

[32] For a convenient and concise listing or rhetorical terminology, see Richard A. Lanham, *A Handlist of Rhetorical Terms* (Berkeley and Los Angeles: University of California Press, 1969). Consult also Heinrich Lausberg,

He foresees the protests to his verdict against *desigualdad:* "Diránme que todo es desigualdades este mundo, y que sigue a lo natural lo moral. ... Pues si el hombre es un otro mundo abreviado, ¿qué mucho que cifre en sí la variedad?," and replies, "Pero no hay perfección en variedades del alma que no dicen con el Cielo. De la luna arriba no hay mudanza" (*D.*, VI, 94). There are instances when the author raises questions which he himself answers (hypophora). Some examples of this are "... ¿qué será, sin ser Davo, en una grave conversación estar chanceando? Será hacer farsa con risa de sí mesmo" (*D.*, IX, 100); "Pero ¿qué remedio habría tan eficaz, que curase a todos estos de figuras, y los volviese al ser de hombres? Pues de verdad que lo hay, y es infalible" (*D.*, XVI, 120). Some of the questions asked have strong moral connotations and are so worded as to elicit the affirmation or denial of the reader (erotesis). Such questions as "Pero, ¿qué desigualdad más monstrosa que la de Nerón?" (*D.*, VI, 94), or "¿Qué aprovecha la fragancia de los ámbares, si la desmiente la hediondez de las costumbres?" (*D.*, XVI, 118), or "Infeliz genio el que se declara por de una sola materia, ... pues, ¿qué si fuera vulgar?" (*D.*, VII, 95) constrain the reader into affirming the author's opinion.

The use of emotional exclamations (exclamatio) to move the listener to a like feeling is ubiquitous in *El Discreto*. These exclamatory statements serve various purposes, which may be enumerated as follows:

(1) To accentuate expressions of praise following descriptions of negative qualities: After the depiction of the "hombre desigual," his opposite is acclaimed — "¡Oh, el prudente! ¡Qué tranquilo costea las puntas y los esteros! ¡Qué señor mide los golfos!" (*D.*, VI, 93); after the disparagement of the "malillas de belleza," Popea is praised — "¡Qué bien conoció este vulgar riesgo, y qué bien supo prevenirlo la celebrada Popea de Nerón, la que mejor supo lograr la mayor belleza!" (*D.*, XI, 105).

(2) To give emphasis to an expression of warning: The exhortation to be an "hombre de buen dejo" is reiterated in

---

Handbuch der literarischen Rhetorik; eine Grundlegung der Literaturwissenschaft (2 vols.; München: M. Hueber, 1960). Also useful on this topic is Sister Miriam Joseph's *Rhetoric in Shakespeare's Time: Literary Theory of Renaissance Europe* (New York: Harcourt, Brace & World, 1962).

various ways, beginning with "¡Oh, cuántos soles habemos visto entrambos nacer con risa de la aurora y también nuestra, y sepultarse después con llanto del ocaso!," continuing with "¡Qué aplaudido comienza un mando, ... Pero ¡qué callado fina!," and ending with "¡Qué adorado, o de la esperanza o del temor, entra un valimiento, si él mismo no se desmintiera a la mitad de la dicción dividida!" (*D.*, XII, 106-107).

(3) To give emphasis to a point which has been otherwise stated: The following paragraphs on the subject of "Del modo y agrado" serve this purpose: "¡Qué de materias graves e importantes se gastaron por un mal modo, y qué dellas, ya desahuciadas, se mejoraron y concluyeron por el bueno!" and "¡Cuántas cosas muy vulgares y ordinarias las pudo realzar a nuevas y excelentes y las vendió a precio de gusto y de admiración!" (*D.*, XXII, 136).

(4) To conclude a paragraph, as an emphatic restatement of the issue: Examples of this are: "Salen otros del torno de su barro ya destinados para la servidumbre de unos espíritus serviles, sin género de brío en el corazón, ... ¡Oh, cuántos hizo superiores la suerte en la dignidad, y la naturaleza esclavos en el caudal!" (*D.*, II, 83) and "Resuelven algunos con extremada sindéresis, decretan con plausible elección, y piérdense después en las ejecuciones, ... ¡Qué de veces degenera de lo heroico y se destina a una vulgarísima nada!" (*D.*, XXI, 134).

The Static Nature of El Discreto—*Rhetoric as a Compensating Factor*

Animation through rhetoric is essential in *El Discreto*. There is a lack of movement and direction in the work as a whole, which is apparent also in its component units. The smaller unit, the paragraph, will be discussed first, and then the larger unit, the *realce*, will be analyzed.

The following analogy may be used to describe a paragraph of *El Discreto:* "... we may compare it with successive flashes of a jewel or prism as it is turned about on its axis and takes the light in different ways." [33]

---

[33] Morris W. Croll, "The Baroque Style in Prose," *Studies in English Philology: A Miscellany in Honor of Frederick Klaeber*, ed. by Kemp Malone

Gracián's use of the Senecan "curt period" is best appreciated if seen in comparison to the Ciceronian "circular period" of Fray Luis de Granada. [34] In order to make such a comparison, I have deliberately not chosen a paragraph in the "genus sublime" where all of Fray Luis de Granada's rhetorical devices would be displayed. A paragraph in the "genus humile" is more closely akin to Gracián's sententiousness. The following paragraph is quoted from the *Guía de pecadores:*

> El tercero pecado es murmuración, la cual algunas veces viene a parar en detracción; porque comenzando a decir de una persona las culpas públicas y livianas, de ay venimos poco a poco a parar en las secretas y graves, con que una persona queda infamada y publicada por mala; lo cual sin duda es grandísimo peligro y perjuicio, pues es contra la fama y la honra, la cual todos tienen en más que la hacienda, y algunos, aun en más que la misma vida. [35]

The paragraph forms a continuous unity, flowing from one clause into the next. The connection of the periods within the paragraph is compact and logical, with the result that the thought is carried forward into each consecutive sentence. In this paragraph the frequent use of the relative pronoun "la cual" or "el cual" (having the force of "que") binds the period tightly to the immediately preceding period which contains the antecedent. Subordinate conjunctions, which are stricter connectives, are preferred over the loose coordinating conjunctions which would allow for greater freedom. Within this short paragraph there are three subordinate conjunctions introducing dependent clauses — "porque" (cause), "con que" (result), and "pues" (cause). This complex interdependence of clauses, which requires the reader to refer backwards to clarify the connections, as well as the amplify-

---

and Martin Ruud (Minneapolis: University of Minnesota Press, copyright 1929; renewed 1957 by Kemp Malone), pp. 207-233, rpt. in *Style, Rhetoric and Rhythm: Essays,* ed. by J. Max Patrick *et al.* (Princeton, N. J.: Princeton University Press, 1966), p. 212.

[34] See Rebecca Switzer, *The Ciceronian Style in Fray Luis de Granada* (Lancaster, Pa.: Lancaster Press, 1927), for a fuller analysis of this author's style.

[35] Ed. by M. Martínez Burgos (Madrid: Espasa-Calpe, 1966), p. 129.

ing use of doublets connected by the coordinate conjunction "y" ("públicas y livianas," "secretas y graves," "infamada y publicada," "peligro y prejuicio," "la fama y la honra") retard the speed of the paragraph. The movement is complex and slow. The thought is carefully worked out, and expands and develops during the course of the paragraph.

In contrast to this is the following example of a paragraph from *El Discreto:*

> Tanto se requiere en las cosas la circunstancia como la substancia; antes bien, lo primero con que topamos no son las esencias de las cosas, sino las apariencias; por lo exterior se viene en conocimiento de lo interior, y por la corteza del trato sacamos el fruto del caudal; que aun a la persona que no conocemos por el porte la juzgamos. (*D.*, XXII, 135)

What is immediately striking in this paragraph is the avoidance of syntactic ligatures. Almost all conjunctions have been replaced by semicolons, with the result that it is not the unity of the paragraph which is emphasized but rather its disjunction into component members. The complex hypotaxis of Fray Luis de Granada is replaced by a spontaneous parataxis, and the slowness of subordination is replaced by the speed of juxtaposition. There is no logical progress within the paragraph, no development of an idea. The paragraph is composed of a series of aphorisms, which in no way add information but simply repeat one another in varying ways. From the initial statement there is merely a shift of emphasis in the reiteration. There is variation form the more abstract dichotomy "circunstancia-substancia" to the more concrete dichotomy "exterior ("porte")-interior" of a person, and a shift from literal to metaphoric statement, with the analogy drawn to "corteza-fruto." But there is no real movement from beginning to end.

This type of paragraph has been analyzed as "... a series of imaginative moments occurring in a logical pause or suspension." [36] Such a description can be extended, in the case of Gracián, to encompass the *Discreto* as a whole.

---

[36] Croll, *loc. cit.*

Most of the *realces* of the *Discreto* are either anatomies of a subject or definitions of a characteristic. Therefore, very little movement is possible other than the subtle dialectic apparent in the *realces* involving *cuestiones,* such as "Hombre de ostentación" (XIII). This quality of dissection rather than movement is especially evident in the *realces* where development of character or the use of narrative would have been feasible. I shall focus on the *diálogos, alegorías,* and *sátiras* because these forms will be integral components of *El Criticón.*

The *diálogos* of *El Discreto* are not so much dialogues as conversations. There is no differentiation of characters or their viewpoints, nor is there development in a point of view from the beginning to the end of the discourse. This lack of any conflict of ideas, this omission of the opposition of two viewpoints, make the *diálogos* a mechanic rather than a dynamic mode. Gracián uses the *diálogos* not to explore the difficulties of a subject but to prove a preconceived idea, with the result that these *realces* could just as easily be subtitled *carta,* or *razonamiento académico,* or *crisis.*

The characters in the dialogue remain undefined and isolated. What communication takes place is accomplished by means of "exterior" stylistic patterns rather than by "interior" conceptual exchange.

The simplest form this takes is of the "grammatical cohesion" formed by a question and answer series. At the end of *Realce* XVII, "El hombre en su punto," the author asks the "Canónigo" three questions, "—¿De modo que se hace un rey?," "—Y pregunto: ese punto a que llegaron, ¿será fijo?," and "—¿De modo que sigue lo moral a lo natural, descaece con la edad la memoria y aun el entendimiento?" (*D.,* XVII, 123). The answers to each question provide a means of refining upon the topic. More subtle means of binding the characters' speeches include word play (agnominatio), as in the following exchange:

> AUTOR. —¿De modo que se *hace* un rey?
> CANÓNIGO. —Sí, que no se *nace* hecho. ... (*D.,* XVII, 123),[37]

---

[37] In this and subsequent citations from *El Discreto,* emphasis added is mine.

an inversion in the order of repeated words to contrast ideas (antimetabole), as in

> Doctor. —Dicen que, *al buen entendedor, pocas palabras.*
> Autor. —Yo diría que, *a pocas palabras, buen entendedor.* ... (*D.,* VIII, 97),

and the use of parallel expressions of equal length and construction (isocolon), an example of which is

> Doctor. —Las verdades que más nos importan vienen siempre *a medio decir.*
> Autor. —Así es, pero recíbanse del advertido *a todo entender.* (*D.,* VIII, 97)

Exact parallelism is, however, usually avoided. In this exchange,

> Autor. —*No hay cosa* más fácil que el *conocimiento* ajeno.
> Doctor. —Ni más dificultosa que el propio (*D.,* VIII, 98),

exact symmetry of the antithetical statements is avoided by the ellipsis of the phrase "No hay cosa" and the substantive "conocimiento" from the second member. In the following lines:

> Autor. —Las motas percibe en los *ojos* del vecino.
> Doctor. —Y las vigas no divisa en los propios (*D.,* VIII, 98),

there is an ellipsis of the substantive "ojos" from the second member. Thus Gracián sacrifices balance for the sake of elegant concision.

This same lack of movement or interplay is discernible in the *alegoría* of *El Discreto*, entitled "Hombre de espera" (*Realce* III). A static, visual quality permeates the *realce*, which begins with a physical description of "la Espera," proceeds to a description of her cortège, first encompassing general types ("hombres," "ancianos," "italianos," etc.), then specific men ("el Gran Capitán," "Alfonso V," etc.).

The possibility of conflict presents itself when an opposing array of Passions confronts the army of Patience. A change in verb tense from the imperfect of description ("iban caminando," "Procedía," "Conducía," "iban," etc.) to the preterite of definite action ("Era esto una muy tarde, cuando vivamente les *comenzó* a tocar arma un furioso escuadrón de monstros, que lo es todo extremo de pasión" [*D.*, III, 86]) indicates the change. But action is deflected towards reflection. "Espera" consults her followers, "consultaba lo hacedero" (*D.*, III, 86), and is duly advised.

The main element of this allegory, the figure of "Espera," is presented in flat, descriptive passages. The personification is established through physical description and identifying objects. The figure does not unfold before the reader nor reveal itself through words and actions. There is no interaction between her and her followers because she uses indirect rather than direct speech: "Mandó hacer alto a la Detención, y ordenó a la Disimulación que los entretuviese mientras consultaba lo hacedero" (*D.*, III, 86).

The possibility of a more vividly conceived personification may be seen in the figure of Fortune in the fable "Arte para ser dichoso" (*Realce* XXIII). Although there is no physical description of her appearance, the details of her actions and her use of direct speech make her representation a more graphic one than that of "Espera." When confronted by Jupiter — "Miróselo la Fortuna de reojo: iba a sonreírse, pero, advirtiendo dónde estaba, mesuróse, y muy caricompuesta, dijo: 'Supremo Júpiter: Una palabra sola quiero que sea mi descargo, y sea ésta: si él es un asno, ¿de quién se queja?'" (*D.*, XXIII, 139). In this case there is a hint of a personality behind the abstract figure. Her actions are not predetermined, for she has a choice of action ("iba a sonreírse") and is capable of deciding which course to take. In this instance Gracián has particularized the abstraction, expanding his use of the personification allegory.

The *realces* which are vituperative include the *sátiras* (*Realces* IX, XI, XX), the *satiricón* (*Realce* XVI), the *crisis* (*Realce* VI), and the *invectiva* (*Realce* XIV).

The aims of a satirist can vary: "A satirist who believes that his society is stuffy, overordered, and convention-ridden employs revolutionary satire, and a satirist who sees his society as chaotic, individualistic, and novelty-seeking tries to rein it by using a defensive satire." [38] The content of Gracián's satires is definitely not revolutionary, for it does not impel to action against a society. On the contrary, he emphasizes order and satirizes any deviation from the norms of established society as extremes from an ideal "center" of moderation.

Neither is the form of the satire conceived of as a dynamic mode. The satires are analytical and consist of an anatomy of the defect under discussion. Their structure is best compared to "... a house of mirrors in which one theme (or vice) is reflected over and over, with distortions and variations but without essential change." [39]

The structure of the satires in *El Discreto* is usually triangular, their pattern being a movement from the general to the specific. In *Realce* XX, "Contra la hazañería," Gracián begins with the all-inclusive term "defectos" — "Grande asunto es el conseguir singulares prendas, pero mayor es el huir vulgares defectos ..." (*D.*, XX, 130). Then he specifies "Uno déstos es la hazañería ..." (*D.*, XX, 131), which is followed by a discussion of specific subtypes within this grouping, such as *soldados* ("Desta suerte hay algunos que no son soldados, pero lo desean ser, y lo afectan y lo procuran parecer ..." [*D.*, XX, 131]), *ministros* ("Muéstranse otros muy ministros afectando celo y ocupación, grandes hombres de hacer siempre negocio del no negocio ..." [*D.*, XX, 131]), *hormiguillas del honor* ("Andan otros mendigando hazañas, hormiguillas del honor, que con un solo grano, que a veces más será paja, van más afanados y satisfechos que los valientes pías que tiran el plaustro de Ceres ..." [*D.*, XX, 132]). In *Realce* IX, "No estar siempre de burlas," the *hombre de burlas* is analyzed by "géneros," mentioned in ascending order, each being worse than the last enumerated. At first they are referred to as "Estos tales" ("Estos tales nunca se sabe cuándo hablan de veras ..." [*D.*, IX, 99]), from which they deteriorate: "Otro género hay aún más enfadoso por lo que tiene de perjudicial. ... Aborrecibles monstros, de quienes huyen todos más que del bruto de Esopo ..." (*D.*, IX, 99-100). The same pattern is followed in

---

[38] Ronald Paulson, *The Fictions of Satire* (Baltimore: The Johns Hopkins Press, 1967), p. 19.
[39] *Ibid.*, p. 43.

Realce XVI, "Contra la figurería," and again the "géneros" of the general defect are listed in ascending gradation. The first group are men who "... siguen una extravagante singularidad y la observan en todo" (*D*., XVI, 117-118); the next group is described as "Otro género hay déstos, que no son hombres, y son aun más figuras, pues si los primeros son enfadosos, éstos son ya ridículos ..." (*D*., XVI, 119); and there is yet another step — "Pero si la singularidad frívola en la corteza del traje es una irrisión, ¿qué será la del interior, digo del ánimo? ... que la mayor figurería es sin duda la del entendimiento" (*D*., XVI, 119). This method of organization through gradation is mentioned in the *Agudeza*: "Cuando van subiendo los asuntos, sale mejor el artificio con la gradación" (*Ag*., LIV, 470).

The vice satirized is depicted against a norm to which it is contrasted. This presentation by contrast may be achieved by the use of antithesis at the level of the sentence or the paragraph.

The sentence construction *no ... sino* is employed repeatedly, with the first part of the clause stating the positive or ideal quality, and the second half, the negative or real quality. Gracián writes of Nero — "No se venció a sí mismo, sino que se rindió" (*D*., VI, 94); his opinion of *hazañería* is that "No nace de alteza de ánimo, sino de vileza de corazón, pues no aspiran a la verdadera honra, sino a la aparente; no a las verdaderas hazañas, sino a la hazañería" (*D*., XX, 131), and adds that "No fueron triunfos los de Domiciano, sino hazañerías; ... triunfaban tal vez por haber muerto un jabalí, que no era triunfo, sino porquería" (*D*., XX, 132); he writes of the *malillas* that "Tropiezan todos en el ladrillo que sobresale a los demás, de modo que no es aquélla eminencia, sino tropiezo; así en muchos el querer campear no viene a ser realce, sino tope" (*D*., XI, 105). Another type of antithetical sentence is found, with a more symmetrically balanced bifurcation: "¿Qué aprovecha la fragancia de los ámbares, si la desmiente la hediondez de las costumbres? Bien pueden embalsamar el cuerpo, pero no inmortalizar el alma" (*D*., XVI, 118-119).

Paragraphs extolling a virtue are interpolated within the satires, serving to emphasize the polarity between the evil presented in the satire and the good praised in the contrast. In the *realce* "No sea desigual" paragraphs concerning the "prudente" and the "varón cuerdo" are interspersed (*D.*, VI, 93); a description of the *malilla* is sharply interrupted by a reference to a discreet man — "Al paso que un varón excelente, ... se retira ..." (*D.*, XI, 105); an account of the actions of the *hombre de figurería* is arrested by a contrasting description — "En las acciones heroicas dice bien la singularidad, ni hay cosa que concilie más veneración que las hazañas" (*D.*, XVI, 118). The juxtaposition of the paragraphs is abrupt. Smoothness of transition is sacrificed for the sake of startling contrast.

Gracián maintains the stance of an omniscient author looking at the objects of his ire. Such a means of presentation is static. Presentation through action and dialogue, rather than through description, would have given a greater sensation of immediacy. These satires are well described as follows:

> In general, the conventional in satire naturally gravitates toward the static and discursive and is always trying to reduce relationships to a static pair of characters, the satirist looking (or railing) at a second man, but without any sense of their conjunction or reciprocity. All the satirist's attention goes into the perception of the satiric observer or the emblematic qualities of the object; the great advantages offered by fictional representation, story, and plot are lost.[40]

Having waived the advantages of representation, the author stresses the use of rhetoric to convince his reader. Gracián's disparaging attitude towards the objects of his attack is achieved linguistically.

The chief means of ridicule is through reduction of the human being. This is achieved by means of "animalization" of the person, as seen in such phrases as "camaleones del aplauso" (*D.*, XX, 131), "hormiguillas del honor" (*D.*, XX, 132), "... es muy de gallinas cacarear todo un día y al cabo poner un huevo" (*D.*, XX, 132), "Quieren algunos ser siempre los gallos de la publicidad, y cantan tanto que enfadan" (*D.*, XI, 105), "... mueren ... éstos como grajos, gracejando mal y porfiando" (*D.*, IX, 101). This method may be related to the fable, in which "Propónese pasar

---

[40] Paulson, *op. cit.*, p. 73.

entre los brutos, árboles y otras cosas inanimadas, por ficción, lo que entre los racionales por realidad. Consiste también el fundamento de su artificio en la semejanza o paridad, pero después el primor está en la entretenida ficción con sus empeños y suspensiones, dándoles la extraordinaria salida" (*Ag.*, LVI, 482). This form of narrative fiction is praised by Gracián, for "Enseñan mucho estos apólogos, y por la semejanza exprimen grandemente la verdad" (*Ag.*, LV, 474).

"Depersonalization" is another reductive mechanism. It consists in negating any individuality to the persons discussed by referring to them by means of nouns and pronouns which connote contempt, such as "Hay sujetos" (*D.*, XI, 104), "Hay algunos" (*D.*, XI, 104), "estos tales" (*D.*, XIV, 115), or by comparing them to inanimate objects. Examples of this include "Otro género hay déstos, que no son hombres, y son aun más figuras ..." (*D.*, XVI, 119), and "Andan de parto, soberbios y hinchados montes ..." (*D.*, XX, 132).

The disparagement of the satirized objects can further be effected through the use of irony, as seen in such remarks as "... usan *graciosísimos* bordones, para ser de todas maneras peregrinos" (*D.*, XVI, 118), and "... en cada ademán o gesto encierran una *profundidad* entre exclamaciones y reticencias ..." (*D.*, XX, 132), and the employment of hyperbolic comparisons. The *hombres de burlas* are "Aborrecibles monstros, de quienes huyen todos más que del bruto de Esopo, que cortejaba a coces y lisonjeaba a bocados" (*D.*, IX, 100); the false soldiers "... meten más máquina en una antojada aventura que el belicoso y afortunado marqués de Torrecusa en un romper las trincheras de Fuenterrabía, en un socorrer a Perpiñán y desbaratar campalmente tantas veces los bravos y numerosos ejércitos de Francia" (*D.*, XX, 131); the *ministros* "... llevan más máquina que el artificio de Juanelo, de igual ruido y poco provecho" (*D.*, XX, 132).

The satirist can also ridicule by showing the discrepancy between his victim's idealized image of himself and the reality projected: "Lo que ellos *presumen* gracia *es* un prodigioso enfado de los que tercian" (*D.*, IX, 100); "... cuando se *presumen* admirados, se *hallan* reídos de todos" (*D.*, XX, 131); "Desta suerte hay algunos que no *son* soldados, pero lo desean ser, y lo afectan y lo procuran *parecer*" (*D.*, XX, 131). Further grounds for ridicule are provided for by the discrepancy between the intended effect of the victim's actions and their real consequences. The *hombres de burlas* "... ganan fama de decidores y pierden el crédito de prudentes; pásase el gusto del chiste, y queda la pena del arrepentimiento: lloran por lo que hicieron reír" (*D.*, IX, 100); the contradictory men "... solicitan la ocasión y andan a caza de empeños, ... todo lo arañan con sus acciones y todo lo desazonan con sus palabras" (*D.*, XIV, 115); the *malilla* suffers the following fate — "Achaque es de todo lo muy bueno que su mucho uso viene a ser abuso ... y, perdiendo aquella primera estimación de raro, consigue el desprecio de vulgar, y es lástima que su misma excelencia le cause su ruina. Truécase aquel aplauso de todos en un enfado de todos" (*D.*, XI, 104). Furthermore, "... la que comenzó a ser una hazañosa vasija, ... viene a rematar en un vilísimo vaso de su ignominia y descrédito" (*D.*, XI, 105). As can be seen, the insistence on the consequences of ill-advised actions provides the satirist with a means of "punishing" his victims.

Intensity of moral condemnation is conveyed to the reader by means of carefully selected adjectives and the use of emphatic synonyms. The author's choice of adjectives is an indication of his attitude towards his subjects. The use of adjectives in Gracián is uncommon, and the "formula" adjective [41] is never employed, for adjectives "... no han de ser continos ni comunes, sino significativos y selectos.... El estilo lacónico los tiene desterrados en primera ley de atender a la intensión, no a la extensión" (*Ag.*, LX, 498). The adjectives used in these satires are not decorative. They are emotional in character, precede the nouns they qualify, and invariably imply moral condemnation. Some examples are "aborrecible frialdad" (*D.*, IX, 100), "prodigioso enfado" (*D.*, IX, 100), "intolerable grosería" (*D.*, XIV, 114), "vanísima hinchazón" (*D.*, XVI, 119), "enfadosa gravedad" (*D.*, XVI, 119), "enfadoso hartazgo" (*D.*, XI, 105), and "Nace la hazañería de una

---

[41] See Wolfgang Kayser, *Interpretación y análisis de la obra literaria*, trans. by María D. Mouton and V. García Yebra (Madrid: Gredos, 1961), p. 142, for distinction between "objective," "affective," and "formula" adjectives.

desvanecida poquedad y de una abatida hinchazón ..." (*D.*, XX, 131).

The pattern of synonymic accumulation of negative terms is extremely effective, as witnessed in the following phrases: "Que es de ver uno destos *destemplados de agudeza, siniestros de ingenio* ..." (*D.*, IX, 101); "... viene a rematar en un vilísimo vaso de su *ignominia y descrédito*" (*D.*, XI, 105); "Pero así como a unos los hace *aborrecibles,* y aun *intratables,* esta enfadosa afectación ..." (*D.*, XVI, 119); "El remedio de todos éstos es poner la mira en otro semejante *afectado, paradojo, extravagante, figurero* ..." (*D.*, XVI, 120).

* * *

The *Criticón,* like the *Discreto,* is an anatomy. In it, however, the author has unified the simple, embryonic structures of the *Discreto* into a continuous and complex movement. The anatomy changes from a static to a dynamic mode, transformed by the search for happiness of the two pilgrims.

Chapter II

EL CRITICÓN AS A NOVEL

Although Gracián had initially intended *El Criticón* to have two parts ("A quien leyere" C., I, 99),[1] the novel consists of three parts (published, respectively, in 1651, 1653, and 1657), entitled "En la primavera de la niñez y en el estío de la juventud," "Juiciosa cortesana filosofía en el otoño de la varonil edad," and "En el invierno de la vejez." Such a division of the life of man had been delineated in the final *realce* of *El Discreto*, entitled "Culta repartición de la vida de un Discreto," in the statement that "Comienza la Primavera en la niñez alegre, tiernas flores en esperanzas frágiles. Síguese el Estío caloroso y destemplado de la mocedad. . . . Entra después el deseado Otoño de la varonil edad coronado de sazonados frutos, en dictámenes, en sentencias y en aciertos. Acaba con todo el Ivierno helado de la vejez . . ." (*D.*, XXV, 142). There are thirteen chapters in each of the first two parts of *El Criticón*, and twelve chapters in the final part. As the chapters in *El Discreto* were called *realces*, so these are denominated *crisis*. This term is mentioned in the *Agudeza* in the discussion of the "crisis juiciosas" and is described as follows: "Las juiciosas calificaciones participan igualmente de la prudencia y de la sutileza. Consiste su artificio en un juicio profundo, en

---

[1] Citations from *El Criticón* are to the critical edition of Miguel Romera-Navarro (3 vols.; Philadelphia: University of Philadelphia Press, 1938-40). Hereafter *El Criticón* will be referred to as *C*. The volume is indicated by capital Roman numerals, the *crisis* by small Roman numerals, and the page by Arabic numerals.

una censura recóndita, y nada vulgar, ya de los yerros, ya de los aciertos" (*Ag.*, XXVIII, 368). [2]

The narrative scheme of the novel is as follows: The aged Critilo, traveling from Goa to Spain in search of his lost wife, Felisinda, is shipwrecked on the island of St. Helena. Here he encounters the young and uncivilized Andrenio, who has been reared since birth by wolves. Critilo and Andrenio establish a relationship as pedagogue and pupil, and only later discover that their true relationship is that of father and son.

They leave the island and begin their journey through the world. The focal point of the first part of *El Criticón*, which encompasses the youth of Andrenio, is Madrid, the courtly center of the world — "... una de sus más célebres ciudades, gran Babilonia de España ..." (I, v, 181). The second part of *El Criticón* deals with middle age, and passage into this stage is symbolized by the travelers' entrance into the province of Aragón, "... de quien dezía aquel su famoso rey ... comparando las naciones de España a las edades, que los aragoneses eran los varones" (I, xiii, 403-404). The pilgrims continue through France into Germany, arriving at the political center of the world, the court of Ferdinand III (1608-1657), where they hope to find Felisinda. They learn that the court has moved to Rome, and therefore they continue south. The crossing of the Alps signifies passage into old age — "... fuéronse encaminando a los canos Alpes, distrito de la temida vejecia (II, xiii, 383). The climax of the last part of the journey is their arrival in Rome, the religious center of the world, which is described as "... el cielo, la coronada cabeça del mundo y mui señora de todo él, la sacra y triunfante Roma, por su valor, saber, grandeza, mando y religión" (II, ii, 58). Here they finally learn that Felisinda, or "Happiness," cannot

---

[2] Romera Navarro, *C.*, I, i, 103, note 2, quotes the definition of *crisis* given by Liñán y Verdugo, *Guía y avisos de forasteros*, 1620, ed. Madrid, 1923: "Crisis es un vocablo de naturaleza griega, de la facultad de la arte médica, que quiere decir juicio, del verbo crino, que es juzgar ..." (p. 215). Otis H. Green relates the term to the definition given in Gabriel de la Gasca y Espinosa's *Manual de avisos del perfecto cortesano...*, published in 1631. See "Sobre el significado de 'crisi(s)' antes de *El Criticón*. Una nota para la historia del conceptismo," *Homenaje a Gracián* (Zaragoza: Institución "Fernando el Católico," 1958), pp. 99-102.

be attained in this world. They confront Death and proceed to the "Isla de la Inmortalidad" which is reserved only for the most deserving of men. Every stage of this allegorical journey is characterized by significant encounters which serve to deepen the pilgrims' understanding of the world and to increase their disillusion.

Theme of El Criticón

Nowhere does Gracián refer to *El Criticón* as a novel. In the prologue to the First Part it is referred to as a "filosofía cortesana" (I, "A quien leyere," 97), and the Third Part is called a "tratado de senectud" (III, "Al que leyere," 14). It can easily be considered a fragmented work whose only unifying factor is the journey of the two main characters. Such a view is expressed by E. Correa Calderón:

> ... pero más que una novela propiamente dicho, es una serie de cuadros sucesivos a los que dan cierta unidad los personajes centrales, un poco a la manera de los *Antojos de mejor vista* de Fernández de Ribera; de *El Diablo Cojuelo*, de Vélez de Guevara; los *Sueños* de Quevedo, y más todavía al modo de los costumbristas de la época, aunque con mayor densidad de pensamiento y mas buída intención en el ingenio.[3]

The two critics who have analyzed the *Criticón* as a novel have reached different conclusions as to its classification. J. F. Montesinos seeks its lineage in the picaresque: "Novela de peregrinación es la suya, novela de camino, de andanzas incesantes remansadas en pocas peripecias. Novela en que el camino determina la marcha, y de la que está ausente la libertad."[4] Francisco Maldonado de Guevara denies this relationship and places it in a different genre: "Así como del *Guzmán*, tanto o más que del *Lazarillo*, procede la novela picaresca europea, o sea la primera novela burguesa, así como también del *Criticón* procede toda la novela pedagógica; el *Telémaco* de Fenelón y las aventuras del

---

[3] *Baltasar Gracián. Su vida y su obra*, p. 193.
[4] "Gracián o la picaresca pura," *Cruz y Raya*, No. 4 (1933), pp. 37-63, rpt. in *Ensayos y estudios de literatura española*, ed. by J. H. Silverman (México: Andrea, 1959), p. 139.

joven Anacharsi, y, a la larga, las novelas educativas de Rousseau y de Goethe." [5] According to Montesinos, the *Criticón* is a novel of "space," the main purpose of which is not the development of a central character but rather the exposure of a world in a multiplicity of scenes and minor characters. According to Maldonado de Guevara, the novel is one of character formation, the main focus of which is the evolution to maturity of Andrenio. [6] The difference is basically one of focus. The events may be viewed objectively on the experiences themselves, or subjectively on the effect of the experiences on the characters.

El Criticón is inherently difficult to classify because of the vastness of its conception. It is a heterogeneous work in which Gracián has incorporated many literary forms:

> En cada uno de los autores de buen genio he atendido a imitar lo que siempre me agradó: las alegorías de Homero, las ficciones de Esopo, lo doctrinal de Séneca, lo juicioso de Luciano, las descripciones de Apuleyo, las moralidades de Plutarco, los empeños de Eliodoro, las suspensiones del Ariosto, las crisis del Boquelino y las mordacidades de Barclayo. (I, 97-98) [7]

---

[5] "La teoría de los géneros literarios y la constitución de la novela moderna," *Estudios dedicados a Menéndez Pidal*, III (1952), 318-319.

[6] Terms used by, Kayser, *op. cit.*, p. 482.

[7] Most of this material was readily available to Gracián in the library of his patron, Vincencio Juan de Lastanosa. The contents of the library are listed in the "Sparvenfeldt" catalog, which has been edited by Karl-Ludwig Selig (see *The Library of Vincencio Juan de Lastanosa, Patron of Gracián*, Travaux d'Humanisme et Renaissance, Vol. XLIII [Genève: E. Droz, 1960]). The library included the following works of the authors mentioned by Gracián: of Homer, *La uligia* (sic) *de Homero* (González Pérez, Amberes, 1550); of Aesop, *Hysopo, su vida y fábulas* (Sevilla, 1590), *Vida y fábulas de Isopo* (Joachim Romero Cepeda, Alcalá, 1590), *Phaedri Aug. Liberti Fabularum Aesopiarum libri V* (Parisijs, 1630); of Seneca, *Proverbios de Seneca* (D. Pedro Díaz de Toledo, Medina, 1555), *Seneca, los siete libros de beneficjs* (Madrid, 1629), *Siete libros* (Licenciado Fernando Navarrete, 1627), *Seneca, sin contradecirse en dificultades políticas* (Diego Ramírez de Avelda, Caragoça, 1653), *Prontuarij iconum pars secunda* and appendix (Lugduni, 1581), *Lucij Annei Senecae opera divi:a in III volumina* (Parisijs, 1640); of Lucian, *Diálogos de Luciano en lengua italiana* (Venecia), *Luciano, sus diálogos traducidos en español* (Don Francisco de Herrera Maldonado, Madrid, 1621); of Apuleus, *El asno de oro* (Madrid, 1601); of Plutarch, *Apotegmas de Plutarco* (Alcalá, 1533), *Morales de Plutarco* (Alcalá de Enares, 1548); of Ariosto, *Discursos sobre los primeros cantos del Orlando en italiano* (Laura Terracina, Venecia, 1550), *El Orlando Furioso en 32 en*

It is more appropriate, therefore, to examine *El Criticón* in relationship to the novel as a genre, rather than to try to classify it within the genre.

The first criterion of the novelistic qualities of *El Criticón* must be Gracián's own judgment concerning the intention of the *epopeya*. He writes in the *Agudeza* that it is a "Composición sublime por la mayor parte, que en los hechos, sucesos y aventuras de un supuesto, los menos verdaderos, y los más fingidos y tal vez todos, va ideando los de todos los mortales. Forja un espejo común y fabrica una testa de desengaños" (*Ag.*, LVI, 477). This stress on disillusion as the principal purpose of the "agudeza compuesta" coincides with a key concept in modern critical theory on the definition of the novel. Some recent statements on the novel include the following: "More than any other form, it was immediately and widely accepted as an instrument for the discovery of truth. More, it was a weapon for the destruction of pretense and unreality. Cervantes wrote *Don Quixote* primarily as an attack on the untruth, the deliberate non-realism, of such romances as *Amadís de Gaula*,"[8] as well as "The novel records the passage from a state of innocence to a state of experience, from that ignorance which is bliss to a mature recognition of the actual way of the world."[9] The same critic

---

italiano (Venecia, 1587); of Boccalini, *Abisos del Parnaso en ytaliano* (Venecia, 1612), *Visos del Parnaso* (Madrid, 1634), *Discursos políticos* (Huesca, 1640), *Pietra del Paragone* (Cormopoli, 1615); of Barclay, *Argenis* (Parisijs, 1625), *El Argenis* (D.n Joseph Pellicer, Madrid, 1626). It is interesting to note the absence from the catalog of Heliodorus, whose *Ethiopica*, or *The Adventures of Theogenes and Chariclea*, was extremely influential in the conception of *El Criticón*. For further information of Boccalini's influence in Spain, consult R. H. Williams, *Boccalini in Spain* (Menasha, Wis.: George Banta, 1946), and for further information on Heliodorus in Spain, see the "Introduction" to Francisco López Estrada's edition of Fernando de Mena's translation, the *Historia Etiópica de los amores de Teágenes y Cariclea* (Madrid: Aldus, 1954). On Gracián's literary preferences, see Karl-Ludwig Selig, "Some Remarks on Gracián's Literary Taste and Judgments," *Homenaje a Gracián* (Zaragoza: Institución "Fernando el Católico," 1958), pp. 155-162.

[8] John Wain, "The Conflict of Forms in Contemporary English Literature," *Essays on Literature and Ideas* (New York and London: Macmillan & Co., 1963), rpt. in *The Novel: Modern Essays in Criticism*, ed. by Robert Murray Davis (Englewood Cliffs, N. J.: Prentice Hall, 1966), p. 292.

[9] Maurice Z. Shroder, "The Novel as a Genre," *The Massachusetts Review* (1963), rpt. in *The Novel: Modern Essays in Criticism*, ed. by Robert Murray Davis (Englewood Cliffs, N. J.: Prentice Hall, 1966), p. 44.

adds that the novel essentially records a "process of disillusionment." [10]

This conflict between illusion and reality which inevitably terminates in disillusionment is considered by Georges Lukacs to be the crucial characteristic of the novel which distinguishes it from the epic. There is a "... faille entre l'intérieur et l'extérieur, significative d'une différence essentielle entre le moi et le monde, d'une non-adéquation entre l'âme et l'action." [11] The ideas of the individual are no longer in conformity with the reality surrounding him, with the result that his situation becomes problematical: "Le danger n'apparaît qu'à partir du moment où le monde extérieur a perdu contact avec les idées, où ces idées deviennent en l'homme des faits psychiques subjectifs: des idéaux.... dès lors qu'elles sont changées en idéaux, l'individualité perd le caractère immédiatement organique qui faisait d'elle une realité non problématique." [12]

The theme of *desengaño* is undoubtedly the central motif of the *Criticón*. [13] As the ideals of the person cannot be satisfied by the reality of the world, the only solution is withdrawal into the solitude suggested by Critilo of "ver, oír y callar" (I, vi,

---

[10] *Ibid.*, p. 46.

[11] *La théorie du roman*, trans. by Jean Clairevoye (Switzerland: Gonthier, 1963), p. 20.

[12] *Ibid.*, p. 73.

[13] The pessimism and disillusion of Gracián have been mentioned by every critic of this author. The connection is frequently made between the author's attitude and the deteriorating historical circumstances of Spain. A typical statement is that of Karl Vossler: "No se le escapaba que el Imperio universal de los Habsburgos se cuarteaba por todos sus flancos. Con ávido mirar contemplaba el desmoronamiento de las provincias, la rebeldía de los catalanes, el derrumbamiento económico, y tenía una sensibilidad agudísima para la mengua de las energías morales. ... Su novela satírica *El Criticón* está llena de presentimientos y ecos sombríos, incluso de honda desconfianza frente a toda la grandeza y magnificencia del mundo, frente a todo el señuelo y la belleza de la vida terrenal." See "Introducción a Gracián," *Revista de Occidente*, CXLVII (1935), 334. Schröder, *op. cit.*, makes a most interesting connection of the theme of *desengaño* and the usual structure of the *crisi*. He shows that the process of *desengaño* proceeds in three stages, from the seduction by a false concept, to close examination of the *bonum*, to final disillusionment. These three stages correspond to three sections in the organization of the *crisi* (p. 83).

213).[14] This is the only stance possible to a superior being in a corrupt world.[15]

In order to illustrate the theme of conflict between the self's illusion and the world's reality, Gracián could have written a didactic, theological work. He eschewed this possibility, however, because of its lack of imaginative appeal. His opinion of the "... teólogos, assí escolásticos como morales y expositivos" is that "... los más de éstos ya no hazen otro que trasladar y bolver a repetir lo que ya estava dicho. Tienen bravo cacoetes de estampar y es muy poco lo que añaden de nuevo; poco o nada inventan" (III, viii, 272-273). Instead he chose to vivify his teachings by means of narrative fiction.

Structural Principle of El Criticón

The predominating structural principle with which Gracián began *El Criticón* is that of the "romance,"[16] in spite of his

---

[14] This is a proverbial statement, the usual form of which is "oír, y ver, y callar." Variations include "Oír, y ver, y callar, hace buen hombre y buena mujer," "Oír, y ver, y callar, recias cosas son de obrar," and "Oír, y ver, y callar, y preguntado, decir verdad con libertad." See Gonzalo Correas, *Vocabulario de refranes y frases proverbiales y otras fórmulas comunes de la lengua castellana* (Madrid: Revista de Archivos, Bibliotecas y Museos, 1924), p. 371. Francisco Rodríguez Marín adds "Oír, ver y callar, vida ejemplar" in his *Los 6.666 refranes de mi última rebusca* (Madrid: Bermejo, 1934), p. 121. Correas defined the statement as "Esto se usa mucho amonestando." Ramón Caballero, in his *Diccionario de modismos de la lengua castellana* (Buenos Aires: Librería el Ateneo, 1942), writes that "Oír, ver y callar" is a "Frase hecha que aconseja discreción, prudencia, etc." (p. 870). The theory presented in the *Agudeza* is thus put into practice, for in the section on the uses of erudition, Gracián notes the usefulness of proverbs: "... hasta los adagios y refranes valen mucho: han de ser comúnmente escogidos por huir la vulgaridad" (Ag., LVIII, 490). The extensive use of *refranes* in the *Criticón* can be appreciated by seeing Romero-Navarra's "Registro de refranes y dichos proverbiales" included as an appendix to Vol. III of his edition of *El Criticón*, pp. 498-506. For more detailed discussion of Gracián's use of proverbs, see especially Samuel Gili Gaya, "Agudeza, modismos y lugares comunes," *Homenaje a Gracián* (Zaragoza: Institución "Fernando el Católico," 1958), pp. 89-97, as well as Francisco Ynduraín, "Refranes y 'frases hechas' en la estimativa literaria del Siglo XVII," *AFA*, VII (1955), 103-130.

[15] See Douglas Bush, "The Isolation of the Renaissance Hero," *Reason and Imagination. Studies in the History of Ideas, 1600-1800*, ed. by J. A. Mazzeo (New York: Columbia University Press, 1962), pp. 57-69.

[16] Northrop Frye uses the term "mythos" to describe the structural principle of a literary work. See "Archetypal Criticism: Theory of Myths,"

condemnation of the novels of knight-errantry as "—Trasto viejo ... de alguna barbería" (II, i, 35).

The ingredients of "romance" concern Andrenio and include the following general features: His birth is mysterious since he is of unknown parentage. As he explains to Critilo: "—Yo —dixo— ni sé quién soy ni quién me ha dado el ser, ni para qué me lo dió" (I, i, 110). Having been abandoned, he is rescued and reared by an animal: "Allí me ministró el primer sustento una de estas que tú llamas fieras y yo llamava madre" (I, i, 111). Critilo, the real father, is not recognized as such until later when the "anagnorisis"[17] or recognition takes place, and adopts the role of a wise guide.

Andrenio's state of innocence regarding the evils of the world and of women makes him comparable to Adam before the Fall: "—¡O lo que te embidio —exclamó Critilo— tanta felicidad no imaginada, privilegio único del primer hombre y tuyo!" (I, ii, 119). From the isolated island Andrenio and his guide proceed into the world on a quest, the goal of which is a feminine figure, defined as a "mother" to Andrenio and "wife" to Critilo. Their destination can be reached only after a long and dangerous journey involving perilous struggles, during the course of which Andrenio must contend with the onslaught of a corrupt world and evil women such as "Falsirena" and "Volusia." His active struggle for temperance against the assault of passions is finally rewarded by the acceptance into the "Isla de Inmortalidad."[18]

There is, therefore, a bond between Gracián's moral allegory and medieval chivalric romance, for in addition to the structural motifs, *El Criticón* shares with the tales of knights-errant the general medieval milieu of castles, hermitages, crossroads, innumerable encounters, and battles. Perhaps the most outstanding example of the transference of chivalric romance into allegory is

---

Anatomy of Criticism: Four Essays (New York: Atheneum Press, 1969), pp. 131-239.

[17] Term used by Aristotle in the *Poetics* (1452 a XI), which, with "peripety" or reversal, constitutes a complex action in a tragic plot. See *The "Poetics" of Aristotle*, trans. by S. H. Butcher (London: Macmillan and Co., 1911), pp. 41-42.

[18] Typical motifs of the "romance" are discussed by Frye in his *Anatomy of Criticism*, pp. 186-206.

Spenser's *Faerie Queene,* which is intimately connected with the Arthurian tales. Rosemund Tuve writes that

> It seems to me that Spenser recognized, from significances given to ancient romance plots in a few great well-known pieces, that romances were a sort of "historicall fiction" naturally amenable to being read as "continued Allegory, or darke conceit," though primarily "historicall" and delighting.
> ... ...
> ... Moreover, romances demonstrate, and Spenser must have observed this, the accepted convention of being *intermittently* allegorically significant—and indeed would be unreadable otherwise. [19]

The tradition of imbuing secular material with religious significance is apparent in Spain in both poetry and prose. [20] An example of such a transference is the publication in 1575 of Sebastián de Córdoba's *Obras de Boscán y Garcilaso trasladadas a materias cristianas y religiosas.* In the same manner, the knight-errant tales were assimilated into versions *a lo divino.*

Another form of spiritualization of secular material is the allegorical interpretation given to Heliodorus' Greek romance, known in seventeenth-century Spain as *Historia Etiópica de los amores de Teágenes y Cariclea.* The first versions of the romance to appear in Spain were the *Historia de los amores de Clareo y Florisea* of Alonso Núñez de Reinoso, published in 1552, and the *Selva de aventuras* of Jerónimo de Contreras, published in 1565. [21] The culmination of these attempts to imitate Heliodorus is Cervantes' *Los trabajos de Persiles y Segismunda, Historia Setentrional,* which appeared in 1617.

---

[19] *Allegorical Imagery. Some Medieval Books and Their Posterity* (Princeton, N. J.: Princeton University Press, 1966), pp. 390-391.

[20] Bruce W. Wardropper terms the process *contrafactum,* and discusses its history in lyrical poetry in Spain as well as other European countries in *Historia de la poesía lírica a lo divino en la cristiandad occidental* (Madrid: Revista de Occidente, 1958). For definition of the term, see Wolfgang Kayser, ed., *Kleines literarisches Lexikon,* Sammlung Dalp, 17, Vol. III (München: Francke, 1966), p. 211.

[21] These works are available in Vol. III of the *B.A.E.,* ed. by D. Buenaventura Carlos Aribau (Madrid: Rivadeneyra, 1846), pp. 431-468 and 469-505, respectively.

In order to understand Cervantes' interest in Heliodorus, it is useful to consider the *Philosophía antigua poética* of Alonso López Pinciano, which was published in 1596 and which had a profound effect on Cervantes' literary theory. [22] In the section on the epic, Pinciano states that verse is not the exclusive characteristic of the epic — "... de manera que los amores de Theágenes y Cariclea, de Heliodoro, y los de Leucipo y Clitofonte de Achiles Tacio, son tan épica como la Ilíada y la Eneyda, ..." [23] and sanctions an allegorical reading of the epic. He says of Heliodorus that although the novel is entitled an *historia* and not a *poema*, "... no hay duda que sea poeta, y de los más finos épicos que han hasta agora escripto; a lo menos, ninguno tiene más deleyte trágico y ninguno en el mundo añuda y suelta mejor que él; tiene muy buen lenguaje y muy altas sentencias; y si quisiessen exprimir alegoría, la sacarían dél no mala." [24]

Cervantes' suggestions for a prose epic which are stated in the *Quixote* (I, 47) are brought to fruition in his *Persiles y Segismunda*. The author refers to this novel as one "... que se atreve a competir con Heliodoro, si ya por atrevido no sale con las manos en la cabeza..." [25] and adds that "... ha de ser o el más malo o el mejor que en nuestra lengua se haya compuesto, quiero decir de los de entretenimiento. ..." [26]

Cervantes' insistence that his last novel is his best work suggests to the critic Walter Boehlich that the author felt that he had not only successfully imitated Heliodorus, but surpassed him. For, just as Tasso, in his *Gerusalemme liberata*, had created a

---

[22] For influence of Pinciano on Cervantes, see E. C. Riley, *Cervantes' Theory of the Novel* (Oxford: Clarendon Press, 1962). Alban K. Forcione, in his *Cervantes, Aristotle and the "Persiles"* (Princeton, N. J.: Princeton University Press, 1970), furthers the discussion of Cervantes' attitude towards neo-Aristotelian literary theory by pointing out instances of the author's anticlassical stance.

[23] Citations are from the edition of Alfredo Carballo Picazo, Vol. III (Madrid: Consejo Superior de Investigaciones Científicas, Instituto "Miguel de Cervantes," 1963), p. 165.

[24] *Ibid.*, p. 167.

[25] "Prólogo al lector," *Novelas ejemplares*, p. 770. All citations of Cervantes are to the text of the *Obras completas*, ed. by Ángel Valbuena Prat (Madrid: Aguilar, 1965).

[26] "Dedicatoria al Conde de Lemos," *Don Quijote de la Mancha*, II, in *Obras Completas*, p. 1271.

Christian verse epic to rival those of Homer and Virgil, so he wished to compose the Christian prose epic and become, as it were, the "Christian" Heliodorus.[27] He accordingly changed the title from *amores* to *trabajos* in order to imply a tale of Christian suffering,[28] and converted the adventurous journey into a pilgrimage from the north, the world of unbelief, to Rome, the center of the world of faith.[29] The symbolic meaning of Rome can be seen in the following statement of Periandro (the name by which Persiles is known in the novel): "Procura, señora, tener salud, que yo procuraré la salida de esta tierra, y dispondré lo mejor que pudiere de este viaje: que, aunque Roma es el cielo de la tierra, no está puesta en el cielo, y no habrá trabajos ni peligros que nos nieguen del todo el llegar a ella, puesto que los haya para dilatar el camino. . . ."[30]

The motif of the pilgrimage to Rome, as well as certain structural features such as beginning *in medias res* and closing in a circle, will be reiterated by Gracián in *El Criticón*. Cervantes' tale is one of purification through suffering; Gracián's tale is one of purification through *desengaño*. Both authors, however, were able to imbue the Greek novel with the spirit of the Counter-Reformation.

Spatial and Temporal Structure of El Criticón

The basic structural principle of *El Criticón* is age, as seen by the titles given to the three parts: "En la primavera de la niñez y en el estío de la juventud," "Juiciosa cortesana filosofía en el otoño de la varonil edad," and "En el invierno de la vejez." The cycle of human life will, therefore, be the basis of the novel, and its pattern will be reiterated by the cyclical rhythm of nature and the rising and falling movement of civilization. The human cycle is presided over by an archetypal female figure. As explained by Northrop Frye:

---

[27] "Heliodorus Christianus. Cervantes und der byzantinische Roman," *Freundesgabe für Ernst Robert Curtius* (Bern: Francke, 1956), p. 106.
[28] *Ibid.*, pp. 108-109.
[29] *Ibid.*, p. 114.
[30] *Los trabajos de Persiles y Segismunda*, in *Obras completas*, p. 1590 (Bk. II, ch. vii).

> To the extent that the encyclopaedic form concerns itself with the cycle of human life, an ambivalent female archetype appears in it, sometimes benevolent, sometimes sinister, but usually presiding over and confirming the cyclical movement. One pole of her is represented by an Isis figure, a Penelope or Solveig who is the fixed point on which the action ends. The goddess who frequently begins and ends the cyclical action is closely related. This figure is Athene in the *Odyssey* and Venus in the *Aeneid;* in Elizabethan literature, for political reasons, usually some variant of Diana, like the Faerie Queen in Spenser. [31]

In *El Criticón* the figure is, of course, Felisinda. Comparable examples in Spanish literature include Amadís de Gaula's Oriana and Quijote's Dulcinea.

Spatial Structure

Like its Greek prototype, Heliodorus' *The Adventures of Theagenes and Chariclea*, and like Cervantes' *Los trabajos de Persiles y Segismunda*, the spatial composition of *El Criticón* is circular.

The action begins on the island of St. Helena. The island, described as "o perla del mar o esmeralda de la tierra" (I, i, 103), uninhabited by human beings except for Andrenio, rich in fruit and abundant in fish, symbol of God's creation, is associated with Eden before the Fall. The novel terminates at the "Isla de Inmortalidad" which is blessed with timelessness. There are no clocks, no aging, no death (III, xii, 371-372). Thus *El Criticón* moves from the innocence of Eden and the timelessness of the prelapsarian state, through the postlapsarian corruption, back to a state of timeless grace. In other words, the initial terrestrial Eden is subsequently redefined as a celestial Utopia.

It is significant that both geographical locations are islands, for passage to them requires a ritualistic journey through water. The waters traversed between St. Helena and the world are corrupted and raped, for man in his greed "... surca los mares y sonda sus más profundos senos solicitando perlas, los ámbares y los corales para adorno de su vizarro desvanecimiento" (I, ii,

---

[31] *Op. cit.*, pp. 322-323.

116). The ships which ride the waters bear gold, the root of all corruption. The waters to the "Isla de Inmortalidad," on the other hand, are traversed only by the chosen "remando y sudando" (III, xii, 377). Instead of denoting man's corruption, they bear witness to his achievement, for the blackness of the river Lethe is reinterpreted as being "... de la preciosa tinta de los famosos escritores que en ella bañan sus plumas" (III, xii, 376). A journey over these waters is pleasing to all the senses: "Recréase el oído con la suave música, los ojos con las cosas hermosas, el olfato con las flores, el gusto en un combite; pero el entendimiento, con la erudita y discreta conversación entre tres o quatro amigos entendidos, y no más, porque en passando de aí, es bulla y confusión" (III, xii, 379).

The terminal points of the geographical movement from island to island do not, however, imply simply cyclical return. The journey also entails progress, for the pilgrims move upwards from earth to heaven. Upon their arrival at the "Isla de Inmortalidad," Andrenio cries "—¡Tierra, tierra!," which the "Inmortal" corrects to "—¡Cielo, cielo!" (III, xii, 382). In order to incorporate both the circular and linear patterns, the journey could be more adequately described as spherical, the point of termination being on a higher, wider plane than the point of departure.

The spiritual progress implied by the journey is expressed by means of geographical symbols. As indicated by W. Krauss: "El viaje de Critilo y Andrenio a través del mundo de las culturas nacionales es, a la vez, un viaje a lo largo de toda la vida humana, de la historia, del desarrollo del hombre natural hasta la perfección universal."[32] The initial and terminal points of the journey are especially significant. The pilgrims begin their pilgrimage in Spain, and end it in Italy, countries to which Gracián attributes the following symbolic significance:

> Porque es de notar que España se está oy del mismo modo que Dios la crió, sin averla mejorado en cosa sus moradores, fuera de lo poco que labraron en ella los romanos: los montes se están oy tan sobervios y zahareños como al principio, los ríos innavegables corriendo por

---

[32] *Op. cit.*, p. 117.

> el mismo camino que les abrió la naturaleza, las campañas se están páramos, sin aver sacado para su riego las azequias, las tierras incultas; de suerte que no ha obrado la industria. Al contrario, la Italia está tan otra y tan mejorada que no la conocerían sus primeros pobladores que viniessen, porque los montes están allanadaos, convertidos en jardines, los ríos navegables, los lagos son vivares de pezes, los mares poblados de famosas ciudades, coronado de muelles y de puertos, las ciudades todas por un parejo hermoseadas de vistosos edificios, templos, palacios y castillos, sus plaças adornadas de brolladores y fuentes, las campañas son Elisios, llenas de jardines. ...
> (III, ix, 295-296)

He also describes Spain as the country of Juno, the Goddess of Fertility, and Italy as the country of Minerva, the Goddess of Wisdom (III, ix, 296-297).

It can be seen that the progress from Spain to Italy is, culturally, a movement from nature to art, and, individually, a movement from passion, or control by the body, to reason, or control by the mind. In the same way that the *hombre* must be molded into an *persona*, nature must be perfected by art:[33]

> Es el arte complemento de la naturaleza y un otro segundo ser que por estremo la hermosea y aun pretende excederla en sus obras. Préciase de aver añadido un otro mundo artificial al primero, suple de ordinario los descuydos de la naturaleza, perficionándola en todo: que sin este socorro del artificio, quedara inculta y grosera.
> (I, viii, 243)

The city where the journey begins is Madrid; the city where it ends is Rome. Rome is the point where the process of forming the *persona* is culminated, for it is "... oficina de los grandes

---

[33] This commonplace that art complements and perfects nature is found in the *Protrepticus* of Aristotle, who also mentions it in reference to education in the *Politics* (VII, 1337, a 2). See J. A. Close, "Art and Nature in Antiquity and the Renaissance," *JHI*, XXX (1969), 472-474. On this subject also see E. W. Tayler, *Nature and Art in Renaissance Literature* (New York: Columbia University Press, 1964). For background material and discussion of the meanings assigned to "nature," see Arthur O. Lovejoy and George Boas, *Primitivism and Related Ideas in Antiquity* (New York: Octagon Books, Inc., 1965).

hombres: aquí se forjan las grandes testas, aquí se sutiliçan los ingenios y aquí se hazen los hombres muy personas" (III, ix, 280). Because it is the most eminent place on earth, it is necessarily the point of meeting of the two spheres where contact is made between the natural world and the supernatural world. As explained by Argos to the travelers: "Essa que te parece a ti andar entre pies de la tierra, es el cielo, la coronada cabeça del mundo y mui señora de todo él, la sacra y triunfante Roma, por su valor, saber, grandeza, mando y religión." Its high obelisks represent the union of earth and sky: "... lo que pretendieron fué coser la tierra con el cielo, empresa que pareció impossible a los mismos Césares, y éstos la consiguieron" (II, ii, 58).

Temporal Structure

The basic temporal structure of the *Criticón* is cyclical, the process of change being endemic to the natural world and contrasting with the divine world, the "Isla de Inmortalidad," where no change occurs.

The cyclical symbols are presented in four phases. In the human world, age determines the four stages, which correspond to the titles of the three parts of the *Criticón* — "niñez" and "juventud," "varonil edad," "vejez." In the vegetable world, the seasons reoccur rhythmically, coinciding with the ages of man — "primavera de la niñez," "estío de la juventud," "otoño de la varonil edad," "invierno de la vejez." [34] The growth pattern of fruits is also seasonal, as explained by Critilo to Andrenio:

---

[34] Man is compared to the seasons in Horace (*Odes*, IV, vii, 9-16):

> frigora mitescunt zephyris, ver proterit aestas
>   interitura, simul
> pomifer autumnus fruges effuderit, et mox
>   bruma recurrit iners.
> damma tamen celeres reparant caelestia lunae;
>   nos ubi decidimus,
> quo pius Aeneas, quo Tullus dives et Ancus
>   pulvis et umbra sumus.

See James Gow, ed., *Carmina* (Cambridge: Cambridge University Press, 1914), p. 110. S. K. Heninger attributes the pervasiveness of the pattern of four in the Renaissance to the influence of the Pythagorean tetrad, which provided an ideological basis for the microcosm-macrocosm analogy: "Pythagoras was the first man in western culture to propose a persistent

> ... pues previno que no todos los frutos se sazonessen juntos, sino que se fuessen dando vez según la variedad de los tiempos y necessidad de los vivientes: unos comiençan en la primavera, ... sirven otros, más frescos, para aliviar el abrasado estío, y los secos, como más durables y calientes, para el estéril invierno; ... de suerte, que acabado un fruto, entra el otro, para que con comodidad puedan recogerse y guardarse, entreteniendo todo el año con abundancia y con regalo (I, iii, 131)

In the world of fire, the celestial spheres, the sun and moon, create the pattern of morning and evening. The sun's disappearance moves Andrenio to say:

> ... la grandeza de mi contento se corvirtió presto en un excesso de pesar al ver, digo, al no verle, trocóse la alegría del nacer en el horror del morir, el trono de la mañana en el túmulo de la noche. ... Creí no verle más, con que quedé muriendo. Pero volví presto a resucitar entre nuevas admiraciones a un cielo coronado de luminarias, haziendo fiesta a mi contento. (I, ii, 123)

The stars also appear and disappear, "... saliendo unas y ocultándose otras" (I, ii, 124). Water creates its own cycle, which corresponds to the age pattern of man: "Es la niñez fuente risueña: ... Precipítase ya la mocedad en un impetuoso torrente.... Sossiégase, ya río, en la varonil edad. ... Mas, ¡ai!, que al cabo viene a parar en el amargo mar de la vejez ..." (II, i, 17-18). The fourth phase of this cycle of brook-river-sea, the rain, is alluded to later: "Hasta las aguas, al cabo de los años mil, bolvían a correr por donde solían ..." (III, x, 308). This whole rotary movement of recurrence is summed up by Critilo:

> —Traçó las cosas de modo el supremo Artífice —dixo Critilo— que ninguna se acabasse que no començasse luego otro; de modo que de las ruinas de la primera se levanta la segunda. Con esto verás que el mismo fin es principio, la destrucción de una criatura es generación de la otra. Quando parece que se acaba todo, entonces comiença de nuevo: la naturaleza se renueva, el mundo

---

pattern that prevails throughout each level of creation — which is, of course, the ideological basis for the entire microcosm analogy" (p. 15). See "Some Renaissance Versions of the Pythagorean Tetrad," *SRen,* VIII (1961), 7-33.

se remoça, la tierra se establece y el divino govierno es admirado y adorado. (I, iii, 139)

It is understood that man's recurrence in this circular scheme is not individual, but generic.

Although the generic relationship of an individual to cosmic time is circular, his personal relationship to historic time is linear.[35] From Andrenio's first awakening to consciousness until the end of the novel, both the protagonists are firmly within the grasp of time without any possibility of escape. The process of aging and death is a continuous threat.

The process of life of the individual described in the beginning parts of *El Criticón* is best depicted by a parabolic curve of ascent, zenith, and inevitable descent to death, a pattern which acts as an insistent *memento mori*. Any allusion to eternal time in the religious sense is subjugated to the pressure of historical time. The sense of time in *El Criticón* may be explained with the following analysis of Hans Meyerhoff:

> With the fading belief in eternal order, time came to be experienced more and more within the context, order and direction of human history. ...
> ... ...
> ... Time, historical time, became the only medium in which human life unfolded and fulfilled itself. Its order was set by the causal relations constituting the history of man or nature, by the things done in and undone by time. It unfolded in one direction only, as a constant challenge or as a source of frustration, moving toward an open future of novelty and creation or toward a closed future of oblivion and death. ... Common to both attitudes was the overwhelming realization, or rediscovery, that time confronted man with nothing but relentless change and transitoriness, that within the constant transformations of nature and society "naught may endure but Mutability." [36]

---

[35] For distinction between "cosmic," "historical," and "existential" time, see John Henry Raleigh, "The English Novel and Three Kinds of Time," *Sewanee Review*, LXII (July-September 1954), rpt. in *The Novel: Modern Essays in Criticism*, ed. by Robert Murray Davis (Englewood Cliffs, N. J.: Prentice Hall, 1966), pp. 242-252.

[36] *Time in Literature* (Berkeley: University of California Press, 1955), pp. 94-95.

Two facets of this analysis are especially relevant to Gracián. The first is his strong awareness of transitoriness. Georges Poulet notes of the seventeenth century that

> Mais de toutes les inquiétudes du siècle la plus fréquente et la plus douloureuse est celle que fait naître le sentiment de la discontinuité de la durée. Réfugiée en le moment où elle existe, la conscience voit ses modes successifs d'existence passer l'un après l'autre et lui échapper. Se sentir vivre, c'est se sentir à chaque instant laisser derrière soi un instant que *était* le moi lui-même. [37]

Gracián feels this so keenly that he considers even truth to be subject to time, for much is simply a question of taste. He writes in the *Agudeza* that "Por raros, por superlativos que sean los conceptos, si no tienen estrella suelen malograrse, que esto de ventura es achaque trascendiente. ¿Qué diré del uso? Que corren unos en un tiempo y arrincónanse otros, y vuelven éstos a tener vez porque no hay cosa nueva para el sol. ... Importa mucho el pensar al uso, no menos que la gala del ingenio" (*Ag.*, LX, 499). This is one reason why history acquires such importance in the thinking of Gracián. History must be depended upon for objective truth, and therefore any books written in adulation must be destroyed — "... no hay cosa que más presto caiga que la mentirosa lisonja que no tiene fundamento; antes solicita enfado" (III, viii, 269).

The other facet of Meyerhoff's statement which applies to Gracián is his attitude toward the future, which is closed and death-oriented. This constitutes a contrast to the Renaissance attitude toward time, when, as described by Poulet:

> La temporalité n'apparaissait donc plus seulement comme la marque indélébile de la mortalité, mais aussi comme le théâtre et le champ d'action où, en dépit de sa mortalité, la créature peut révéler son authentique divinité, et conquérir une immortalité personnelle. Nul besoin d'une aide supplémentaire et surnaturelle. Solidaire de toutes les époques, possesseur, par la pensée, de l'univers histo-

---

[37] *Études sur le Temps Humain* (Edinburgh: Edinburgh University Press, 1949), p. 22.

rique comme de l'univers spatial, l'homme se sentait créateur, si pas de son être, au moins de son destin. [38]

Gracián expresses man's finiteness by means of metaphoric comparisons to the natural cycle. Withered flowers are described as a

> —Retrato al fin —ponderó Critilo— de la humana fragilidad. Es la hermosura agradable ostentación del començar; ... mas todo viene a parar en la tristeza de un marchitarse, en el horror de un ponerse, y en la fealdad de un morir, haziendo continuamente del ojo la inconstancia común al desengaño especial. (I, iii, 133)

In this statement, the steady yet insistent cadence of the isocolons ("... en la tristeza de un marchitarse, en el horror de un ponerse, y en la fealdad de un morir") accentuates the inexorability of death. These phrases are synonymic and therefore emphatic, and their effect is enhanced by the gradation within the series. For, although all the infinitives ("marchitarse," "ponerse," morir") refer to death, the impact of the first two is mitigated by metaphoric comparisons, to flowers that wither and to the sun that sets. The final infinitive, "morir," is, however, stark and direct. There is a distinct lack of movement in the passage becaues of the scarcity of transitive verbs and the preponderance of verbal nouns. The verbs have, as it were, been frozen into nouns. They have lost their dynamic characteristics, and have acquired a rigidity relevant to the meaning of the passage.

There is also a comparison to the water cycle to symbolize man's movement toward death:

> Acertadamente discurría quien comparava el vivir del hombre al correr del agua, quando todos morimos y como ella nos vamos deslizando. Es la niñez fuente risueña: nace entre menudas arenas, que de los polvos de la nada salen los lodos del cuerpo, brolla tan clara como sencilla, ríe lo que no murmura, bulle entre campanillas de viento, arrúllase entre pucheros y cíñese de verduras que le fajan. Precipítase ya la mocedad en un impetuoso torrente, corre, salta, se arroja y se despeña, tropeçando

---

[38] *Ibid.*, p. 15.

> con las guijas, rifando con las flores, va echando espumas, se enturbia y se enfurece. Sossiégase, ya río, en la varonil edad, va passando tan callado quan profundo, caudalosamente vagaroso, todo es fondos sin ruido; dilátase espaciosamente grave, fertiliza los campos, fortaleze las ciudades, enriqueze las provincias y de todas maneras aprovecha. Mas ¡ai!, que al cabo viene a parar en el amargo mar de la vejez, abismo de achaques, sin que le falte una gota. ... (II, i, 17-18)

Gracián's initial resonance of Jorge Manrique prompts the reader to compare the use of the same metaphor in the two authors. In Jorge Manrique "Nuestras vidas son los ríos / que van a dar en el mar / que es el morir," there is simply a comparison A is to B. But this does not satisfy Gracián, and he proceeds to dissect this metaphor, to analyze it as far as he can go. To the synthetic A-B comparison he adds its analytical extension: A^1-B^1 *(niñez-fuente)*, A^2-B^2 *(mocedad-torrente)*, A^3-B^3 *(varonil edad-río)*, A^4-B^4 *(vejez-mar)*. Once the conceit has been established, it harmoniously develops into a set of correspondences.[39]

The essence of the meaning of the paragraph is delivered by the verb, always in initial position. In the first age ("Es la niñez"), the verbs are mainly onomatopoeic, "brolla," "ríe," "bulle," referring to cheerful, active sounds; in the second age ("Precipítase"), there is an asyndetic accumulation of verbs of action, which well express the furious waters; in the third age "Sossiégase"), the serenity of the expanded waters is revealed by the use of adverbs, "caudalosamente," "espaciosamente," and the calm symmetry of the last phrases ("fertiliza ... fortaleze ... enriqueze"); in the final age ("Mas ¡ai!"), the effect of movement cut short is given by the confrontation of the active "viene" and the static "parar" in the expression "viene a parar." The movement of the imagery in the paragraph from life to death can be foreseen from the very beginning in the violent "hysteron proteron," where Gracián, by reversing the normal order in the phrase "quando todos morimos y como ella nos vamos deslizando," implies that death precedes life.

---

[39] For relationship between the conceit and the doctrine of correspondence, see Mazzeo, "Metaphysical Poetry and the Poetic of Correspondence."

What is significant about these images, based on the similitude of the aging process of man to the vegetable and water cycle, is that they terminate by being images which differentiate. Gracián has deliberately omitted the final step in the natural cycle which converts the parabolic curve into a circle, for the flowers are reborn in the spring and the water returns as rain.

The *memento mori* is restated in the scenes of the dinner feast and the ball game, both of which are given allegorical interpretations. The dinner feast shows that "... el tiempo buela, la vida se acaba, la muerte le coge, la sepultura le traga, la tierra le cubre, la pudrición le deshaze, el olvido le aniquila: y el que ayer fué hombre, oy es polvo, y mañana nada" (I, vii, 242). In this description the speed of oncoming death is accentuated by the nervous rapidity of the short, parallel phrases, each with the verb in a final, emphatic position. The asyndetic enumeration isolates and makes final each step of the descending gradation which leads to man's annihilation, the finality of which is reiterated in the abrupt summation, where the juxtaposition of the adverbs of time, "ayer" "oy" and "mañana," and the ellipsis of the final verb, "será," express the nearness of death.

The result of the ball game is similar: "... ya está el hombre miserable entre unos, ya entre otros, ya abatido, ya ensalçado; todos le sacuden y le arrojan, hasta que rebentado viene a parar entre la açada y la pala, en el lodo y la hediondez de un sepulcro" (I, viii, 257).

In a similar passage — "... que todos son hijos del barro y nietos de la nada, hermanos de los gusanos, casados con la pudrición: que si oy son flores, mañana estiércol, ayer maravillas y oy sombras, que aquí parecen y allí desaparecen" (III, vii, 224), the initial and frequently used biblical metaphor "hijos del barro" is extended to create a series of paradoxical familial relationships, emphasizing man's reduction to nothingness. The second part of the passage, which summarizes and restates the initial thought, consists of a series of antitheses, created by converting a word into its opposite. Thus "flores" become "estiércol," "maravillas" turn into "sombras" and the verb "parecen" becomes "desaparecen," forming a series of "ingeniosas transposiciones." As Gracián explains: "Consiste su artificio en transformar el objeto y convertirlo en lo contrario de lo que parece; obra grave la inventiva y una pronta tropelia del ingenio" (*Ag.*, XVII, 311). This transformation is from the present to the future, for "No sólo se transforma el caso ya pasado, sino el que ha de suceder, y se hace la transmutación en lo venidero" (*Ag.*, XVII, 316). The propinquity of the words referring to time — "oy" and "mañana," "ayer" and "oy," "aquí" and "allí," the use of the verb "ser" to express the transition, and its ellipsis in the subsequent phrases have the effect of juxtaposing life and death, neglecting the intermediary process of living.

Only in the final stages of the Third Part of *El Criticón* is there a suggestion of a circular relationship of man to cosmic time. In the discussion of the seven ages of man [40] presided over by the seven planets, infancy is ruled by the moon, and in old age "... vuelve a presidir la Luna y buelve a niñear y a monear el hombre decrépito y caduco, con que acaba el tiempo el círculo, mordiéndose la cola la serpiente: ingenioso geroglífico de la rueda de la humana vida" (III, x, 302-303). [41] This concept of circular time is a way of obviating the directional time to death, and is a premonition of the "salvation" from ultimate death achieved by the pilgrims in the "Isla de Inmortalidad." As they contemplate the Wheel of Time, they see that things "... siempre eran las mismas, sólo que unas passavan, otras avían passado y bolvían a tener vez. Hasta las aguas, al cabo de los años mil, bolvían a correr por donde solían ..." (III, x, 308).

Civilization, like mankind, is considered to have a direct relationship to time. As in the case of man's relationship to time,

---

[40] The division of life into seven stages is found in the *De Septemmadis* (or *De Septimanis*) of Hippocrates. See ed. *Œuvres complètes d'Hippocrate*, trans. by E. Littré, Vol. VIII (10 vols.; Paris: Baillière, 1853), p. 636. This division as well as other systems are mentioned in Censorinus, *De Die Natale*, trans. by William Maude (New York: Cambridge Encyclopedia Co., 1900), pp. 11-13, Ch. III, "Various stages of life." By means of analogy between the microcosm and macrocosm, these seven stages in the life of man correspond to the seven planets.

[41] Here Gracián refers to the image of the snake biting its tail found in Alciato's emblem CXXXII, which reads "Ex litteratum studijs immortalitatem acquiri." For this and many other references in Gracián to the *Emblemata*, see Karl-Ludwig Selig, "Gracián and Alciato's *Emblemata*," *CL*, VIII (Winter 1956), 1-11.

the linear downward direction is emphasized in the first parts, and the cyclical acquires importance in the final part.

The linear pattern describing civilization is not parabolic, as is that of man, but descending. The high point of civilization is the mythical Golden Age, and the low point is the present.[42] This is to be expected, as any form of *laus temporis acti* implies a critique of the present. Gracián's vision of the mythical past lacks certain features of the *topos* which are found in Don Quijote's speech. For instance, Don Quijote alludes to a form of "Christian socialism,"[43] saying "... ignoraban estas dos palabras de *tuyo y mío*, ..." and mentions the leisure of the epoch, "... a nadie le era necesario para alcanzar su ordinario sustento tomar otro trabajo que alzar la mano y alcanzarle de las robustas encinas ..." and "... aún no se había atrevido la pesada reja del corvo arado a abrir ni visitar las entrañas piadosas de nuestra primera madre. ..." An important part of his view is the pastoral peacefulness — "Entonces sí que andaban las simples y hermosas zagalejas de valle en valle y de otero en otero, ..." and innocent freedom — "Las doncellas y la honestidad andaban, como tengo dicho, por dondequiera, solas y señeras, sin temor que la ajena desenvoltura y lascivo intento las menoscabasen, y su perdición nacía de su gusto y propia voluntad."[44]

Gracián's stance is firmly that of the Chrisitan moralist, similar to that of Antonio de Guevara in his *Reloj de príncipes*, where "... a new note is sounded; the golden age is ascetic and industrious; labor, albeit common, is habitual from the outset; it is not a penance for a later falling-off; once deprecated by the classical hedonists, it is now extolled by Christian moralists."[45]

In Gracián's eyes, the Golden Age was one of heroic virtue, no longer possible: "Qué, ¿pensavais hallar aora un don Alonso

---

[42] For discussion of the Golden Age myth, see Harry Levin, *The Myth of the Golden Age in the Renaissance* (Bloomington: Indiana University Press, 1969); and Lovejoy and Boas, *Primitivism and Related Ideas in Antiquity*, especially Ch. 2, "Chronological Primitivism in Greek and Roman Mythology and Historiography," pp. 23-102.

[43] Term used by Levin, p. 28.

[44] *Don Quijote de la Mancha*, I, ch. xi, in *Obras completas*, pp. 1066-1067.

[45] Levin, *op. cit.*, p. 29.

el Magnánimo en Italia, un Gran Capitán en España, un Enrico Quarto en Francia haziendo corona de su espada y de sus guarniciones lises? Ya no ay tales héroes en el mundo ni aun memoria dellos" (I, vi, 185-186).[46] It was characterized by sobriety in intellectual taste: "Solemnizávanse en otro tiempo las graves sentencias, los heroicos dichos de los príncipes y señores; pero aora, la frialdad del truhán y el chiste de la cortesana" (III, vii, 222).

There was also sobriety of dress and manner, which is symbolic of a lack of deception and hypocrisy. The women "Parecían de otra especie, porque eran muy calladas, no andariegas, honestas, hazendosas; al fin, mugeres para todo y no como agora para nada" (III, x, 312), and the men were "... buenos y llanos, sin artificio ni embeleco, tan sencillos en el vestido como en el ánimo, sin pliegues en las capas y sin doblezas en el alma, con el pecho desabrochado mostrando el coraçón, la conciencia a ojo, con el alma en la palma, y por esso vitoriosa ..." (III, x, 317).

What is interesting about Gracián's use of the *topos* is that, while employing it to show a deterioration from the ideal, he is sufficiently aware of its being a *topos* to employ it ironically on several occasions. It can be used falsely by the envious "vulgo" against "Artemia," whose artifice has had the following consequences:

> De aquí es que los hombres no son ya los que solían, hechos al buen tiempo y a lo antiguo, que fué siempre lo mejor. ... ¿Qué se hicieron aquellos buenos hombres,

---

[46] This use of the indefinite article "un" before the proper nouns is considered by Leo Spitzer to be a characteristic of the *conceptista* style. The same effect is achieved by using proper names in the plural. Both these uses "... indique d'ailleurs que ce n'est pas le personnage individuel ... mais le *type* du personnage puissant. ..." He adds that Gracián "... aime à donner un sens nouveau aux mots, à leur insuffler pour ainsi dire un nouvelle âme sémantique: le nom propre employé comme appellatif acquiert une acception nouvelle ... le nom propre ne doit pas seulement avoir, chez Gracián, la fonction de dénommer un être, mais aussi de le dépeindre et caractériser." See "'Betlengabor' — Une erreur de Gracián? (Note sur les noms propres chez Gracián)," *RFE*, XVII (1930), 177, 179. This article also appears under the title of "Uber die Eigennamen bei Gracián," in the *Romantische Stil-und Literaturstudien*, Vol. 2 (Marburg a. Lahn: N. G. Elwert'sche Verlagsbuchhandlung, 1931), pp. 181-188.

con aquellos sayos de la inocencia, aquella gente de bien? ... Aora, todo al contrario, no toparéis sino hombrecillos maliciosos y bulliciosos, todo embeleco y fingimiento, y ellos dicen que es artificio. (I, ix, 286)

Another way of undermining the *topos* is by showing that it does not contain any objective truth. Distance can create a deceptive perspective, and Critilo comments as he climbs the Ladder of Fortune that "Todos los passados nos parece que fueron grandes hombres, y todos los presentes y los que vienen nos parecen nada: que ai gran diferencia en el mirar a uno como superior o inferior, desde arriba u desde abaxo" (II, vi, 210). Age can have a particularly significant effect, and invalidates many aspects of the *topos*. As a group of old men are complaining of present times, and extolling the past: "... Llegóse en esto el Sabio y díxoles bolviessen la mira atrás y viessen otros tantos viejos que estavan diziendo mucho más mal del tiempo que ellos tanto ablavan; y detrás de aquéllos, otros y otros, encadenándose hasta el primer viejo su vulgaridad" (II, v, 176).

The author himself comments ironically on the myth. He writes that "De la mucha canalla que de adentro redundava se descomponían por allí cerca muchos otros corrillos, y en todos estavan murmurando del govierno, y esto siempre y en todos los reinos, aun el siglo de oro y de la paz" (II, v, 175).

The ironic supposition that life was once peaceful and beatific is further undermined by word plays with the metallic epithets which are applied to the ages. The use of the adjectives "golden," "silver," "brazen," and "iron" applied to successive generations seems to have first been used by Hesiod, and established as a *topos* by Ovid.[47] Gracián attains the "de-mythification" of the terms, as it were, by using them in the literal "metallic" sense as well as in the figurative moral sense of the *topos*. The purpose of the word play, or *equivocación*, is stated in the *Agudeza* — "Suele comúnmente la equivocación terciar a la malicia y torcer el sentido" (*Ag.*, XXXIII, 395). The Frenchman encountered by the pilgrims reverses the *topos* by insisting that the present is the "golden age" because

---

[47] Levin, *op. cit.*, pp. 14-24.

> —Sólo el oro es el estimado, el buscado, el adorado y querido. No se haze caso de otro, todo va a parar en él y por él; y assí dize bien, quando más mal, aquel público maldiciente: *Tuti tiramo a questo diabolo di argento.* (II, iii, 106) [48]

His reinterpretations of the meaning of "golden" emphasize the disparity between the spirituality of the past and the materialism of the present.

Critilo's opinion is that it is either the iron or brazen age:

> —Yo diría —respondió Critilo— que en el de hyerro: con tantos, todo anda errado en el mundo y todo al rebés: si ya no es el de bronze, que es peor, con tanto cañón y bombarda, todo ardiendo en guerras; no se oye otro que sitios, assaltos, batallas, degüellos, que hasta las mismas entrañas parece se han buelto de bronze. (II, iii, 105-106)

This statement contains two word plays — "hierro" as metal and as error and "bronze" as an age and as the metal of war weapons. Andrenio contributes to the reinterpretation of the *topos* by adding a new "age":

> —Más yo digo que el de lodo, quando todo lo veo puesto dél: tanta inmundicia de costumbres, todo lo bueno por tierra, la virtud dió en el suelo con su letrero *Aquí yace,* la vasura a cavallo, los muladares dorados, y al cabo al cabo, todo hombre es varro. (II, iii, 106)

The homonymic ring in the sounds of "oro" and "lodo" classify it as a *retruécano,* the value of which is enhanced because of its moral intention: "Si el retruécano dice con lo moral del sujeto, alcanza proporcional correspondencia, que es el más vistoso artificio" (Ag., XXXII, 391). The effect of Andrenio's statement is further enhanced by the concretization of the abstract concept *virtud,* which has been personified as a corpse buried beneath

---

[48] Throughout the *Criticón* Gracián deliberately misspells the Italian phrases he employs, thereby imitating and satirizing the imperfect combinations of Italian and Spanish heard frequently during that period. See Romera-Navarro, *C.,* I, xiii, p. 398, note 135, for quote from Cristóbal de Villalón's *Viaje de Turquía,* which criticizes the mixture of the two languages as an "ensalada."

a tombstone. This same vivid image will much later be utilized by Larra, when he writes in his "Día de difuntos de 1836" that "Aquí yace media España: murió de la otra media."

This ambiguous presentation of the golden age myth predominates in the first two parts of *El Criticón*. Only in the final stage of the novel is the downward movement of civilization arrested by a suggestion of cyclic regeneration. As they contemplate the Wheel of Time, the "Cortesano" encourages the distressed pilgrims: "¡Ea, alégrate! que aún bolverá la virtud a ser estimada, la sabiduría a estar muy valida, la verdad amada y todo lo bueno en su triunfo" (III, x, 325). The wait, however, may be long — "... detiénense y mucho en bolver los siglos de oro, y adelántanse los de plomo y de hierro. Son las calamidades más ciertas en repetir que las prosperidades" (III, x, 323-324), and Critilo laments that he will die before this cosmic regeneration: "—Y quando será esso —suspiró Critilo— ya estaremos nosotros acabados y aun consumidos" (III, x, 325).

The nature of Gracián's "Isla de Inmortalidad" indicates that he believes that civilization is degenerating,[49] and that the only possible arrest of its inexorable decay is the effort of superior beings.

Novelistic Devices

An important aspect in the consideration of *El Criticón* as a novel are the devices Gracián uses to maintain interest and to

---

[49] The concept of the decadence of Spain is a critical topic in its seventeenth-century literature. Bernardo Blanco González, in a carefully documented study, analyzes the causes of the decadence. He feels that the imperialist expansion of Charles V has been exaggerated as a cause, and seeks the roots of the decay in the economic failure of Spain to develop a capitalist system. Instead of manufacturing wool products, Spain continued to export the raw wool and import manufactured goods, thereby never accumulating any capital and maintaining a basically agricultural economy. The author relates the economic problems to the function of the court and of the *hidalgo* and *cortesano*. The *hidalguía* originally had a definite military function, but as early as the fifteenth century they were becoming more of an adornment than a useful group. By the time of Charles V, the *cortesano*, the cosmopolitan courtier, was active in court decisions, and was influential in Spain's fatal decision to follow an imperialist destiny. See *Del Cortesano al Discreto. Examen de una "decadencia,"* Vol. I (Madrid: Gredos, 1962).

create suspense. These include addressing the reader and making him a participant of the action, interrupting the narration of a protagonist, arranging each *crisi* so that expectations are aroused to continue to the next *crisi*, creating tension by means of describing sights and sounds which are only later identified, using a counterpoint technique of narration while the protagonists are separated, and presenting allegorical characters who are only subsequently identified. Many of these techniques are found in Cervantes and are a direct inheritance from the *Orlando furioso* of Ariosto.[50]

Each of these techniques will be discussed separately, and examples of their use quoted from the text.

(1) *Author's addresses to the reader:* The change in Gracián's method of comunicating with his reader is one of the essential differences between the novelistic form of *El Criticón* and the aphoristic form of his previous treatises. In these the reader is treated impersonally and addressed in concise imperatives, as seen in such examples from the *Oráculo manual*: "Nunca apresurarse ni apasionarse" (*O.*, 166); "No todo se ha de conceder, ni a todos" (*O.*, 170); "Hanse de sellar los afectos, cuanto más los defectos" (*O.*, 185); "Saber usar de los amigos" (*O.*, 194); "Traer qué alabar" (*O.*, 201). The infinitive formulation of these maxims emphasizes their atemporal and abstractly intellectual quality.[51]

In *El Criticón,* however, Gracián makes a concerted effort to keep his reader interested and alert by appealing to him emotionally. There is an instance when Gracián makes a direct apostrophe to the reader:

> ¡O tú, que hazes mofa del fabulosamente necio, advierte que eres el verdadero, tú eres el mismo de quien te ríes, tanta y tan solemne es tu demencia! Pues, instándote

---

[50] See Maxime Chevalier, *L'Arioste en Espagne (1530-1650), recherches sur l'influence du "Roland furieux"* (Bordeaux: Institut d'études ibériques et ibéro-americaines de l'Université de Bordeaux, 1966), especially pp. 461-491.

[51] According to J. M. Blecua, "Para que la sentencia sea válida universalmente, tendrá que ofrecer siempre un carácter intemporal e inespacial, lo que se consigue perfectamente con el infinitivo." See *op. cit.*, p. 23.

que dexes los riesgos del vicio y te acojas a la vanda de la virtud, respondes que aguardas acabe de passar la corriente de los males. (II, ix, 281)

This vehement and impassioned warning reminds the reader of the allegorical relevance of the story to his own life, and acts as an incitement to active virtue. The exhortation is especially effective because it coincides with a moment of heightened tension in the progress of the pilgrims, who for the first time are called "guerreros" rather than "peregrinos" (II, ix, 282).

More frequently Gracián appeals to the reader by establishing a tone of confidence with him and by making him a participant in the action. This correspondence between the author and his public is evidenced in the use of the first person plural form of the verb to indicate the course of the narration. Some examples of this procedure are "Pero *dexémosle* tan bien entretenido y *sigamos* un rato al prudente anciano ..." (I, viii, 254); "Cómo se desempeñó el varón halado, cómo logró Critilo su dicha, *veremos* después de dar noticia ..." (II, iv, 166). The author-reader correspondence is also seen in the use of the first person plural form of the possessive adjective — "*nuestros* dos peregrinos del vivir" (II, i, 18); "*Nuestros* dos peregrinos del mundo" (II, iii, 99), and the first person plural form of the pronoun — "En qué parte, y lo que en él les sucedió, *nos* lo ofrece la crisi siguiente" (I, iv, 165). [52]

Gracián shows concern for his reader by trying to make his characters more "real" and believable. At times he comments on the psychological reactions of the pilgrims. When Andrenio witnesses the horrifying sights in the "Plaça Mayor," the author notes "¡Qué passo éste para Andrenio!" (I, vi, 204), and when Critilo withdraws from the difficult ascent to power, Gracián interprets his reaction with humor: "Mas Critilo, anteviendo tantos y tan inaccessibles dificultades, tratava de retirarse, consolándose

---

[52] (Emphasis added.) Chevalier, *op. cit.*, p. 484, notes that this formula is used frequently at first in the *Quijote*, but is dispensed with later: "Cette manière familière d'intéresser le lecteur à l'action a séduit le romancier dans les premiers chapitres du *Quichotte*, où les expressions du genre de 'notre hidalgo,' 'notre bon chevalier,' 'notre errant' reviennent avec fréquence. Elles disparraissent ensuite du livre, sans doute parce que l'auteur, toujours soucieux de variété, redoute qu'elles ne deviennent monotones et lassantes."

a lo çorro de los razimos y diziendo ..." (II, xii, 350). On one occasion Gracián insists that the story is true, thus appealing to the reader's need for veracity.[53] When Critilo and Andrenio are in the Court of Death, he writes "Esto estavan viendo y oyendo, no en sueños ni por imaginación fantástica, sino muy en desvelo y muy de veras, olvidados de sí mismos ..." (III, xi, 367).

A frequently used method of adding interest are Gracián's parenthetical exclamations which, by interrupting the flow of the sentence, serve to heighten tension. Some examples of this are: "Pero donde mostró su eficacia el licor pestilencial fué en aquellos que bevieron dél, porque al mesmo punto que le tragaron (¡cosa lastimosa, pero cierta!) todo el interior se les rebolvió ..." (I, vii, 226); "Pero ¡o cosa estraña! que no se veía quién gorgeava ni quién tañía; con ninguno topavan, nadie descubrían ..." (II, x, 307). Parenthetical comments employing word plays are used by the author to clarify the dichotomy between the *ser* and the *parecer* of the topic being discussed. Examples of this include "Apenas (digo, a glorias) estuvieron dentro ..." (II, x, 307); "Y fué de suerte (digo, desdicha) que no quedó rostro sin lunar ..." (II, xi, 332). More explicitly personal comments are "Cuentan que un cierto curioso, mas yo le difiniera necio, dió en un raro capricho ..." (III, ix, 275); "Y si dizen que el sueño es un ensayo de la muerte, yo digo que no es sino un olvido de ella" (III, xi, 341). Through the use of such parenthetical apostrophes, the author not only establishes a confidence with the reader, but also facilitates his comprehension of the narration.

Thus it can be seen that, though Gracián's usual point of view is that of an omniscient author who maintains a neutral stance, there are instances when the author intrudes in the text and makes comments to the readers. The purpose of the change from "neutral" omniscience to "editorial" omniscience[54] is to heighten the interest and relevancy of the story.

---

[53] Harry Sieber mentions that the insistence on the truth of the narration is a characteristic of the picaresque novel, the purpose of which is to make more believable the *pícaro* and his narration. See "Apostrophe in the *Buscón:* An Approach to Quevedo's Narrative Fiction," *MLN,* LXXXIII (March 1968), 193-194.

[54] Terms used by Norman Friedman, "Point of View in Fiction: The Development of a Critical Concept," *PMLA,* LXX (1955), rpt. in *The Novel:*

(2) *Narration of protagonist interrupted to create suspense:* [55] The clearest example of this is Critilo's recounting to Andrenio of the tragedy of his life, which is interrupted by the arrival of the ships and postponed for the voyage: "Quede doblada la hoja para la primera ocasión, que no faltarán muchas en una navegación tan prolixa" (I, iv, 154). Even once he has begun, the completion of the tale is impeded — "... mas ¿cómo lo podré dezir?; no sé si acertaré: mejor será dexarlo" (I, iv, 159), until Andrenio insists that it be completed. Once again Critilo finds it hard to continue because of the emotional content of the story: "Aquí interrumpieron las palabras los sollozos, ahogándose la voz en el llanto" (I, iv, 161).

The more usual method of interruption is from one *crisi* to the next. For instance, "Artemia" asks: "—Una cosa deseo mucho oírte— le dixo a Andrenio, —y es, entre tantas maravillas como viste, entre tantos prodigios como admiraste, ¿quál fué el que más te satisfizo? Lo que respondió Andrenio nos lo diga la otra crisi" (I, viii, 264). Salastano's [56] servant announces the beginning of the tale of his search for true friendship: "—Oíd, señores— començó el criado, —la más portentosa maravilla de quantas avéis visto ni oído. Pero lo que él refirió diremos fielmente después de aver contado lo que le passó a la Fortuna con los Bragados y Comados" (II, ii, 84-85). Critilo questions the "Hermitaño," "—Dime, por tu vida larga, si no buena, con esta virtud

---

Modern Essays in Criticism, ed. by Robert Murray Davis (Englewood Cliffs, N. J.: Prentice Hall, 1966), pp. 152-157. For more on this topic, consult Wayne C. Booth, "Distance and Point-of-View. An Essay in Classification," *Essays in Criticism,* XI (1961), rpt. in *The Novel: Modern Essays in Criticism,* pp. 172-189. In his *The Rhetoric of Fiction* (Chicago: University of Chicago Press, 1961), Booth expands the concept of the author's commentary to include all the techniques of manipulation available to the author to control his reader's response and mold his beliefs.

[55] See Chevalier, *op. cit.,* p. 461, for Cervantes' use of this technique of Ariosto: "Le désir de ne pas lasser l'attention du lecteur apparaît d'abord dans le découpage des ensembles que l'on pourrait juger pesants: le long discours de don Quichotte sur les armes et les lettres est interrompu à deux reprises. ... La nouvelle dramatique du *Curieux malavisé* s'arrête brusquement. ... Cervantes jouera de ce procédé avec une virtuosité consommée dans l'aventure de la duègne Doloride. ..."

[56] This is an anagram for the name of Gracián's friend and patron, Don Vincencio Juan de Lastanosa (1607-1684).

fingida ¿podremos nosotros conseguir la felicidad verdadera?" and he replies "—¡O pobre de mí!— respondió el Hermitaño, —en esso ai mucho que dezir: quédese para otra sitiada" (II, vii, 246).

(3) *Narration of plot development interrupted:* This is an obvious way that the author can manipulate the reader, urging him forward to the next *crisi* so that he may find out the conclusion of an adventure. This technique for arousing expectations was used by Ariosto,[57] and was so typical of the novels of chivalry that it was satirized by Cervantes in the battle of Don Quijote and the *vizcaíno*. Gracián states his admiration of these "suspensiones del Ariosto" (I, "A quien leyere," 98), and uses them to such an extent that his critic Matheu y Sanz comments that "... los fines de las *crisis* son imitaciō de los *Amadises* y *Esplandianes,* pues quando mas engolfado en la narraciō la dexas en calma diziendo *que lo ha de dezir la crisi siguiente.*"[58] In spite of this criticism, the technique produced the desired effect in the readers of the day, "... trayéndolos suspensos la gustosa peregrinación de los héroes que introduce ..." (II, "Censura," p. 3).

It is an easily recognizable method of heightening the tension, because very frequently the narration is interrupted midway and replaced by suspension points which lead to the next *crisi*. For example, at their entrance into the world Critilo and Andrenio look for *hombres* in vain — "Iban por una y otra parte solíci-

---

[57] This technique of Ariosto and its use by Cervantes is discussed by Chevalier, *op. cit.,* pp. 461-463, and by Helmut Hatzfeld, *El "Quijote" como obra de arte del lenguaje,* RFE, Anejo LXXXIII (Madrid: Consejo Superior de Investigaciones Científicas, Instituto "Miguel de Cervantes," 1966), pp. 127-129. Chevalier insists that the technique is derived from Ariosto and not from the novels of chivalry: "L'emploi ironique du procédé montre assez clairement que Cervantès le doit à l'Arioste, qui en fait le même usage, et non pas aux romans de chevalerie, où les formules de ce genre, assez couramment employées, sont dues au simple désir d'aider le lecteur à s'orienter dans une action complexe et ne prennet jamais l'accent enjoué qu'elles avaient dans le *Roland furieux* et qu'elles recouvrent dans le *Quichotte* ..." (p. 462).

[58] See edition of Romera-Navarro, I, p. 98, note 23, as quoted from *Crítica de reflección y censura de las censuras. Fantasía apologética y moral* (Valencia: Bernardo Nogués, 1658), p. 70. For information on author's pseudonym and background, see Romera-Navarro's "Introducción," *C.,* I, p. 12, note 44.

tamente buscándolos sin poder descubrir uno tan solo, hasta que
... Pero cómo y dónde los hallaron, nos lo contará la otra crisi"
(I, v, 183); Andrenio, in despair about survival in the world,
looks for a solution: "—Yo te le he de dar —dixo el Quirón —tan
fácil como verdadero si me eschuchas en la crisi siguiente" (I, vi,
214). The answer is interrupted by the introductory passage in
the next *crisi*, then related in the past tense: "Iba muy consolado
Andrenio con el único remedio que le diera para poder vivir, y
fué que mirasse siempre el mundo, ... al contrario de los
demás ..." (I, vii, 216); Critilo seeks to lure Andrenio away from
"Falimundo's" court — "No cessava Critilo de pensar en su remedio, pero el extraordinario modo como lo consiguió diremos adelante, entretanto que se da noticia de las maravillas de la celebrada Artemia" (I, vii, 242); Andrenio searches for a way out of
"Volusia's" deceptive House of Pleasure — "Cómo baxó y por
dónde, adelante lo veremos" (I, x, 317).

Other examples include the announcement of the "premática"
of "Vejecia" — "Quien los quisiere lograr, estienda el gusto a
la crisi siguiente" (III, i, 49) and the explanation of a way of
avoiding death — "Éste único remedio, tan plausible quan deseado, será el asunto de nuestra última crisi" (III, xi, 368).

A larger use of this technique of suspense is the extension of
El Criticón from two parts to three parts. Gracián describes his
original plan in the prologue:

> He dividido la obra en dos partes, treta de discurrir lo
> penado, dexando siempre picado el gusto, no molido; si
> esta primera te contentare, te ofrezco luego la segunda,
> ya dibujada, ya colorida, pero no retocada, y tanto más
> crítica quanto son más juiziosas las otras dos edades de
> quienes se filosofa en ella. (I, "A quien leyere," 99-100)

Until the end of the Second Part the original plan is maintained.
Critilo begs their guide to lead them to Felisinda: "El mayor
favor sería guiarnos a casa de aquel ínclito marqués embaxador
de España, cuya casa es nuestro centro, donde pensamos poner
término a nuestra prolixa peregrinación hallando nuestra felicidad deseada" (II, xii, 360). In the last *crisi*, the "Gigantinano" —
"... aviéndoles desengañado de que el marqués embaxador que
ellos buscavan no assistía ya en la corte imperial, sino en la

romana, ... y aviendo ellos resuelto, después de mucha desazón y sentimiento, proseguir el viaje de su vida hasta conseguir su alejada felicidad y marchar a la astuta Italia" (II, xiii, 363), they proceed to the Alps, and the author announces: "Lo que por allá les sucedió, ofrece referir la tercera parte, en el erizado Invierno de la Vejez" (II, xiii, 383).

(4) *Sights and sounds which are identified later:* There are several examples of this technique which Hatzfeld, in his analysis of *Don Quijote*, calls "expectativa impresionista": [59]

> Oyeron en esto un gran ruido, como de pendencia, en un rincón de la plaça, entre diluvios del populacho. Era una muger, origen siempre del ruido, muy fea, pero muy aliñada. ... (I, vi, 201)

> Oyóse en esto una confusa vozería, vulgar aplauso de una insolente turba que assomava. Pararon al punto y repararon en un chabacano monstruo que venía atrancando sendas, seguido de inumerable turba. ... (II, iv, 128)

> Esto les estava ponderando, quando de repente interrumpió su discurso una viva arma que se començó a tocar por todas partes. Acudieron prontos a tomar las armas y a ocupar sus puestos. Lo que fué, y lo que les sucedió, nos dirá la crisi siguiente. (II, viii, 280)

> En llegando aquí se sintieron tirar del oydo, y aun arrebatarles la atención. Miraron a un lado y a otro, y vieron sobre un vulgar teatro un valiente *decitore* rodeado de una gran muela de gente. ... (III, iv, 137)

(5) *Counterpoint technique:* On several occasions Andrenio and Critilo are separated, whereupon the adventures of each are related in consecutive order. [60] For instance, Critilo goes to "Arte-

---

[59] *Op. cit.*, p. 100.
[60] This technique is used extensively in *El Quijote*, when Sancho leaves Don Quijote at the palace of the Dukes to become governor of the *Insula Barataria*. Chevalier, *op. cit.*, disagrees with Hatzfeld on the purpose of the separation: "Nous ne pensons pas que le romancier ait été contraint à cette narration parallèle par le départ de Sancho, comme l'estime Hatzfeld. ... Le découpage savant et amusé auquel el se livre obéit une fois de plus au goût de l'auteur pour la variété et à un désir malicieux de rivaliser avec l'art du *Roland furieux*" (p. 463).

mia's" court, leaving Andrenio in the court of "Falimundo." After giving Critilo's impressions of "Artemia's" court, the author writes: "Pero dexémoslo tan bien entretenido y sigamos un rato al prudente anciano que camina en busca de Andrenio a la corte del famoso rey Falimundo" (I, viii, 254). After Critilo and Andrenio have been reunited and have engaged in a prolonged discussion of the "moral anatomía del Hombre," the scene switches: "Desta suerte fué la sabia Artemia filosofando, y ellos aplaudiendo. Pero dexémoslos aquí tan bien empleados, mientras ponderamos los estremos que hizo el engañoso y ya engañado Falimundo" (I, ix, 284). Much later on, as the pilgrims are approaching "Vejecia" by means of different paths: "Encontraron ya los crudos criados con el no bien maduro Andrenio: agarraron dél. Pero antes de dezir lo que con ellos le passó o le hizieron passar, demos una vista a Critilo, que aviendo entrado por la puerta de los honores, avía llegado a la mayor estimación" (III, i, 45).

Many separations of the two protagonists serve an intellectual purpose of thematic importance, showing the different decisions and reactions of passion (Andrenio) as opposed to reason (Critilo). They can also serve a structural purpose, providing a suspenseful interlude until the protagonists may once again be reunited. The separation motivates an energetic quest for a reunion, as Critilo anxiously searches for Andrenio. When Andrenio remains in the court of "Falimundo," Critilo searches for a way to help him out — "No cessava Critilo de pensar en su remedio ..." (I, vii, 242) — and eventually the "Sabio" from "Artemia's" court finds Andrenio and returns him to Critilo. Having left Andrenio with "Falsirena," Critilo returns to find them both missing and bemoans his companion's absence: "—¡O Andrenio mío! dixo suspirando, —dónde estarás! ¡dónde te podré yo hallar! ¡en qué avrás parado!" (I, xii, 364). The desperation of Critilo's search is conveyed by a rapid succession of verbs — "Buscóle por toda la casa.... Dió mil bueltas a la corte.... Perdía el juizio alambicándole en pensar traças.... Resolvió al cabo bolver a consultar a Artemia.... Salió de Madrid ..." (I, xii, 364).

As the journey continues, Andrenio is tempted by the "Saber Falso," and before Critilo can continue on his journey he insists, "—Quisiera hallar primero — replicó Critilo — aquel mi camarada que te he dicho que echó por la vereda de la Necedad"

(II, vi, 201), and finally finds him on the Ladder of Fortune. Here they become reunited: "Conoció a Critilo, que no fué poco desde tan alto y de donde muchos desconocieron a sus padres y hijos, mas fué llamada de la sangre. Dióle luego la mano y levantóle, y entre los dos pudieron ayudar a subir los demás" (II, vi, 209). Once again Andrenio falls into error as he loses himself in the "Casa de Alegría," and Critilo refuses to continue without him — "... que no me dexasse la mitad, pues otro yo allá queda, Andrenio, aun más amigo que hijo, nada suyo y todo ageno, rendido a una brutal vinolencia" (III, iii, 86), and seeks the help of the "Zahorí" in order to find him.

6) *Posterior identification of allegorical characters:* According to Rosemund Tuve, this subsequent recognition of a character is one of the appeals inherent to the reading of allegory:

> This is a pleasure native to allegorical reading. So basic is it that those who find little enjoyment in deliberate reflection upon the meanings of *any* type of experience, had best avoid the form. It asks of us a most catholic interest in every sort of moral experience.... Many qualities of allegorical writings (some criticized as figurative excesses) depend from this expectation that readers enjoy recognizing and realizing what they have long known; it is to be distinguished from taking in information or receiving instructions, overstressed as aims of literary allegory, though present. [61]

Gracián was well aware of the value of any form of enigma, realizing that "... quien dice misterio, dice preñez, verdad escondida y recóndita, y toda noticia que cuesta, es más estimada y gustosa" (Ag., VI, 260).

As the pilgrims enter the world, they encounter a woman leading a squadron of children, whom she attacks and begins to kill until they are saved by another woman. Only after they have witnessed the event does Critilo explain to the astonished Andrenio that the first woman was "nuestra mala inclinación, la propensión al mal" (I, v, 172) and that the second was "Razón," described as "reyna de la luz, madre del desengaño" (I, v, 173).

---

[61] *Op. cit.*, p. 162.

The personification of hypocrisy, "Falimundo," is not named until long after his initial presentation. He is first described by "Proteo" as "un gran rey, y con toda propiedad monarca" whose main attribute is that "... el hazer parecer las cosas, que es el arte de las artes" (I, vii, 219), but is not named until "Artemia" realizes that Andrenio "... queda sin duda en la Babilonia, que no corte, de mi grande enemigo Falimundo" (I, viii, 250). A similar procedure is followed in the identification of "Volusia," who is first the "salteadora" described as a "gallarda hembra, entre muger y entre ángel" (I, x, 303), and later named: "Aquella agradable salteadora es la famosa Volusia, a quien llamamos nosotros delectación y los latinos *voluptas* ..." (I, xi, 320).

During the middle stage of their journey, Critilo and Andrenio are exposed to the "Anfiteatro de monstruosidades." The climax of this visit is an encounter with Satan, who is surrounded by the three enemies of the soul. Each is vying with the other for importance, and in so doing describes itself. Only after these descriptions, however, does Satan identify his cohorts by name, pointing out "Tú, ¡o Carne! ... Y tú, ¡o Mundo! ... Mas tú, Demonio ..." (II, ix, 296-297). After this experience, Critilo and Andrenio accomplish the difficult ascent to Virtue, and are instructed to proceed to the court of "Honoria." Here they see "... un hombrecillo tan no nada que aun de ruín jamás se veía harto; tenía cara de pocos amigos y a todos la torcía, mal gesto y peor parecer ..." (II, xi, 327), who only later is identified as being Momus, the evil spirit of blame and mockery.

Once the pilgrims, by this time in their old age, have crossed the Alps, they continue on their journey to Rome. At one point their way is obstructed by a frantic crowd, all of whom are fleeing from the Truth who is about to give birth. Critilo and Andrenio ask their guide, the "Acertador," why they fear the offspring of Truth. He is about to give an answer as to who the firstborn is, "... yo diría que el primero es ..." (III, iii, 107) but is interrupted and completes his identification in the following *crisi*: "—Pues hágote saber que era el Odio, el primogénito de la Verdad ..." (III, iv, 118). He promises to take them to the second born immediately — "A esse os quiero yo llevar agora para que le conozcáis y gozéis de su buen trato" (III, iv, 119), but he is not identified until much later as "Desengaño" (III, v, 153). After their guide, known as the "Descifrador," has left them, Critilo and Andrenio learn with great surprise from the "Zahorí" that "—Pues ésse era el Desengaño, el querido hijo de la Verdad por lo hermoso y lo lucido; ésse el que causa los dolores después de averle sacado a luz" (III, v, 153).

They proceed on their journey, and when Andrenio inquires about a fantastic palace they are approaching, the "Ocioso" responds: "—Estos — dixo — son los célebres desvanes de aquella tan nombrada reyna, la Hija sin padres" (III, vii, 223). After further questions, Andrenio finally guesess her identification: "—Según esso — dixo Andrenio, — esta vana reyna es o quiere ser la inchadíssima Sobervia" (III, vii, 224).

Gracián's increased awareness of the effectiveness of this technique may account, in part, for his removal of the marginal notes used in the first two parts. These "márgenes desembaraçadas "(III, "Al que leyere," 14) leave the reader free to experience the pleasure of recognition, uninterrupted by the "aids" of the author or editor's guidelines. [62]

---

[62] Romera-Navarro comments that "En todo caso, estos títulos marginales del *Criticón*, que muestran a veces en algún detalle menos cultura que la del texto, y aun cierta ligera incongruencia, estoy muy inclinado a creer que los puso el impresor, y no Gracián" (*C.*, I, xi, 344, note 159).

Chapter III

ALLEGORY IN *EL CRITICÓN*

We have seen that *El Discreto* was an initial attempt at using varying modes of exposition, all of which are incorporated into the *Criticón*. There is no doubt, however, that the primary modes encountered are satire and allegory, and Gracián describes his novel as a union of "... lo picante de la sátira con lo dulce de la épica ..." (I, "A quien leyere," 97).

It is significant that allegory constitutes the predominant structure of the novel. Other forms of fiction could have been employed, for "Una mesma verdad puede vestirse de muchos modos ..." (Ag., LV, 473). This decision to use allegory as the structural principle can be explained by two reasons.

The first is that the genre of the epic was interpreted as being allegorical. Gracián praises the epic as a "Composición sublime por la mayor parte, que en los hechos, sucesos y aventuras de un supuesto, los menos verdaderos y los más fingidos y tal vez todos, va ideando los de todos los mortales" (Ag., LVI, 477). He writes of Homer that "... pinta al vivo la peregrinación de nuestra vida por entre Cilas y Caribdis, Circes, cíclopes y sirenas de los vicios" (Ag., LVI, 477).

The second reason is that it served Gracián's tactical purposes. The definition of allegory inherited from antiquity is that *Allegoria est enim, sicut saepe jam dictum est, quando aliud dicitur, et aliud significatur*.[1] Etymologically the term is a composite

---

[1] Robert Worth Frank, Jr., "The Art of Reading Medieval Personification-Allegory," *ELH*, XX (December 1953), 239. The author quotes from Cassiodorus on Psalm XXXI, 13 Migne, PL 70, col. 223.

of *allos* (other) and *agoreuein* (speaking openly). Thus if *agoreuein* means open, public speaking, the prefix *allos* inverts its meaning.[2] It is in its ability to disguise that allegory offers a tactical advantage. Gracián describes it in these terms as "... afectado disfraz de la malicia, ordinaria capa del satirizar" (*Ag.*, LVI, 479). Unlike political allegory, its purpose is not to disguise dangerous material. As moral allegory it disguises bitter, difficult truths which would otherwise be unpalatable to the reader: "Son las verdades mercadería vedada, no las dejan pasar los puertos de la noticia y desengaño, y así han menester tanto disfraz para poder hallar entrada a la razón, que tanto la estima" (*Ag.*, LVI, 479).

Although the definition of allegory as "speaking otherwise than one seems to speak" suggests that it is a difficult, baffling mode, its intent is the opposite. It seeks to facilitate communication by transforming intangible concepts into tangible images. As expressed by Gracián, the method of allegory "Consiste también en la semejanza, con que las virtudes y los vicios se introducen en metáforas de personas, y que hablan según el sujeto competente. Las cosas espirituales se pintan en figura de cosas materiales y visibles, con invención y traza de empeños y desempeños en el suceso" (*Ag.*, LVI, 479).

Allegory was widely used in seventeenth-century Spain, especially in the theatre. It is interesting to compare Gracián's statements on allegory and Pedro Calderón de la Barca's theoretical statements on the use of allegory in the *auto sacramental*. Unlike Gracián, Calderón does not explore the possibilities that allegory offers for duplicity as a "capa" or "disfraz." He is interested in the duality of allegory, in the double levels of meaning that it is capable of expressing simultaneously. In the *Loa* to *El Sacro Parnaso*, the personified figure of Allegory explains:

>   ... soy
> (si en términos me defino)
> Docta Alegoría, Tropo
> Retórico, que expresivo,

---

[2] Angus Fletcher, *Allegory. The Theory of a Symbolic Mode* (Ithaca, N. Y.: Cornell University Press, 1964), p. 2.

> debajo de una alusión
> de otra cosa, signifìco
> las propiedades en lejos
> los accidentes en usos,
> pues dando cuerpo al concepto
> aún lo no visible animo ... [3]

The phrase "dando cuerpo al concepto" is comparable to Gracián's previously mentioned statement that "Las cosas espirituales se pintan en figura de cosas materiales y visibles. ..." Calderón further states that the use of allegory in drama is a method of theological instruction which helps to make comprehensible difficult doctrinal matters. In *Sueños hay que verdades son* he writes:

> Y pues lo caduco no
> puede comprender lo eterno
> y es necesario que, para
> venir en conocimiento
> suyo, haya un medio visible
> que en el corto caudal nuestro
> del concepto imaginado
> pase a práctico concepto:
> Hagamos representable,
> a los teatros del tiempo ... [4]

Thus, both novelist and dramatist have in common the desire to instruct their readers in moral truths. Calderón uses allegory primarily as a means of clarification,[5] while Gracián also uses it as a strategy to convince his readers of bitter preceptos.

Symbol-Allegory in El Criticón
Characterization in El Criticón *and the* Quijote

The fact that allegory is the predominant mode of *El Criticón* affects the characterization. The characters are rigidly in control

---

[3] In *Autos sacramentales, alegóricos y historiales del Phénix de los poetas*, ed. by Don Juan Fernández de Apontes (6 vols.; Madrid: Viuda de Fernández, 1760), VI, 3.

[4] *Ibid.*, V, 282.

[5] For a detailed discussion of Calderón's theories of the *auto*, see A. A. Parker, *The Allegorical Drama of Calderón* (Oxford: Dolphin Book Co., 1968), especially Ch. 2.

of the author and, in Parts I and II, Andrenio and Critilo react according to the precise patterns necessitated by their allegorical nature. Only in Part III is there a change in Gracián's presentation of the characters.

By Part III the "flatness" [6] of the characterization begins to acquire a fuller elaboration as the characters react in an unexpected manner, surprising both reader and author: "Mas Andrenio, porque no se dixesse que siempre tomava la contraria y quería salir con la suya, se dobló esta vez, diziendo que se rendía más al gusto de Critilo que al acierto" (III, vii, 217); "Hasta el mismo Critilo, ¿quién tal creyera?, llevado del vulgar escándalo, quando no exemplo, se metió en fuga" (III, iii, 116). At the same time that Gracián allows greater freedom to his characters, he, as an author, becomes more removed and views the work from a more detached perspective. The following statement of the "Cortesano" is indicative of this: "—Esto bastará por agora —les dixo el Cortesano—, y baxemos a comer, no diga el otro simple letor: '¿De qué passan estos hombres, que nunca se introducen comiendo ni cenando, sino filosofando?'" (III, x, 335). This comment, which parodies the romance form of the novel by pointing out its lack of realistic content, [7] would not have been possible unless Gracián had adopted an attitude of ironic detachment from his work.

This lack of freedom of the characters is one of the chief factors which differentiates *El Criticón* from *Don Quijote*. As analyzed by Américo Castro, one of Cervantes' major achievements was that "... se hizo incluir en la estructura del personaje el proceso del 'hacerse' de su vida, y la proyección en esa vida de un estímulo incitante, capaz de expandirla a su vez en una proyección poética, hecha y creada desde dentro de su experiencia vital." [8] In *El Criticón* the action takes precedence over the character, whose reaction is inevitable and predeterminado by his allegorical significance (except, as we have said, in Part III where there is more flexibility). In contrast to this, "Un rasgo estructural

---

[6] Term used by E. M. Forster, *Aspects of the Novel* (New York: Harcourt, Brace & World, 1927), p. 103.

[7] Frye, *op. cit.*, mentions this type of parodic irony as an ingredient of *Don Quijote*. See p. 223.

[8] *Hacia Cervantes* (Madrid: Taurus, 1967), p. 312.

del *Quijote* es que *el quién de la acción importe más que el contenido de lo que se haga o acontezca:* estas figuras humanas existen como un 'estar siendo.' " [9]

In spite of the great differences in the characterization of *El Criticón* and *Don Quijote,* Gracián's use of two principal protagonists has frequently been compared to Cervantes' creation of Don Quijote and Sancho Panza. [10] The validity of such a comparison depends on the interpretation assigned to Cervantes' characters. It is, for instance, an accurate analogy according to Knud Togeby's study of the composition of *Don Quijote,* in which he analyzes Don Quijote as the "soul" and Sancho Panza as the "body," a divided entity which is reunited during the course of the novel, thus allowing for the salvation of both. [11] Even the relevancy of this comparison is doubtful, however. It depends for its veracity on an allegorical interpretation of Cervantes' characters, which thus automatically approximates it to Gracián's openly allegorical characterization.

The precariousness of any comparison to Cervantes is emphasized when Gracián's attitude towards this author is realized. Although he never directly mentions Cervantes, when he alludes to him it is always with disdain. In the satire "Contra la hazañería" of *El Discreto,* he mentions that "... no todos los ridículos andantes salieron de la Mancha" (*D.,* XX, 131). In the "Reforma de los libros" in *El Criticón* he first condemns the "libros de cavallerías" and adds that

> Replicaron algunos que para passar el tiempo se les diesse facultad de leer las obras de algunos otros autores que avían escrito contra estos primeros burlándose de su quimérico trabajo. Y respondióles la Cordura que de ningún modo, porque era dar del lodo en el cieno, y avía sido querer sacar del mundo una necedad con otra mayor. (II, i, 35)

Such an antipathy towards Cervantes' novel is comprehensible both on ideological and stylistic grounds. In Gracián's view, Don

---

[9] *Ibid.,* p. 320.
[10] Correa Calderón, *op. cit.,* p. 223; and Coster, *op. cit.,* p. 159.
[11] "La composition du roman *Don Quijote,*" *Orbis Litterarum,* Supplementum 1 (Munksgaard, 1957).

Quijote was merely a "ridículo andante," the opposite of his own ideal of *discreción* and *cordura*. The stylistic divergence between Cervantes and Gracián is considerable. The comments of Francisco Navarro y Ledesma in his biography of Cervantes vividly express the different effect on the reader of each of these styles of writing:

> De igual modo Gracián el abrumador, Gracián el macizo, Gracián el berroqueño, el genial Gracián, amigo de los espíritus enrevesados y tortuosos, ¿cómo había de perdonar a Cervantes su mediterránea claridad, la transparente sencillez con que dice cuanto quiere, sin envolver el concepto en hábitos y más hábitos de carpida y cardada y abrigos de lana conventual, toda sólida, tupida y tramada sin resquicios, agujeros ni costuras? Gracián es igualmente implacable, no tropieza nunca, no se descuida jamás; es hermético y sin mechinales, resquebrajaduras ni rendijas por donde entre el aire de fuera. [12]

It is doubtful that Cervantes could have inspired Gracián's use of two protagonists. It is possible, on the other hand, that the romances served as a source of inspiration. Beginning with Heliodorus' Theagenes and Chariclea, the pair of lovers is a characteristic of all these novels. Cervantes writes of Persiles and Segismunda, and John Barclay of Poliarchus and Argenis in his *Argenis*, admired by Gracián when he inquires "¿Qué cosa más ingeniosa y perfecta que el *Argenis* de Barclayo?" (*Ag.*, LV, 477). [13]

Another likely source for Gracián's use of two protagonists may be found in the *Agudeza*, in one of his examples of allegory:

> Consideremos, dice, una manera de imaginación como la que fingió Platón cuando dijo que era un carro la voluntad del hombre, que le tiraban dos caballos, el uno blanco y el otro negro; el blanco, el apetito racional, y el negro, el irracional, a quien llamó San Agustín porción superior y inferior. (*Ag.*, LVI, 479)

---

[12] *El ingenioso hidalgo Miguel de Cervantes Saavedra* (Madrid: Sucesores de Hernando, 1915), p. 376.

[13] The *Argenis*, published in 1621, was translated into Spanish in 1626 by José Pellicer de Salas y Tovar, and formed part of Lastanosa's library. See Selig, *The Library of Vincencio Juan de Lastanosa, Patron of Gracián*.

That the representation of the rational and irrational sides of man was the initial intent of the author can be seen in his selection of the characters' names. Both names have Greek origins, "Critilo" being related to the word for *el crítico* and Andrenio to the word for *hombre*.[14] Names are of utmost importance in allegory, for they are clues to the essential nature of the character. Thus, the relationship of the two pilgrims begins with an exchange of names: "Començó por los nombres de ambos, proponiéndole el suyo, que era el de Critilo, y imponiéndole a él el de Andrenio, que llenaron bien, el uno en lo juizioso, y el otro en lo humano" (I, i, 110). The phrase "llenaron bien" is indicative of the allegorical procedure. The name indicates established contours, which the subsequent behavior of the character "fills." In this way it is a limiting factor, because it establishes a predetermined pattern which restricts the actions of the characters.

The Protagonists as Symbol-Allegories

Opinions on the degree of interest generated by Andrenio and Critilo as characters vary. In comparing *Pilgrim's Progress* to *El Criticón*, L. B. Walton concludes of Bunyan that "His characters are little more than allegorical figureheads. Gracián's work, on the contrary, is rich in subtle psychological insight."[15] In contrast to this, Krauss writes that "Únicamente los dos peregrinos son incapaces de provocar tensión. El interés por ellos es, en realidad, un interés por sus vivencias. ... Este es el procedimiento seguido en todas las novelas alegóricas. ... El sujeto de la acción queda reducido a una simple figura formal. ..."[16] The difference of opinion is based on the fact that while the former critic views the protagonists as novelistic "characters" capable of psychological motivation, the latter considers them allegorical figures, whose pattern of action is predetermined and inflexible.

The ambiguity in the judgments of Andrenio and Critilo as protagonists is due to the fact that they can neither be considered "rounded" novelistic characters nor "flat" allegorical abstractions.

---

[14] Romera-Navarro, *C.*, I, i, p. 110, notes 45 and 46.
[15] "Two Allegorical Journeys. A Comparison Between Bunyan's *Pilgrim's Progress* and Gracián's *El Criticón*," *BHS*, XXXVI (1959), 29.
[16] *Op. cit.*, p. 50.

In the *Criticón* two types of allegorization are employed. Characters such as "Virtelia" (Virtue), "Sofisbella" (Wisdom), "Falimundo" (Hypocrisy), etc., are "personification-allegories," defined as follows: "Its essential characteristic is that it uses abstractions as though they were concrete substances — people, places, things." [17] These characters are "literal" because they mean what their names say they mean. There is no need to interpret them and imbue them with a second meaning. Critilo and Andrenio are, on the other hand, "symbol-allegories." They are concrete beings, whose past is described and whose future is projected, yet they also have a second level of meaning. They require a different type of reading than do the personification-allegories:

> The fundamental difference between the method used in reading symbol-allegory and that used in reading personification-allegory may be stated as follows. In symbol-allegory, the reader must make two interpretations before he can understand the "other" meaning of the narrative. He must interpret, first, the symbols, and second, their pattern of relationship and activity. ... In personification allegory, on the other hand, the reader must make at most one translation to understand the allegory. He does not have to find a second meaning for the personifications in the allegory, for they have none. [18]

In relation to Gracián's terminology, personification-allegory coincides with his definition of allegory: "Consiste también en la semejanza, con que las virtudes y los vicios se introducen en metáfora de personas, y que hablan según el sujeto competente" (*Ag.*, LVI, 479). Symbol-allegory, on the other hand, coincides with his description of the *epopeya* as "Composición sublime por la mayor parte, que en los hechos, sucesos y aventuras de un supuesto, los menos verdaderos y los más fingidos y tal vez todos, va ideando los de todos los mortales. Forja un espejo común y fabrica una tela de desengaños" (*Ag.*, LVI, 477).

Because Critilo and Andrenio are symbol-allegories rather than personification-allegories, their significance and relationship are

---

[17] Distinctions between types of allegory made by Frank, *op. cit.*, p. 242.
[18] *Ibid.*, p. 244.

more complex than would initially appear. The relationship between the protagonists, and, correspondingly, the symbolic significance of each, changes during the course of the novel. The change indicates an ever-increasing awareness on the part of the author of the possibilities inherent in the use of two main characters.

Initially Critilo and Andrenio symbolize the rational-irrational dichotomy of man, implied by their allegorical names. This is reinforced by the adjectives used to describe the characters: "... el *advertido* [19] náufrago emprendió luego el enseñar a hablar al *inculto* joven" (I, i, 109); "... dixo el *sagaz* Critilo al *incauto* Andrenio" (I, v, 167). While Andrenio's statements are usually introduced by "dixo" or "prosiguió," Critilo's are more often prefaced by "ponderó." The few references to their physical appearance stress the dichotomy symbolized in the age difference. All we know of Critilo is that he is old, "... cisne ya en lo cano y más en lo canoro" (I, i, 104), while Andrenio is young and in his prime — "un gallardo joven" (I, i, 107). Further details describing Andrenio — "lo rubio y tendido de su cabello, lo perfilado de su rostro" (I, i, 108) — contribute not to the individual outline but to intensify Andrenio's type-cast as a European "Everyman." His lack of clothing, "... del traje no se podían rastrear indicios, pues era sola la librea de su inocencia" (I, i, 108), is symbolic both of his irrational nature and his innocence. He is "bestial" — "... que parecía entenderse mejor con los brutos que con las personas ..." (I, i, 108) — and therefore untutored in the ways of men. This innocence from evil is borne out in the comparison of Andrenio to Adam when Critilo admires the "... privilegio único del primer hombre y tuyo ..." (I, ii, 119).

As can be seen, details of physical description are negligible. As pointed out by K. L. Selig, there is a "... lack of emphasis on the 'visual' in the composition of the imagery in the work of Gracián. Gracián, also, for example, mentions relatively few painters and pays little attention to the plastic and visual arts. The exception is, of course, his reference to Hieronimus Bosch,

---

[19] Unless otherwise stated, emphasis added in these and subsequent textual citations from *El Criticón* are mine.

obviously due to our author's preoccupation with the grotesque." [20] As Gracián's intention was not to impress *Ut pictura poesis*, the characterization is accomplished not by means of the description of appearance, action, and gesture, but rather by means of language usage.

In *El Criticón* the speech of Andrenio and Critilo reflects the rational-irrational dichotomy established by their age differentiation. M. C. Gariano distinguishes the protagonists as follows: "Vivir para Andrenio es un acto de síntesis, un asociarse con todo lo que se le ocurre: pero Critilo se disocia de los hechos con que se encara y trata de captar el otro lado de la medalla para que, a través de lo que ve, logre entender cuanto se oculta a su mirada." [21] Schröder differentiates the sensual, spontaneous amazement of Andrenio from the critical distance and judgment of Critilo. [22] This difference is reflected in their manner of speaking, especially during their first encounter. Here they relate directly to each other without the presence of a third character, the inevitable "guide" who in various forms leads them through the world.

Andrenio functions primarily through his instincts. He expresses hunger and food has a soothing effect:

> A mis voces y a mis llantos acudían enternecidas las fieras, cargadas de frutas y de caça, con que se templava en algo mi sentimiento y me desquitava en parte de mis penas. (I, i, 113)

---

[20] "Some Remarks on Gracián's Literary Taste and Judgments," p. 159, note 12. Gracián's reference to Bosch occurs in the statement: "—Hazed cuenta —dixo el Quirón— que soñáis despiertos. ¡O qué bien pintava el Bosco!; aora entiendo su capricho" (I, vi, 192). For further information on Bosch in Spain, see Xavier de Salas, *El Bosco en la literatura española*, Discurso leído en la Real Academia de Buenas Letras de Barcelona y contestación de Carlos Sanllehy (Barcelona: Imprenta J. Sabater, 1943), and Ricardo del Arco y Garay, "Estimación española del Bosco en los siglos XVI y XVII," *RIE*, X (1952), 417-431. Also useful are articles on Francisco de Quevedo and Bosch. See Margherita Morreale, "Quevedo y el Bosco. Una apostilla a *Los Sueños*," *Clavileño*, VII (1956), 40-44, and Margarita Levisi, "Hieronimus Bosch y los *Sueños* de Francisco de Quevedo," *Filología*, IX (1963), 163-200.

[21] "Simbolismo y alegoría en *El Criticón* de Gracián," *Asomante*, XXII, No. 2 (1966), 45.

[22] *Op. cit.*, p. 13.

He expresses pain, which is described physically:

> Probé muchas vezes a seguir aquellos brutos arañando los peñascos, que pudieran ablandarse con la sangre que de mis dedos corría: valíame también de los dientes; pero todo en vano y con daño, pues era cierto el caer en aquel suelo regado con mis lágrimas y teñido en mi sangre. (I, i, 113)

His responses are emotional, as expressed by the verbs "sentía," "me salteó" (I, i, 112), "me atormentava" (I, i, 113), and this causes him to express himself hyperbolically: "Lo que llegó ya a ser ansia de rebentar y agonía de morir ..." (I, i, 114), or "... y el deseo de ver y de saber quién era ... me traía a extremos de morir" (I, i, 114).

This emotionality encompasses Andrenio's feeling of identification with nature: "Pero si las mismas peñas temblavan, ¡qué haría yo!— prosiguió Andrenio —Todas las partes de mi cuerpo parecieron quererse desencasar también, que hasta el coraçón, dando saltos, no hize poco en detenerlo ..." (I, ii, 118); "Pues, ¿qué diré quando sentía el horrísono fragor de los nublados y sus truenos? Ellos se resolvían en lluvia, pero mis ojos en llanto" (I, i, 114). He focuses on the extremes of nature, its grandiosity of beauty or terror, its size and magnificence:

> —Aunque todo para mí era una *prodigiosa continuada novedad* —dixo Andrenio—, renové la admiración al esplayar el ánimo con la vista por essos *inmensos* golfos ... me llamava atento a que empleasse otra gran porción de mi curiosidad en su *prodigiosa grandeza*. Cansado pues yo de caminar, que no de discurrir, sentéme en una de estas más *eminentes* rocas, repitiendo tantos pasmos quantas el mar olas. (I, iii, 135-136)

Andrenio is equally aware of the destructive power of nature:

> ... pues me lo interrumpió un *extraordinario* ruido que parecía salir de las más *profundas* entrañas de aquel monte: conmovióse todo él, temblando aquellas firmes paredes, bramava el *furioso viento vomitando* en tempestades por la boca de la gruta, començaron a desgajarse con *horrible* fragor aquellos *duros* peñascos y a caer con

tan *espantoso estruendo* que parecían quererse venir a la nada toda aquella gran máquina de peñas. (I, ii, 117)

The impact of the passage is enhanced by the unusual number of adjectives employed, by the placement of the adjectives before the nouns they modify, as well as by the use of alliteration in the phrases "viento vomitanto" and "espantoso estruendo." The emotional content of the description is increased by the use of hypallage, for adjectives such as "furioso" applied to "viento," or "horrible" to "fragor," and "espantoso" to "estruendo" express not an inherent quality of the noun but rather Andrenio's reaction to the event described.

Andrenio's speech is characterized by a quality of enthusiasm. One indication of this is an almost excessive use of adjectives. Another is the use of sentences in ascending gradation, each phrase of which impels the reader forward to the climax: "... començava abrir el día, día claro, día grande, día felicíssimo, el mejor de toda mi vida" (I, ii, 118). The repetition of a word in succeeding clauses (conduplicatio) contributes to the effect of excitement: "*Mirava* el cielo, *mirava* la tierra, *mirava* el mar ..." (I, ii, 119); "Lo que yo mucho celebrava era el ver *tanta* multitud de criaturas con *tanta* diferencia entre sí, *tanta* pluralidad con *tan* rara diversidad ..." (I, iii, 130). An accumulation of verbs creates the rapid staccato rhythm of exhilaración: "... y en cada objeto de éstos me transportava sin acertar a salir dél, viendo, observando, advirtiendo, admirando, discurriendo y lográndolo todo con insaciable fruición" (I, ii, 119); "Cogía esta y aquella flor, solicitado de su fragancia, lisonjeado de su belleza, no me artava de verlas y de olerlas, descogiendo sus hojas y haziendo prolija anatomía de su artificiosa composición" (I, iii, 131-132). A similar effect is achieved by a rapid accumulation of nouns: "Ibame escuchando sus regalados cantos, sus quiebros, trinos, gorjeos, fugas, pausas y melodía, con que hazían en sonora competencia bulla el valle, brega la vega, trisca el risco y los bosques vozes, saludando lisonjeras siempre al sol que nace" (I, iii, 133).

Andrenio's passionate spontaneity continues upon his entrance into the world, and is expressed primarily by means of short exclamatory sentences. The sight of the enthroned "esclavos de sí mismos" elicits a strong reaction from the amazed Andrenio:

"—¡O quién pudiera llegar— dezía —y barajar aquellas suertes! ¡O cómo derribara yo a puntillazos aquellas mal empleadas sillas y las trocara en lo que avían de ser y ellos tan bien merecen!" (I, vi, 198-199). The sight of "Falimundo" disconcerts him to such an extent that he begs "—¡Basta— dixo Andrenio—, que rebiento!" (I, viii, 259). Some exclamations are ironic, such as "—¡O qué bueno va el mundo!— dixo Andrenio" (I, vi, 199). Eventually, however, his spontaneity and enthusiasm are curtailed by "Quirón's" admonition that he be silent: "—No grites— dixo Quirón—, que nos perdemos" (I, vi, 199).

In contrast to Andrenio, Critilo is rational and interpretive. His initial relationship with Andrenio is that of the pedagogue, reflecting the influence of what is considered to be a possible source of *El Criticón*, Ibn Tufayl's *El filósofo autodidáctico*.[23]

Critilo responds to Andrenio's subjectivity and personal anecdote with objectivity and impersonal generalization. In an allegory there are two levels of meaning, the literal and the figurative. In this initial phase of *El Criticón* Andrenio narrates the literal and Critilo then proceeds to give it the figurative, or second level of meaning. To Andrenio's account of the wolf who nurtured him, Critilo responds: "—Muy propio es— dixo Critilo —de la ignorancia pueril el llamar a todos los hombres padres y a todas las mujeres madres" (I, i, 111). To Andrenio's reaction to nature he warns "... mas no seas tú uno de aquellos que freqüentan cada año las flores tan atentos no más que a recrear los materiales sentidos, sin emplear el alma en la más sublime contemplación" (I, iii, 132). To Andrenio's intimation of God, Critilo replies: "—Es muy connatural— dixo Critilo —en el hombre la inclinación a su Dios, como a su principio y su fin, ya amándole, ya conociéndole" (I, iii, 142). All these responses have in common the transformation of a personal statement into a general one, serving to expand Andrenio, the individual, into Andrenio, the

---

[23] For biographical details on this source, see Romera-Navarro, *C.*, I, i, pp. 111-112, note 56. For stylistic comparison between Gracián and Ibn Tufayl, see Klaus Heger, *Baltasar Gracián; estilo lingüístico y doctrina de valores. Estudio sobre la actitud literaria del conceptismo* (Zaragoza: Institución "Fernando el Católico," 1960), Ch. I, pp. 19-30, with a summary of conclusions on p. 27.

"Everyman." The experience of one man becomes the experience of every man.

In his dialogue with Andrenio, Critilo never speaks on a personal level. He raises all experience to the level of abstract eternal verities, frequently stated in a form resembling *sententiae:* "—Bien lo creo— dixo Critilo—, que quando los ojos ven lo que nunca vieron, el coraçón siente lo que nunca sintió" (I, ii, 119); "Fáltanos la admiración comúnmente a nosotros porque falta la novedad, y con ésta la advertencia" (I, ii, 119); "Los mayores prodigios, si son fáciles y a todo querer, se envilecen; el uso libre haze perder el respeto a la más relevante maravilla, y en el mismo sol fué favor que se ausentase de noche para que fuesse deseada a la mañana" (I, ii, 120); "No es tanto la noche para que duerman los ignorantes quanto para que velen los sabios. Y si el día executa, la noche previene" (I, ii, 123-124).

Because Critilo's function is to teach Andrenio, much of his speech has the quality of an explanation, as seen in the frequent use of the formula "Es que" to begin his portion of the dialogue: "—Es que atendió— ponderó Critilo ..." (I, iii, 130); "—Es que las aves— acudió Critilo ..." (I, iii, 133). To succeed in his didactic role of explaining the world to Andrenio, Critilo employs various methods of explanation by definition that have a persuasive effect. They may be classified as follows: (1) *Definition by citing the praise of authorities,* as in the summation of his analysis of the universe:

> Assí que con razón definió un filósofo este universo espejo grande de Dios. Mi libro, le llamava el sabio indocto, donde en cifras de criaturas estudió las divinas perfecciones. Combite es, dixo Filón Ebreo, para todo buen gusto donde el espíritu se apacienta. Lyra acordada, le apodó Pitágoras, que con la melodía de su gran concierto nos deleyta y nos suspende. Pompa de la magestad increada, Tertuliano, y armonía agradable de los divinos atributos, Trismegisto. (I, iii, 143)

(2) *Definition by etymology:* "Llámase sol porque en su presencia todas las demás lumbreras se retiran: él solo campea" (I, ii, 121). (3) *Definition by metaphor:* Critilo describes the sun as "... coraçón del lucimiento ... el más luciente espejo en quien las

divinas grandezas se representan" (I, ii, 121-122); the moon is "... segunda presidente del tiempo. ... Tiene a medias el mando con el sol ..." (I, ii, 126); the mountains are "... firmes costillas del cuerpo muelle de la tierra ..." (I, iii, 140); the world is an "edificio" the architect of which is God: "... assí aquel divino Arquitecto de esta gran casa del orbe no sólo atendió a su comodidad y firmeza, sino a su hermosa proporción" (I, iii, 132).[24] (4) *Definition by contrast:* The moon is defined by contrast to the sun: "... si él haze el día, ella la noche; si el sol cumple los años, ella los meses; calienta el sol y seca de día la tierra, la luna de noche la refresca y humedece; el sol govierna los campos, la luna rige los mares: de suerte que son las dos valanças del tiempo" (I, ii, 126). (5) *Definition by analogy:* Man's inclination to God is explained by drawing analogies to more concrete, known phenomena: "... si el imán busca el norte, sin duda que le ay donde se quiete, si la planta al sol, el pez al agua, la piedra al centro y el hombre a Dios, Dios ay que es su norte, centro y sol a quien busque, en quien pare y a quien goze" (I, iii, 142); God's creation of the world is explained by analogizing it to an architect's construction of a building:

> Haz el argumento de lo muerto a lo vivo, y de lo pintado a lo verdadero; y advierte que, qual suele el primoroso artífice en la real fábrica de un palacio no sólo atender a su estabilidad y firmeza, a la comodidad de la habitación, sino a la hermosura también y a la elegante sinmetría para que la pueda gozar el más noble de los sentidos, que es la vista, assí aquel divino Arquitecto de esta gran casa del orbe no sólo atendió a su comodidad y firmeza, sino a su hermosa proporción. (I, iii, 132)

Unlike Andrenio, Critilo does not subjectively identify with nature, but rather uses it objectively as a means of instruction in moral verities. He accomplishes this by indicating analogical correspondences between the macrocosm (the cosmos) and the microcosm (man). Gracián alludes to this concept when, in *El Discreto*, man is called "otro mundo abreviado" (*D.*, VI, 94), and

---

[24] Many of these metaphors are *topoi*. Specifically for "God as Maker," see Ernst Robert Curtius, *European Literature and the Latin Middle Ages*, trans. by Willard R. Trask (New York: Harper & Row, 1963), pp. 544-546.

when Critilo says of man that "... por lo que tiene de mundo, aunque pequeño, todo él se compone de contrarios" (I, iii, 138). According to this "doctrine of correspondences," "... there are in reality three worlds: the *sublunary*, the fallen world in which we live, subject to change and decay; the *celestial*, the unchanging world of the planets and stars; the *supercelestial*, the dwelling of angels and the Godhead. These three worlds are held together by God's love and are analogically correspondent." [25] This distinction between sublunary and celestial is expressed in *El Criticón* in the description of the moon: "... es la ínfima de los planetas en el puesto y en el ser, puede más en la tierra que en el cielo: de modo que es mudable, defectuosa, manchada, inferior, pobre, triste, y todo se le origina de la vecindad con la tierra" (I, ii, 126). On the same subject, Gracián had written in *El Discreto*: "Pero no hay perfección en variedades del alma que no dicen con el Cielo. De la luna arriba no hay mudanza" (*D.*, VI, 94).

Within this immense web of corresponding planes arranged in hierarchical order, any thing or occurrence in one "world" could be paralleled by any thing or occurrence in another "world." [26] There is one example of a comparison of celestial powers, the Sun and God: "—Es el sol— ponderó Critilo —la criatura que más ostentosamente retrata la magestuosa grandeza del Criador" (I, ii, 121), but usually the comparisons are between higher and lower spheres.

Because observable phenomena in nature can be analogized to man's life, they provide a suitable means of moral instruction. Thus, the comparison between man and the moon — "Pero lo más digno de notarse es que, assí como el sol es claro espejo de Dios y de sus divinos atributos, la luna lo es del hombre y de sus humanas imperfecciones ..." (I, ii, 126) — adumbrates the relationship between man and God. Similarly, the appearance and disappearance of the stars correspond to the life-death pattern of

---

[25] Thomas P. Roche, Jr., "The Nature of Allegory," *The Kindly Flame* (Princeton, N. J.: Princeton University Press, 1964), pp. 3-31, rpt. in *Elizabethan Poetry: Modern Essays in Criticism*, ed. by Paul Alpers (New York: Oxford University Press, 1967), p. 404.

[26] For discussion of major correspondences appearing in Renaissance literature, see E. M. W. Tillyard, *The Elizabethan World Picture* (London: Chatto & Windus, 1952), Ch. 7.

man. When Andrenio notices the stars "... saliendo unas y ocultándose otras," Critilo responds "—Ideando— dixo Critilo —las humanas, que todas caminan a ponerse" (I, ii, 124). The warring elements of nature are indicative of the dissidence within man: "Assí es —respondió Critilo—, que todo este universo se compone de contrarios y se concierta de desconciertos: uno contra otro, exclamó el filósofo... de lo natural passa la oposición a lo moral; porque ¿qué hombre ay que no tenga su émulo? ¿dónde irá uno que no guerree?" (I, iii, 137).

Critilo's stately, ornamental style of speech reflects the magnitude of the topic with which he deals, the order and grandeur of God's creation. Such an effect is produced chiefly by various techniques of amplification. These include verb accumulations, such as "... todo lo baña, alegra, ilustra, fecunda y influye ..." (I, ii, 122), as well as noun accumulations, such as "... llegar a ver con novedad y con advertencia la grandeza, la hermosura, el concierto, la firmeza y la variedad desta gran máquina criada" (I, ii, 119), or in the following synonymic phrasing: "De suerte que sola una omnipotencia divina, una eterna providencia, una inmensa bondad pudieran aver dispuesto una tan gran máquina, nunca bastantemente admirada, contemplada y aplaudida" (I, iii, 140). There are several examples of the use of the epiphonema which repeats and summarizes the content of Critilo's explanation. His description of the sun terminates with the following summation: "... él es, al fin, criatura de ostentación, el más luciente espejo en quien las divinas grandezas se representan" (I, ii, 122). Similarly, the discussion of the moon ends with "... de modo que es mudable, defectuosa, manchada, inferior, pobre, triste y todo se le origina de la vecindad con la tierra" (I, ii, 126), and the explanation of the maturation rhythm of fruits is summarized in the following words: "... de suerte, que acabado un fruto, entra el otro, para que con comodidad puedan recogerse y guardarse, entreteniendo todo el año con abundancia y con regalo" (I, iii, 131).

Critilo's speech is distinctly rhythmic, reflecting the rhythmic cycle of nature which he is explaining to Andrenio. This is expressed in a gemination pattern of adjectives, nouns, and verbs throughout the initial speeches. Examples of this include: "Impropios nombres la dió la vulgar ignorancia llamándola *fea y desaliñada,* no aviendo cosa más *brillante y serena,* ... siendo *descanso* del trabajo *y alivio* de nuestras fatigas" (I, ii, 123); "... distílense las aguas *saludables y odoríferas,* que *recreen* el olfato *y conforten* el coraçón: tengan todos los sentidos *su gozo y su empleo*" (I, iii, 132); "Las aguas *limpian y fecundan,* los vientos *purifican y vivifican* ..." (I, iii, 140).

Rhythmic fluidity is also achieved by means of a succession of phrases of equal duration and construction (isocolon): "Quando parece que se acaba todo, entonces comiença de nuevo: *la naturaleza se renueva, el mundo se remoça, la tierra se establece* y el divino govierno es admirado y adorado" (I, iii, 139); "... los montes ... en ellos *se recogen* los tesoros de las nieves, *se forjan* los metales, *se detienen* las nubes, *se originan* las fuentes, *anidan* las fieras, *se empinan* los árboles para las naves y edificios, y donde *se guarecen* las gentes de las avenidas de los ríos, *se fortaleçen* contra los enemigos y *gozan* de salud y de vida" (I, iii, 140). In this example, the successive lengthening of the phrases has the effect of retarding the speed of the passage, terminating it at a more stately pace.

Another means of achieving a flowing rhetorical effect is the use of antithesis, as in Critilo's description of the moon: "Tiene a medias el mando con el sol: si él haze el día, ella la noche; si el sol cumple los años, ella los meses; calienta el sol y seca de día la tierra, la luna de noche la refresca y humedece; el sol govierna los campos, la luna rige los mares: de suerte que son las dos valanças del tiempo" (I, ii, 126). As can be seen, strict symmetry is avoided and is found only in short sequences, such as the phrases comparing the moon to man: "... ya crece, ya mengua; ya nace, ya muere; ya está en su lleno, ya en su nada ..." (I, ii, 126).

Critilo's ornate form of speech in the first chapters of *El Criticón* demonstrates Gracián's adherence to the principle of stylistic variety:

> Descendiendo a los estilos en su hermosa variedad, dos son los capitales: redundante el uno y conciso el otro, según su esencia; asiático y lacónico,[27] según la auto-

---

[27] Croll explains the use of the terms "Attic" or "laconic" and "Asiatic" in seventeenth-century theories of style: "For in the controversies of the

ridad. Yerro sería condenar cualquiera, porque cada uno tiene su perfección y su ocasión. (*Ag.*, LXI, 499)

It also illustrates Gracián's concern with decorum. These *crisis* deal with subjects of magnitude with religious significance, "El gran teatro del Universo" (I, ii) and "La hermosa Naturaleza" (I, iii), for which the asiatic style is appropriate: "El dilatado es propio de oradores; el ajustado de filósofos morales" (*Ag.*, LXI, 499-500). As wit would be inappropriate to the theme, it is sacrificed to oratorical grandeur:

> Tienen sus engastes los pensamientos, y no se deben barajar las crisis y ponderaciones de un grave historiador con los encarecimientos y paranomasias de un poeta. Pide muy diferentes pensamientos, y aun palabras, una carta familiar que una oración; ni merece ser asunto principal de un sermón el concepto que es brillante para un soneto. (*Ag.*, LX, 497)

Critilo and Andrenio's relationship of pedagogue-pupil changes when they leave the island of St. Helena and enter the world. As the functions of definition and interpretation are relinquished to the various guides, Critilo's role is increasingly reduced to an admonitory one. This is accompanied by a corresponding change in his communication with Andrenio, which becomes restricted to stark imperatives, formulated in the simplest manner so as to give a sense of urgency. For instance, at the "Fuente de los Engaños" Critilo exclaims "—¡Aguarda, espera, mira primero si es agua!" (I, vii, 221), and as Andrenio is being misled by "Proteo" he warns "—¡Abre los ojos primero, los interiores digo, y porque adviertas donde entras, mira!" (I, vii, 228). The imperatives may also have a negative formulation, and be repeated for the sake of dynamic emphasis: "No te apartes un punto de mi lado, si no

---

Anti-Ciceronians, 'Attic style' means to all intents and purposes the *genus humile* or *subtile*, 'Asiatic' describes the floral, oratorical style of Cicero's early orations or any style ancient or modern distinguished by the same copious periodic form and the Gorgian figures that attend upon it. 'Attic' is always associated with philosophy and the *ars bene vivendi*, 'Asiatic' with the *cultus* of conventional theory." See "Attic Prose in the Seventeenth Century," *Studies in Philology*, XVIII (April 1921), 79-128, rpt. in *Style, Rhetoric and Rhythm: Essays*, pp. 68-69.

quieres perderte. Nada creas de quanto te dixeren, nada concedas de quanto te pidieren, nada hagas de quanto te mandaren" (I, vii, 229). In general terms, the *lento* pace of the initial theoretical discussion is transformed into the *staccato* speed of the subsequent practical action. The change in the dialogue reflects the pilgrims' change of situation: "... si allí lo mirava de lexos y aquí tan de cerca, allí contemplando, aquí experimentando: que todas las cosas se hallan muy trocadas quando tocadas" (I, v, 182).

Yet a further step is discernible in the relationship between the pilgrims. As the novel progresses into its Second Part, Critilo's admonitory role changes gradually into a supportive one. Ascending the mountains of the "varonil edad" is difficult for Andrenio:

> Hazíasele mui cuesta arriba a Andrenio, como a todos los que suben a la virtud, que nunca hubo altura sin cuesta; iba azezando y aun sudando; anímavale Critilo con prudentes recuerdos y consolávale en aquella esterilidad de flores con la gran copia de frutos de que se veían cargados los árboles. ... (II, i, 19)

The arduous path to virtue "Causóle grima a Andrenio ..." (II, x, 302), whereupon Critilo propels him onward, exclaiming "—¡Ea, resuélvete! ..." "—¡Ea, Andrenio, anímate! ..." (II, x, 303). When Andrenio is on the brink of despair, Critilo and "Lucindo" help him: "Diéronle la mano, con que pudo vencer la dificultad" (II, x, 304).

Only towards the end of *El Criticón* does Andrenio achieve equality of stature with Critilo, permitting a union between the two separate entities. As Andrenio is accosted by the "Ocioso" and Critilo by the "Fantástico," they become aware of their mutual dependency:

> Fatales ambos escollos de la vejez, tan por estremo opuestos que en el uno suele peligrar de ociosa y en el otro de vana. Pero fué único remedio darse ambos las manos, con que pudieron templarse y hazer un buen medio entre tan peligrosos estremos. (III, ix, 278)

The evolution in the relationship of Critilo and Andrenio is accompanied by a development in the symbolic significance of each of the protagonists. On the literal level of the narration, Critilo and Andrenio represent the dichotomies of father-son, age-youth, experience-innocence. On the figurative level of the narration, Critilo and Andrenio represent initially a rational-irrational dichotomy, which at the end of the novel acquires more clearly the characteristics of a body-soul dichotomy. In their final stages of life, Andrenio, the "body," falls prey to the temptations of gluttony (drunkenness) and sloth, while Critilo, the "mind," must defend himself against the sin of pride.

What is apparent is that Gracián's conception of the characters underwent a change during the course of writing the novel. While the literal level of the allegorical protagonists predominates in the First Part, the significance of these protagonists becomes increasingly more abstract until, by the end of the Third Part, it is the figurative level which is in the ascendancy.

The "realistic" motifs of the novel include the father-son relationship of the protagonists, their past history, and the object of their quest, the wife-mother figure of Felisinda. All the details corresponding to these motifs are found in the First Part of *El Criticón*.

Critilo's history has the components of a *drama de capa y espada* —a beautiful lady, "noble," "hermosa," "discreta" (I, iv, 156), problems of inheritance, an ominous rival, who "... a más de ser moço, galán y rico, era sobrino del virrey ..." (I, iv, 158), a duel, and an imprisonment. The reality of his narration is enhanced by concreteness of time (reign of Philip II) and of place (Goa), as well as by the adherence to psychological motivation for the events: The duel is the result of jealousy; the imprisonment is the result of greed for Critilo's wealth; and Critilo's weakness of character is caused by the faulty upbringing of a doting mother. This latter point is interesting because of its affinity to one aspect of the picaresque novel. As the picaresque novel developed, the concern for education was stressed, as, for example, in Vicente Espinel's *La vida de Marcos de Obregón*, where such passages as the following are encountered:

> —Acerca de la materia —dijo— de criar los hijos, hay tantas cosas que advertir, y tantas que observar, que aún de los propios padres que los engendraron no se puede

muchas veces confiar la doctrina que ellos han menester: porque las costumbres, corrompidas o mal arrayadas en el principio de los padres, destruyen los sucesores de las casas nobles y ordinarias.[28]

In the case of Andrenio, the mysteriousness of his birth, subsequently clarified by "Falsirena" (I, xii, 354), his search for his mother, and the "anagnorisis" that occurs between him and his "father," Critilo, are all realistic motifs.

After Part One of *El Criticón* these literal components of the protagonists' lives disappear from the narration. It is the symbolic significance of the "peregrinos" which is stressed in statements such as the following: "Con esto se dieron por entendidos nuestros dos peregrinos Critilo y Andrenio, y con ellos todos los mortales ..." (III, ix, 294).

The same transformation from literal to figurative meaning occurs with Felisinda, the wife-mother figure who provides the motivation for the pilgrims' journey. Heger points out that this quest provides the main structural principle of the novel, and moves from a "querencia real" to a union with the "querido irreal."[29] Felisinda maintains a literal significance until the protagonists' arrival in Rome. Andrenio seeks his mother, who, as "Falsirena" promises, "... os restituirá las caricias en abraços que allí os negó, violentada de su honor" (I, xii, 354), and Critilo longs for his wife — "Suspirava Critilo por su deseada Felisinda ..." (I, xii, 359). Once in Rome, however, her abstract, figurative interpretation is clearly stated by the "Cortesano." Upon hearing that they are searching for Felisinda, the "Cortesano" comments, "Dudo que la halléis, por lo que dize de felicidad" (III, ix, 281), and later reiterates the symbolic significance of Felisinda:

---

[28] *La novela picaresca española*, ed. by Ángel Valbuena y Prat (Madrid: Aguilar, 1966), p. 945. George Haley, in his *Vicente Espinel and Marcos de Obregón. A Life and Its Literary Representation*, Brown University Studies, Vol. XXV (Providence, R. I.: Brown University Press, 1959), carefully documents Espinel's life, and points out the ambiguity inherent in a work which is an autobiography of the author cast as an autobiography of the protagonist, Marcos de Obregón. Such a combination of history and fiction affects a comment such as that quoted above, for the reader is uncertain whether it is to be attributed to Espinel or Obregón.

[29] *Op. cit.*, p. 45.

En vano, ¡o peregrinos del mundo, passageros de la vida!, os cansáis de buscar desde la cuna a la tumba esta vuestra imaginada Felisinda, que el uno llama esposa, el otro madre: ya murió para el mundo y vive para el cielo. Hallarla heis allá, si la supiéredes merecer en la tierra. (III, ix, 294)

This interpretation of the figure of Felisinda is reinforced by the polemic on the definition of happiness, the conclusion of which is: "—De verdad, señor, que estos vuestros sabios son unos grandes necios, pues andan buscando por la tierra la que está en el cielo" (III, ix, 293).

Because of their increased abstraction during the course of the novel, the protagonists never break from the isolation of their allegorical being. They are isolated from their past after Part One, and therefore have no history, no depth in time. Neither do they have any depth in space, for they are isolated from the other protagonists. Their meetings with the allegorical personifications and with their guides are brief and transitory. No interaction occurs between them and the outside world because their role is that of passive receptors of information. Neither can it be said that Critilo or Andrenio change or develop as individuals, for Andrenio is just as susceptible to error at the end of the novel as he was at the beginning. The protagonists' eventual recognition of their actual unity and mutual dependence is not the result of any change of character or "epiphany." It is, rather, a fulfillment of their essential symbolic function hinted at from the beginning when they refer to each other as "este otro yo" (I, viii, 249), or "la mitad" (I, viii, 261).

The Protagonists and Perspectivism

The change in the relationship and significance of the protagonists during the course of the novel is accompanied by a development in the author's use of the structural dualism made possible by having two protagonists.

Critics have stressed the importance of perspectivism in *El Criticón*. Mariano Baquero Goyanes writes that "La consideración de que según el color con que se mira, el mundo resulta movedizo, cambiante e inseguro, es fundamental en *El Criticón*, está en la base y entraña de su estructura y propósito."[30] Heger asserts that this perspectivism is a functional one, and does not indicate a relativism on Gracián's part, as the perspectives invariably dissolve into a higher unity.[31] It can be seen, however, that Gracián's use of perspectivism changes as his grasp of the dual structure developed and matured in the process of writing the novel, reaching its culmination in the final book.

The use of the structural device of two characters to express antithetical ideas on a subject begins in Part One with a very brief exchange, when the protagonists confront Madrid:

> —Veo —dixo él— una real madre de tantas naciones, una corona de dos mundos, un centro de tantos reynos, un joyel de entrambas Indias, un nido del mismo fénix y una esfera del Sol Católico, coronado de prendas en rayos y de blasones en luzes.
> —Pues yo veo —dixo Critilo— una Babilonia de confusiones, una Lutecia de inmundicias, una Roma de mutaciones, un Palermo de volcanes, una Constantinopla de nieblas, un Londres de pestilencias y un Argel de cautiverios.
> —Yo veo, dixo el Sabio —a Madrid madre de todo lo bueno mirada por una parte, y madrastra por la otra, que assí como a la corte acuden todas las perfecciones del mundo, mucho más todos los vicios. ... (I, xi, 332)

Neither point of view is an error, and the antithesis is unified into a synthesis, although Baquero Goyanes sees a deeper significance when he writes that the "... juego perspectivístico permite, pues, el escritor lamentar la situación actual de la monarquía española y presentar poco menos que con engañoso espejismo el recuerdo de las glorias imperiales, sólo captables desde la perspectiva ingenua, pueril y alucinada de Andrenio."[32]

In Part II there are two dialogues based on a difference in point of view, comparing impressions of Spain and France (II, iii,

---

[30] "Perspectivismo y sátira en *El Criticón*," *Homenaje a Gracián* (Zaragoza: Institución "Fernando el Católico," 1958), p. 41.
[31] *Op. cit.*, pp. 67-68.
[32] *Op. cit.*, p. 41.

100-103 and II, viii, 251-254). Here the technique of antithesis is more refined.

In the previous dialogue quoted from Part I, each protagonist expresses himself in a string of consecutive synonymous phrases, one stating the positive and the other the negative view, which has a static effect. In Part II, the positive and negative aspects are stated in rapid succession, forming an interlacing pattern with a *staccato* rhythm. The antithesis is expressed sharply in radically short sentences, frequently reduced to exclamatory phrases, such as "—¡Qué industriosa!," or even single words, such as "—Oficiosos" (II, viii, 252). Each positive-negative pair is independent from the other members, tightly bound within itself by means of word plays. These include semantic plays: "—¡Qué poblada de gentes! / —Pero no de hombres" (II, viii, 252), as well as plays with words of similar terminations in consecutive phrases (homoioptoton), such as "rayo" — "desmayo," "dóciles" — "fáciles," "tontos" — "doctos," "laboriosos" — "codiciosos" (II, viii, 252-253). Although stylistically different, the intellectual meaning is the same. As in the first example, these oppositions are not mutually exclusive. The synthesis of the two perspectives receives a linguistic formulation in the hybrid adjective "agridulce" used by Critilo to explain his impression of Spain (II, iii, 100).

By Part III the number of such dialogues has increased and their content has expanded in range to include not only reactions to countries but also to personified entities. The antithetical views more consciously parallel the contrast established between the two protagonists, corresponding more to moral than to physical verities. For example, in the discussion of Germany, the body-soul antithesis represented by Andrenio and Critilo is recreated in the exchange of impressions. Andrenio's statements correspond to physical realities, and Critilo's retorts to moral truths. When Andrenio says "—Tiene dos cuerpos de un español cada alemán," Critilo responds: "—Sí, pero no medio coraçón." To Andrenio's exclamation "—¡Qué corpulentos!," the reply is "—Pero sin alma," and to Andrenio's admiring remark, "—¡Qué altos!," the undercutting comment is that they are "—Nada altivos" (III, iii, 98-99).

Critilo and Andrenio's reactions to the personifications of Truth (III, iv, 119) and Death (III, xi, 350) are also in keeping with the essential nature of each protagonist, and, as occurred previously, the opposing views are united by means of a third interpretation of the opposing reaction. Truth has two sides: "—Advertid que la verdad en la boca es muy dulce, pero en el oydo es muy amarga; para dicha no ay cosa más gustosa, pero para oyda no ay cosa más desabrida" (III, iii, 114) Death also has two faces: "—Es —dixo el ministro que estava en medio de ambos— que la miráis por diferentes lados, y assí haze diferentes visos, causando diferentes efectos y afectos" (III, xi, 350).

The last dialogue on death is important because it shows an advanced method of presentation on the part of the author. The process is one of radical contraction. The interlocutory forms such as "dijo" or "exclamó" are removed; the verbs are elided; a discussion of any sort, even complete sentences, is dispensed with and replaced completely by interjections. The emotional intensity is further reinforced by the anaphoric repetition of the exclamation "¡Qué!" at the beginning of each phrase, as well as by the strict parallelism of the phrases themselves. The parallelism of the phrases, in addition to their shortness in length, has the effect of dramatically juxtaposing opposing views, as in:

—¡Qué pobre!
—¡Qué rica!
—¡Qué triste!
—¡Qué risueña!   (III, xi, 350)

In this short exchange of the protagonists' impressions of death, Gracián has been able to combine the tension of dramatic conflict in the content with the tension of compression in the form.

There is a correspondence between the relationship of the protagonists and the use of perspectivism in the *Criticón*. The greater use of perspectivism as the novel progresses parallels the author's increased awareness of his antithetical protagonists, expressed in the comment of the "Descifrador": "—Paréceme —dixo el Descifrador— que vivís ambos muy opuestos en genio: lo que al uno le agrada, al otro le descontenta" (III, iv, 120). Furthermore, the pattern of antithetical views unified into a synthesis is repeated in the final union of the protagonists into one entity.

Personification-Allegory in El Criticón

Allegory as Dynamic Direction

The allegorical movement in the novel is of thematic importance. Because *El Criticón* is an allegory, the theme of each stage of the novel, or of each book in this case, can be described in terms of the personifications encountered.

The movement in *El Criticón* is from the cyclical order of nature upward to the apocalyptic world. [33] The cyclical pattern of mankind and civilization represents man's integration in the rhythm of nature. It is, so to speak, his tie to the earth. But man has a unique position in the chain of being, for he is an intermediary between heaven and earth:

> Pero unos y otros, árboles y animales, se reduzen a servir a otro tercer grado de vivientes mucho más perfectos y superiores que sobre el crecer y el sentir añaden el raciocinar, el discurrir y entender; y éste es el hombre, que finalmente se ordena y se dirige para Dios, conociéndole, amándole y sirviéndole. (I, iii, 135)

Although bound to nature and partly bestial, man is also partly divine and capable of directing himself upward, as explained by Gracián in the following similitudes: Critilo asks Andrenio:

> ¿No reparaste en aquella estrellita que haze punto en la gran plana del cielo, objeto de los imanes, blanco de sus saetas? Allí el compás de nuestra atención fixa la una punta, y con la otra va midiendo los círculos que va dando en bueltas (aunque de ordinario rodando) nuestra vida. (I, ii, 125)

He explains that

> —Es muy connatural —dixo Critilo— en el hombre la inclinación a su Dios, como a su principio y su fin, ya amándole, ya conociéndole. ... Si la planta al sol, el pez al agua, la piedra al centro y el hombre a Dios, Dios ay

---

[33] Frye, *op. cit.*, pp. 161-162, discusses the cyclical order of nature and the dialectical movement upward as the two fundamental movements of a narrative.

> que es su norte, centro y sol a quien busque, en quien pare y a quien goze. (I, iii, 142)

The apocalyptic world is the goal towards which the pilgrims move, and represents the ideal. The road to this goal is through the demonic, or fallen world, which represents the real. Edwin Honig discusses the many forms that this ideal can take in literary allegory, and writes:

> In these versions the ideal gauges the spiritual or psychological distance that men have fallen. The task of the hero, whose career is made to cover this distance, is obviously to pick up clues and find a way out of the predicament by exploring the realm that separates the earthly from the divine, or to insist on seeking "the true way," however unattainable it is. [34]

As the protagonists explore "the realm that separates the earthly from the divine" and move from one realm into another, they are controlled by one idea. Andrenio, and especially Critilo, are obsessed with their search for Felisinda, who provides the impulse that propels the pilgrims forward to Spain, through France to Germany, finally to Rome, and eventually to death when they realize that she is not attainable in this world. The journey through the fallen world requires great strength of will. When imprisoned in the "Cárcel de interés," Critilo and Andrenio are told that the way to freedom is simple, "—Todo es que queráis" (II, iv, 125); the *ayo* of a complaining second-born son informs his charge that he can, in effect, accomplish much simply "—Queriendo" (III, viii, 264). It is this will which propels the individual forward to fulfill the purpose of his life. This dynamic conception of life is expressed in the phrase "... la definición de la vida es el moverse ..." (III, viii, 259).

In keeping with this dynamic concept of life, the concept of virtue is also active. Critilo notes that among God's chief gifts to man is his "... natural instinto para conocer el bien y el mal, buscando el uno y evitando el otro, donde son más de admirar

---

[34] *Dark Conceit. The Making of Allegory* (Evanston, Ill.: Northwestern University Press, 1959), p. 152.

que de referir las exquisitas habilidades de los unos para engañar y de los otros para escapar del engañoso peligro" (I, iii, 135). It is the inexorable willfulness of an allegorical protagonist in his striving towards virtue that prompts Fletcher to call him "daemonic" because "... it would appear that he did not control his own destiny, but appeared to be controlled by some foreign force, something outside the sphere of his own ego." [35] This obsession imbues the protagonists with an energy, defined as follows: "It may help, in the case of moral energy, to think of each virtue, acquired or lacking, as a kind of moral energy, not, as Aristotle's *Ethics* would define virtue, as a state of being, but an equivalent in the moral world of a tuned-up missile in the physical world." [36]

The driving force of the quest provides for the straight line movement of the allegorical action. Each stage of the journey is marked by battles which must be won before progress can occur. Because these spiritual struggles are presented allegorically, the personifications are of central importance in the expression of the theme.

Secondary Personification-Allegories: "Generalization" and "Spectator" Allegories in El Criticón

The primary allegory of *El Criticón* consists of the incarnations of various virtues and vices which are encountered by Critilo and Andrenio along the route. These may be called "participation" allegories and have a thematic and structural importance. Before these are discussed, however, the many secondary allegories merit attention, as do their differing means of incorporation into the larger framework during the course of the three parts.

The difference in their use from the first to the last parts shows the author's change from a concentration on variety to a concentration on unity. Gracián writes in the prologue to Book Three:

> Sola una cosa quisiera que me estimasses, y sea aver procurado observar en esta obra aquel magistral precepto de Horacio, en su inmortal Arte de todo discurrir, que

---

[35] *Op. cit.*, p. 40.
[36] *Ibid.*, p. 47.

dize: *Denique sit quod vis simplex dumtaxat et unum.* Qualquier empleo del discurso y de la invención, sea lo que quisieres, o épica o cómica u oratoria, se ha de procurar que sea una, que haga un cuerpo, y no cada cosa de por sí, que vaya unida, haziendo un todo perfecto. (III, "Al que leyere," 14)

It is very likely that he is referring in part to a more integrated way of incorporating allegory into the text.

The First Part is the most illustrative of Gracián's initial concern for variety. In the *Agudeza,* the brilliant flashes of the "agudeza suelta" were in strong competition with the "agudeza compuesta" — "... Un ingenio anómalo siempre fue mayor, porque se deja llevar del conatural ímpetu en el discurrir y de la valentía en el sutilizar; que el atarse a la prolijidad de un discurso, y a la dependencia de una traza, le embaraza y limita" (*Ag.*, LI, 459), and Gracián insisted on the need for variety: "A más de que está expuesto todo discurso continuado al riesgo inevitable de que, si quiebra la atención, que acontece de ordinario, perece todo el trabajo y se malogra" (*Ag.*, LI, 459).

One means of achieving variety was the inclusion of many secondary allegories in the narration. There are basically two ways in which the secondary allegories are incorporated. These may be designated as "generalization" allegories and "spectator" allegories.

The "generalization" allegories constitute thematic definitions of a *crisi*. They particularize a generalization by means of a personification, and are the result of a three-step process. As explained by Bertrand Bronson, first the "personal" experience, in this case of Critilo and Andernio, is generalized into a wider statement, raising the concrete to the abstract level. Once this depersonalization has taken place, it is "reparticularized" by means of a personification.[37] These allegories, are, therefore, means of raising the narrative from the literal, personal level of allegory to the figurative, "everyman" level, without sacrificing the appeal of the particular over the general and maintaining the dramatic interest inherent in personified characters. Examples

---

[37] "Personification Reconsidered," *ELH*, XIV (September 1947), 174.

of "generalization" allegories initiating chapters include "El gran teatro del Universo" (I, ii, 116-117), "El despeñadero de la Vida" (I, iv, 145-148), and "La fuente de los Engaños" (I, vii, 215-216).

In "El gran teatro del Universo," the dialogue between the "supremo Artífice" and man dramatizes a doctrinal statement concerning man's attitude toward nature, summarized as

> Todo lo has de ocupar con el conocimiento tuyo y reconocimiento mío; ésto es, reconociendo en todas las maravillas criadas las perfecciones divinas y passando de las criaturas al Criador. (I, ii, 117)

The same statement is echoed on the level of personal narration when Critilo warns Andrenio

> ... mas no seas tú uno de aquellos que freqüentan cada año las florestas atentos no más que a recrear los materiales sentidos, sin emplear el alma en la más sublime contemplación. Realça el gusto a reconocer aquella beldad infinita del Criador que en esta terrestre se representa, infiriendo que si la sombra es tal, ¡quál será su causa y la realidad a quién sigue! (I, iii, 132)

In this introduction the animation of what could be a dry doctrinal statement is accomplished by means of description of action on a visual level and intensification through rhetoric. When the "soberano dueño" speaks, the contact is increased by a parenthetical statement which adds dramatic interest: "Pero entiende, ¡o hombre! (aquí hablando con él) ..." (I, ii, 117). Auditorily the effect is intensified by amplification through repetition. Man's greed is stressed in rhythmic verbal doublets: "Corta le parece la superficie de la tierra, y assí *penetra* y *mina* sus entrañas ... *ocupa* y *embaraça* el ayre ... *surca* los mares y *sonda* sus más profundos senos ..." (I, ii, 116). The warning against such greed is strengthened by a succession of imperatives in ascending gradation: "—Mirad, advertid, sabed. ..." More imperatives follow in a series of juxtaposed antitheses: "Pero entiende, ¡o hombre! (aquí hablando con él), que esto ha de ser con la mente, no con el vientre, como persona, no como bestia. Señor has de ser de todas las cosas criadas pero no esclavo de ellas: que te sigan, no te arrastren" (I, ii, 117).

In "El despeñadero de la Vida" (I, iv, 145-148), the dialogue between "Amor" and "Fortuna" prefaces Critilo's narration of his past love affair. The relevance of the general statement to the personal experience is clearly indicated: "Quien quisiere ver esta filosofía confirmada con la experiencia, escuche esta agradable relación que dedica Critilo a los floridos años y más al escarmiento" (I, iv, 148). In this personification-allegory, the interest is maintained by a technique of suspense, as "Fortuna" tries to guess the complaint of "Amor": "—¿Es acaso el prohijarte a un vil herrero ...?" (145), "—¿Tampoco será el llamarte hijo de su madre?," "—Que sientes mucho el hazerte heredero de tu abuelo ..." (146), until finally the real reason, the accusation of blindness, is arrived at (146). There is also an example of a "pronta retorsión." When "Amor" asks "¿Qué te parece?" "Fortuna" replies. "—Que me pareces ..." (147), an exchange which duplicates the example given in the *Agudeza* for an "ingenioso equívoco" (*Ag.,* XXXIII, 394).

In "La fuente de los Engaños" (I, vii, 215-216) once again the relevance of the general theory or "philosophy" to the particular or "experiential" is stated: "Quánta verdad sea ésta, confírmelo lo que les sucedió a Critilo y Andrenio a poco rato que se avían despedido del sagaz Quirón" (I, vii, 216). This introductory allegory crystallizes the significance of the *crisi,* the theme of which is *engaño,* first seen at the *fuente* and later in the court of "Falimundo." The interest of its construction is based on one of the methods suggested in the *Agudeza* and used in *El Discreto* — the "discurso por cuestión," in which "... consiste la unión en ir discurriendo por las partes y términos entre quienes está la duda" (*Ag.,* LIV, 471). In this allegory the deadly sins dispute their eminence, when Discord "... movió una reñida competencia sobre quien avía de llevar la vanguardia, no queriendo ceder ningún vicio esta ventaja del valor y del valer" (I, vii, 215). The decision in favor of "Mentira" or "Engaño" is reinforced by a hyperbolic description of this personification in an accumulation of damaging metaphors:

> Ella es la autora de toda maldad, fuente de todo vicio, madre del pecado, arpía que todo lo inficiona, fitón que todo lo anda, hidra de muchas cabeças, Proteo de muchas

formas, centimano que a todas manos pelea, Caco que a todos desmiente. ... (I, vii, 215)

The evil deeds of this vice are exaggerated by means of their synonymic enumeration:

> La Mentira, pues, con el Engaño embisten la incauta candidez del hombre quando moço y quando niño valiéndose de sus invenciones, ardides, estratagemas, assechanças, traças, ficciones, embustes, enredos, embelecos, dolos, marañas, ilusiones, trampas, fraudes, falacias y todo género de italiano proceder. ... (I, vii, 216)

Another form of this "generalization" allegory is the "story" which is interpolated into the narrative. An example of this is the "Sabio's" allegorical account of "Contento" and "Descontento," based on the narration in the *Guzmán de Alfarache* (I, i, vii), which Gracián had already duplicated in the *Agudeza* (Ag., LV, 475-476). Here the method differs in that instead of preceding the narrated incident, it follows it. In this case it serves to generalize the experiences of the travelers in the house of "Volusia," the moral being: "—Dios os libre —ponderava el Sabio— de todo lo que comiença por el contento, nunca os paguéis de los principios fáciles; atended siempre a los fines dificultosos y al contrario" (I, xi, 321).

It is interesting to compare briefly Mateo Alemán's and Gracián's versions of the allegorical tale. While the tale in the *Guzmán* is a simple one of Jupiter's anger with mankind for worshipping "Contento" instead of himself, Gracián's is developed into a "plot." It begins with the unhappiness of "Descontento" and his resolve to seek the aid of "Engaño," proceeds to the plans of the two conspirators, which incorporate an aspect of the picaresque, for "Engaño" is to be introduced into the house of Fortune as a *mozo de ciego*, and the final details of the exchange of the garments are described in detail.

There is a difference also in the way in which the allegorical tale is incorporated into the body of the text. The tale in the *Guzmán* is summarized in the moral: "Creyeron los hombres habelles el Contento quedado y que lo tienen consigo en el suelo, y no es así; que sólo es el ropaje y figura que le parece y el

Descontento está metido dentro." Then the author insists on the practical application of this moral to the reader's life and addresses his audience directly: "Ajeno vives de la verdad si creyeres otra cosa o la imaginas. ¿Quiéreslo ver? Advierte: Considera del modo que quisieres las fiestas. ..." He proceeds with a mock dialogue with his reader: "Si te preguntare '¿Adónde vas?,' podrásme responder muy orgulloso: 'A tal fiesta de contento,'" until he convinces him: "Ves ya cómo en la tierra no hay contento y que está el verdadero en el cielo?" [38] After this the adventure of the *pícaro* commences abruptly.

In contrast to Mateo Alemán, Gracián is less personal, more general in his relationship with his reader, addressing him not as "tú" but as "los que abraçan la maldad" and "los que desengañados apechugan con la virtud" (I, xi, 330). The moral application of the tale is extended into a sermon formulated in highly rhetorical terms. There is a series of parallel exclamatory phrases where the *ser* and the *parecer* are juxtaposed:

> ¡Qué florida le parece a éste la hermosura, y qué lastimado queda después con mil achaques! ¡Qué lozana al otro la mocedad, pero quán presto se marchita! ¡Qué plausible se le representa al ambicioso la dignidad, ... más qué pesado le halla después gimiendo so la carga! ¡Qué gustosa imagina el sanguinario la vengança, ... y después, si le dexan, toda la vida anda basqueando lo que los agraviados no pueden digerir! (I, xi, 330-331)

This enumeration is followed by contrasted exclamations on the rewards of virtue in which the *ser — parecer* order is reversed:

> Pero, al contrario, ¡qué dificultosa y cuesta arriba se le haze al otro la virtud, y después, qué satisfación la de la buena conciencia! (I, xi, 331)

At the end the moral of the allegorical tale is once again reiterated in summary:

---

[38] In *La novela picaresca española*, ed. by Ángel Valbuena y Prat, Vol. I (Madrid: Aguilar, 1966), p. 271.

De suerte que desde entonces la Virtud anda vestida de espinas por fuera y de flores por dentro, al contrario del Vicio. Conozcámoslos y abracémonos con aquélla a pesar del engaño tan común quan vulgar. (I, xi, 332)

In summary, it can be said that Gracián took care both to entertain his reader, as seen in the addition of plot complications to the story, and to instruct him, as seen in the extended sermon following the story. Continuity in the narration is not, however, sacrificed, for the tale is made relevant to the adventures of the protagonists in the House of Pleasure.

The "spectator" allegories in Part I correspond to what M. C. Gariano calls an "alegoría mixta." [39] This term describes the usual structure of these allegories, in which first the literal account is given and then the figurative explication follows, usually given by Critilo or one of the guides. The purposes of the "spectator" allegory are twofold: As far as the protagonists are concerned, it allows for different kinds of reactions — the subjective, emotional reaction on the literal level of the narration, and the objective, intellectual analysis on the figurative level of the narration. As far as the reader is concerned it adds suspense, because the "meaning" of the incidents is not disclosed immediately.

One example of a "spectator" allegory is the "Entrada al Mundo" (I, v). The allegory is preceded by a *razonamiento* delineating the theme of man's arrival into the world already deceived: "Parece que le introduze en un reyno de felicidades, y no es sino un cautiverio de desdichas" (I, v, 166). This theory is borne out in practice in the encounter of Critilo and Andrenio with Passion, who leads the children to slaughter, and Reason, who saves them.

The allegory is presented in stages of description followed by the emotional reactions of the protagonists. To the initial sight of the woman and children Andrenio experiences a sentimental, positive reaction: "—Lo que más me admira —ponderó Andrenio— es el indecible afecto desta rara muger: ¿qué madre como ella? ¿puédese imaginar tal fineza?" Critilo, on the other hand, feels an instinctive wariness: "—No embidies —dixo Critilo—

---

[39] *Op. cit.*, p. 43.

lo que no conoces, ni la llames felicidad hasta que veas en qué para" (I, v, 169). The subsequent betrayal elicits a violent denunciation on the part of Andrenio: "—¡O traydora, o bárbara, o sacrílega muger, más fiera que las mismas fieras! ... ¡O inocentes corderillos! ... ¡O mundo engañoso! ..." (I, v, 171). After Reason has saved the children from Passion Critilo explains the meaning of the allegory. It is evident that Andrenio reacts incorrectly because of a lack of knowledge. When he asks, "¿No me dirás, Critilo, quién es aquella primera para aborrecerla, y quién esta segunda, para celebrarla?" (I, v, 172), we see how correct "naming" is vital in structuring a reaction.

Gracián uses cunning devices to control the expectations of the reader and "deceive" him as Andrenio is deceived. Especially important is the description of the matron Passion: "... de risueño aspecto, alegres ojos, dulces labios y palabras blandas, piadosas manos, y toda ella caricias, alhajas y cariños" (I, v, 168). The use of diminutives adds tenderness to the scene, and the children are referred to as "pequeñuelos" and "mayorcillos." Certain warning notes are, however, introduced to inform the alert reader. Her indulgence is mentioned — "... atendiendo a su gusto y regalo, y para esto llevava mil invenciones de juguetes con que entretenerlos" — as is her prejudice in favor of the wealthy — "... con especialidad cuydava de los que iban mejor vestidos, que parecían hijos de gente principal, dexándoles salir con quanto querían" (I, v, 168). Gracián interjects his own doubtful comment in the phrase "al parecer": "Era tal el cariño y agasajo que esta *al parecer* ama piadosa les hazía ..." (I, v, 168-169). Only when the description of "Razón" is given is the reader undeceived. The false sweetness of Passion contrasts with the open clarity of the newcomer, whose face is "muy sereno y grave" and who is surrounded by light: "... que de él y de la mucha pedrería de su recamado ropaje despedía tal inundación de luzes, que pudieron muy bien suplir, y aun con ventajas, la ausencia del rey del día" (I, v, 171).

The clarity and light of Reason are opposed to the confusion and darkness of Passion, who is surrounded by "confussión y vozería" (I, v, 168) and is associated with night: "Era noche, y muy oscura, con propiedad lóbrega" (I, v, 170). Her slaughter takes place in a valley of caves and wild vegetation, populated by dangerous beasts (I, v, 170). The adjectives describing her actions are selected so as to have an optimum of emotional impact. The slaughter is a "lastimoso teatro," an "espectáculo verdaderamente fatal y lastimero," an "horrible estrago y sangrienta carnicería" (I, v, 170).

Another "spectator" allegory is the fight between "Verdad" and "Mentira" (I, vi). It is considerably less developed or pictorially realistic than the previous allegory. Visual description is substituted by conceptual word play. "Mentira" is introduced as "... una muger, origen siemper del ruido, muy fea, pero muy aliñada: mejor fuera *prendida*. Servíala de adorno todo un *mundo*, quando ella le descompone todo" (I, vi, 201-202). In this description there are two *equívocos*: "prendida," meaning both "ataviada" and "presa," and "mundo," meaning both a crowd as well as one of the three enemies of the soul.[40] As can be seen, the conceptual mode is much more economical than the visual mode, as two meanings are enclosed in one word. It is also a means of adding suspense, for, as stated in the *Agudeza*: "Consiste su artificio en usar de alguna palabra que tenga dos significaciones, de modo que deje en duda lo que quiso decir. ... Úsase de la dicción equívoca algunas veces, para exprimir mayor misterio y profundidad" (*Ag.*, XXXIII, 394-395).

It is interesting to compare the allegory of truth and falsehood which appears in the *Guzmán de Alfarache* (I, Bk. III, ch. vii) and which Gracián had duplicated in the *Agudeza* (*Ag.*, XXVIII, 371-373).

While Alemán introduces the allegory with a passage explaining its spiritual significance — "A la Verdad aconteció lo mismo. También tuvo su cuándo. ... Mas como lo bueno cansa y lo malo nunca se daña, no pudo entre los malos ley tan sana conservarse"[41] — Gracián enters the allegory abruptly, and its significance is only later given by "Quirón." Alemán is more descriptive of physical appearance, less conceptual than Gracián, and each description is followed by a generalizing interpretative comment. Thus he writes of "Verdad":

---
[40] Romera-Navarro, *C.*, I, vi, p. 201, notes 95 and 96.
[41] *Op. cit.*, p. 359 (I, Bk. III, ch. vii).

> Iba sola, pobre, y —cual suele acontecer a los caídos, que tanto uno vale cuanto lo que tiene y puede valer, y en las adversidades los que se llaman amigos se declaran por enemigos—. ...[42]

Instead of hinting at the discrepancy between the *ser* and the *parecer* of "Mentira," Alemán juxtaposes the two sides, thus clearly presenting the dichotomy to the reader:

> ... el rostro hermosísimo, pero cuanto más de cerca, perdía de su hermosura, hasta quedar en extremo fea. Su cuerpo, estando sentada, parecía muy gallardo; más puesto en pie y andando descubría muchos defectos. ...[43]

Because the allegory in the *Guzmán* is totally independent from the narration of the *pícaro*, the author feels a constant need to integrate the two, which he does by means of generalizations, such as — "Quien buscara a la Verdad, no la hallará con la Mentira ni sus ministros; a la postre de todo está y allí se manifiesta" [44] — as well as by transforming the allegorical tale into a metaphorical comparison: "Mas, a mi parecer, pinto en la imaginación que la Verdad y la Mentira son como la cuerda y la clavija de cualquier instrumento. ..." [45]

Gracián, on the other hand, greatly condenses the allegorical narration, concentrating not on the battle between "Verdad" and "Mentira" but rather on the effect of the battle on the protagonists. The tight integration of this "spectator" allegory with the principal allegorical framework is seen in the rapidity with which the narration gives way to dialogue, as "Quirón" restrains Andrenio from interfering in the fight. The allegory is extended not by metaphor but by means of an enumeration of examples of "Mentira" in action. Judges, soldiers, doctors, etc., appear before the pilgrims and their hypocrisy is condemned by "Quirón." Gracián has taken great care to maintain narrative unity to prevent the text from becoming a series of "... discursos amorcillados, sin principio ni fin, y todo confusión" (*Ag.*, LIV, 469).

---

[42] Alemán, *op. cit.*, p. 359.
[43] *Ibid.*, p. 360.
[44] *Ibid.*
[45] *Ibid.*, p. 361.

Two other incidents in Book I may be classified as "spectator" allegories, although they differ from the rest in that they do not involve personifications, but are events which are interpreted allegorically. These are the mock-feast (I, vii, 237-242) and the ball game (I, viii, 256-257). The same procedure is utilized, for first the primary literal level is described, and then this is interpreted on the secondary figurative level. Thus the specific stranger at the feast becomes an "everyman" when Critilo says "Sabe, pues, que aquel desdichado estrangero es el hombre de todos, y todos somos él" (I, vii, 241), and the balls in the game are transformed into human heads representing all of mankind: "... ya está el hombre miserable entre unos, ya entre otros, ya abatido, ya ensalçado; todos le sacuden y le arrojan, hasta que rebentado viene a parar entre la açada y la pala, en el lodo y la hediondez de un sepulcro" (I, viii, 257).

A glance at the "generalization" and "spectator" allegories in Books II and III shows a difference in their usage.

In Book II there is an example of the deliberate application of an introductory "generalization" allegory to the main body of the text. The allegory of Fortune facing the representatives of greedy nations (II, iii, 86-89) is followed by a didactic intrusion of the author:

> Quán incurable sea esta hidropesía del oro, intenta ponderar esta crisi después de averse desempeñado de aquel plausible portento que el criado de Salastano, con gran gusto de todos, refirió desta suerte. (II, iii, 89)

This type of connection is, however, unusual. The other introductory allegories are bound to the text more tightly because they are narrated by either Critilo or a guide. For instance, the allegory of the Three Graces (II, ii, 49-54) is told by "Argos" to Critilo and Andrenio:

> Este crítico sucesso les iba contando el noticioso Argos a nuestros dos peregrinos del mundo, y les asseguró avérselo oído ponderar al mismo cortesano. (II, ii, 54)

The allegory of Fortune's vengeance on knowledge and beauty is also related by a character (II, vi, 198-200):

> Esto le ponderava un enano al melancólico Critilo, desengañándole de su porfía en querer ver en persona la misma Sofisbella. ... (II, vi, 200),

and the same is true of the allegory of Valor and the nations (II, viii, 247-251):

> Esto les iba exagerando a Critilo y Andrenio, a la salida de Francia por la Picardía, un hombre que lo era, y mucho. ... (II, viii, 251)

In the allegory of Fortune and the petitioners, one for wisdom and the other for foolishness (II, v, 167-168), the final statement of "Fortuna" that

> Los ignorantes son los muchos, los necios son los infinitos; y assí, el que los tuviere a ellos de su parte, ésse será señor de un mundo entero (II, v, 168)

is immediately linked to the principal narration:

> Sin duda que estos dos fueron Critilo y Andrenio, quando éste, guiado del Cecrope, fué a ser necio con todos. (II, v, 168)

In addition to the greater integration of the allegory with the text, other differences are apparent. There is greater thematic unity in the "generalization" allegories. Fortune is the subject of three of the allegories (II, iii, v, and vi), and the virtue of friendship (II, ii, and the servant's tale, ii, 89-99) is another main topic. In general the allegories prove the ephemeral nature of external possessions such as power or wealth, at the mercy of fortune, as opposed to the eternal nature of internal achievements, such as virtue and friendship.

Furthermore, variety is achieved not by means of a diversity of topics, but rather through a maintenance of suspense and a variation in the recurring personification of "Fortuna." The element of suspense is achieved in various ways: the first is by means of an interruption which is then resumed. The narration accompanying the allegory of Fortune and the greedy nations

(II, iii) is continued only after the tale of the search for true friendship. Another method of suspense lies in structuring the allegory itself in such a way so as to create maximum interest in the reader. This is especially true of the tale of the Three Graces (II, ii) and the search for true friendship (II, iii). In the servant's search for true friendship, the difficulty of the quest is augmented by means of hyperbolic comparisons. The soldier admits that he has witnessed strange sights: "... he visto cosas bien raras, como los gigantes en la tierra del fuego, los pigmeos en el aire, las amazonas en el agua de su río, los que no tienen cabeça, ..." but "... yo no he topado con esse gran prodigio que aora oigo" (II, iii, 91-92). In the allegory of the Three Graces, the suspense is due to the enigma of their identification. They are first described as "Tres soles, digo tres Gracias ..." (II, ii, 49), and later each describes herself in turn and is recognized and named by the "Cortesano" as Dawn, Truth, and Friendship, respectively.

The characterization of Fortune varies. In one allegory (II, iii) she has a positive and direct temperament, obviously excitable, for she does not simply "say" things, but "exclamó" (II, iii, 87) or "alçó la voz la Fortuna" (II, iii, 89). She is demanding, speaking in imperatives: "Venid acá" (II, iii, 87), or "Hablá claro, acabá, dezí" (II, iii, 88). She expresses herself in ironic exclamations: "¡—O qué lindo— alçó la voz la Fortuna, —bueno por mi vida!" (II, iii, 89). In the next allegory (II, v) she is sad, reacting "... con semblante mesurado y aun triste..." (II, v, 167), and in her final appearance (II, vi) acts serious and revengeful: "—¿Es possible— dezía con profundo sentimiento —que nunca aya él oído dezir: 'Ventura te dé Dios, hijo, ...' ni ella, 'Ventura de fea? ...'" (II, vi, 199).

By Book III there is even a further reduction in the use of the secondary allegories. The battle of the virtues and vices for man, related humorously in a satire of doctors and their plethora of useless remedies (III, iii, 82-84), is related by a character: "Ibale ponderando a Critilo este suceso de cada día un varón de ha mil siglos" (III, iii, 84). Critilo himself connects it with the main text: "De esse achaque le vino a la torpe Vinolencia hazer estanco de vicios: ¡y qué feos, qué abominables!" (III, iii, 84), which statement refers to their recent experiences in the "Casa de Alegría."

There are two examples of "generalization" allegories in the form of stories. One is the allegory of the flight of Truth, told by the "Acertador" (III, iii, 110-113) on their way to the Court of Truth, and the other is an allegory of Death. This one is especially interesting because it is, in a sense, two dimensional. The allegorical character of Death narrates it herself (III, xi, 356-361). The double facet allows for the creation of a "personality," because Death can react subjectively during the course of the narration. She makes side comments: "Aveís de saber que quando yo vine al mundo (hablo de mucho tiempo, allá en mi noviciado) ..." (III, xi, 356). She reacts emotionally: "... confiesso que tuve algún horror al matar y anduve en contemplaciones a los principios ..." (III, xi, 356); "Pero al fin, yo me resolví con harto dolor de mi coraçón, aunque dizen que no le tengo ..." (III, xi, 356). Because she relates the vituperations of others, and her own reactions to their comments, this tale is much more dramatic than any other in the novel in the vivacity of its dialogue.

The "spectator" allegories are reminiscent of those mentioned in Book I in that they involve incidents rather than personifications, and are used as a *memento mori*. They are, however, handled in a more sophisticated fashion. In Book I, the figurative interpretation mechanically followed the literal narration, while here the figurative level is incorporated within the dialogue encompassing the reactions to the sight. Andrenio is astounded by the sight of the man walking a tightrope (III, xi, 339), and the significance of the scene is stated in the dialogue:

—¿De éste te espantas tú? —le dixo el Cortesano.
—Pues ¿de quién, si déste no?
—De ti mismo.
—¿De mí, y porqué?
... ...
—Dime, ¿no caminas cada hora y cada instante sobre el hilo de tu vida, no tan gruesso ni tan firme como una maroma, sino tan delgado como el de una araña, y aun más, y andas saltando y baylando sobre él? (III, xi, 339)

Primary Personification-Allegory: "Participation" Allegory in El Criticón

Because *El Criticón* is an allegory, the theme of each stage, or, in this case, of each book, can be described in terms of the personifications encountered. As Robert Worth Frank, Jr., explains:

> The names also may give the reader a key to the theme or problem being dramatized. The writer of a personification-allegory did not choose his abstractions at random. His choice was governed by the body of ideas or the facts of the situation which he was treating. Like any writer dramatizing a theme or problem, he considered the aspects of that theme and gave each its place in the narrative, presenting it in the form, usually, of an abstraction. The meanings stated in the characters' names, when considered as a unit, will help the reader to see the central issue of the personification-allegory. [46]

The names of the personifications acquire added significance in Gracián's writing because of his awareness of their importance. In the *Agudeza* there is a section entitled "De la agudeza nominal" (*Ag.*, XXXI, 385-390), in which Gracián states that

> El nombre ocasiona los reparos y ponderaciones misteriosas. ... Es como una hidra bocal una dicción, pues a más de su propia y directa significación, si la cortan o trastruecan, de cada sílaba renace una sutileza ingeniosa y de cada acento un concepto. (*Ag.*, XXXI, 386)

Herman Iventosch comments that

> Gracián has availed himself of the *primor* of the "agudeza nominal" to symbolize man and his main concerns on earth. His invented names have highlighted the main aspects of the moral message and have offered us an onomastic passage through the nature of man and his moral life itself. [47]

---

[46] *Op. cit.*, p. 246.
[47] "Moral-Allegorical Names in Gracián's *Criticón*," *Names*, IX (December 1961), 232.

In several instances the chief allegorical figures will have a name of onomastic significance, which portrays them more personally and vividly, and other members of their "court" will be mere personifications, as in the case of "Falimundo," whose palace is populated by "Ignorancia," "Malicia," "Necedad," etc. (I, viii, 260-261). This procedure has been called a homiletic method, whereby the main thesis is stated by an *agudeza* and then expanded in the personifications.[48]

The thematic definition by means of personifications has as its base the problem of temptation.[49] The psycho-social evolution from *hombre* to *persona* involves successive encounters with temptations which must be experienced before the next step in the progress toward virtue may be accomplished. Every successful encounter is a move away from the slavery of passions towards the freedom of asceticism.

This is especially apparent in the encounters with Lasciviousness and Greed, whose enslavement is symbolized by chains. "Volusia" is referred to as "aquella dulce tirana" (I, xi, 306), and her method of assault is unique, for

> Era de reparar que a cada uno le aprisionavan con las mismas ataduras que él quería, y muchos se las traín consigo y las prevenían para que los atassen. Assí, que a unos aprisionavan con cadenas de oro, que era una fuerte atadura; a otros, con esposas de diamantes, que era mayor. (I, x, 304)

In the "Palacio de Interés" the pilgrims are chained:

> ... yendo en fuga cayeron en una dissimulada trampa cubierta con las limaduras de oro de la misma cadena, tan apretado laço, que quanto más forcejavan por librarse más le añudavan. (II, iii, 122)

When freed, their liberator leads them to the palace of "Sofisbella" "... donde él iba y dónde hallarían la perfecta libertad" (II, iv, 127).

---

[48] *Ibid.*, p. 225, note 20.
[49] According to Fletcher, *op. cit.*, this is the basic theme of allegory.

Even political ambition is condemned as a form of slavery. The rules of holding power include "... la primera, no ser suyo, sino de todos, no tener hora propia, todas agenas, ser esclavo común, no tener amigo personal ..." (II, xii, 357). A candidate for the office rejects the crown, saying: "—Basta— dixo—, que yo también me acojo al sagrado de la libertad, y desde aora renuncio una corona, que se llamó assí del coraçón y sus cuidados ..." (II, xii, 358). The "Gigantinano" summarizes Gracián's asceticism in the following words:

> Asseguróos que no ai tiranía como la de una passión, y sea qualquiera, ni ai esclavo sugeto al más bárbaro africano como el que se cautiva de un apetito. ... ¡Eh!, que no ai en el mundo señorío como la libertad del coraçón: esso sí que es ser señor, príncipe, rei y monarca de sí mismo. (II, xiii, 363-364)

The temptations encountered serve to strengthen the protagonist and increasingly approach him to perfection and purity. There is a suggestion that the victories in this battle for flawless virtue are accompanied by moments of illumination, which we may call "epiphanies" of self-knowledge. In the *Criticón*, self-knowledge is considered a prerequisite for the attainment of virtue:

> Pero ¿de qué sirve conocerlo todo, si a sí mismo no se conoce? Tantas veces degenera en esclavo de sus esclavos quantas se rinde a los vicios. No ay salteadora Esfinge que assí oprima al viandante (digo, viviente) como la ignorancia de sí, que en muchos se condena estupidez, pues ni aun saben que no saben, ni advierten que no advierten. (I, ix, 265)

Because of this, the pilgrims' ascent is accompanied by inward realizations. These illuminations are expressed as sudden realizations, or as finding oneself after having been lost. For example, Critilo's departure from the court of "Falimundo" in search of "Artemia" is described as: "Rompió con todo, que es el único medio, y saltó por el portillo de dar en la cuenta, aquél que todos quantos abren los ojos le hallan" (I, viii, 246); Andrenio's salvation from the lure of "Falsirena" is stated as: "Salieron todos a la luz de dar en la cuenta, desconocidos de los otros, pero conocidos de sí. Encaminóse cada uno al templo de su escarmiento a dar gracias al noble desengaño, colgando en sus paredes los despojos del naufragio y las cadenas de su cautiverio" (I, xii, 374); the protagonists' conversion from *moços* into *hombres* is explained as: "Con esto, les dieron licencia de passar adelante a ser personas, y fueron saliendo todos de sí mismos, lo primero para más bolver en sí" (II, i, 47); Critilo's and Andrenio's escape from the "Palacio del Interés" is interpreted as follows: "Preguntáronle a su remediador halado dónde estavan, y él les dixo que mui hallados, pues en sí mismos" (II, iv, 127). These moments of vision inevitably constitute a *desengaño*. For instance, when the "Sabio" asks Andrenio if he is pleased to have seen "Falimundo," he replies: "Contento no, pero desengañado, sí. Vamos, que los instantes se me hazen siglos" (I, viii, 261).

The representation of these primary personifications frequently occurs in pairs of a vice and its corresponding virtue. This is done not only to create the dramatic interest of a "battle" but also to facilitate the understanding of the abstract concepts under discussion. Kenneth Burke notes the distinction between positive and dialectical terms:

> ... the former being terms that do not require an opposite to define them, the latter being terms that do require an opposite. "Apple," for instance, is a positive term, in that we do not require, to understand it, the concept of "counter-apple." But a term like "freedom" is dialectical, in that we cannot locate its meaning without reference to some concept of enslavement, confinement, or restriction. [50]

By the same token, truth is more readily understood in terms of its opposite, falsehood, or virtue in terms of its opposite, vice.

In Book I the main personifications encountered by Critilo and Andrenio are "Falimundo," "Artemia," "Volusia," and "Falsirena." We have already seen that in the "generalization" and "spectator" allegories the themes were the battles between Truth and Falsehood (I, vi, 201-202 and I, vii, 225-226) and Passion and

---

[50] *The Philosophy of Literary Form. Studies in Symbolic Action* (New York: Vintage Books, 1957), pp. 93-94, note 7.

Reason (I, v, 168-173). These two themes are reiterated in the *psychomachia* of the personifications of the "participation" allegories.

The main "emotional" theme in Book I is the passion of lasciviousness, appropriate to youth and therefore in keeping with the age structure of the novel as a whole. The lure of this sin is represented by "Volusia" as well as by "Falsirena," both of whom cause the pilgrims to err from their true path. The main "intellectual" theme is deception as opposed to truth, represented, respectively, by "Falimundo" and "Artemia." The two themes are linked by the figures of "Falsirena" and "Artemia," who are opposed to each other as the evil and the good females, one representing art used for good purposes and the other art used for the bad purpose of deception. Of "Artemia" it is said:

> Muy diferente de la otra Cirçe, pues no convertía los hombres en bestias, sino al contrario las fieras en hombres. No encantava las personas, antes las desencantava. (I, viii, 244)

"Falsirena" is described to Critilo by a neighbor:

> Es verdad que ha vivido aí algunos días una Cirçe en el çurcir y una sirena en el encantar, causa de tantas tempestades, tormentos y tormentas, porque a más de ser ruin, asseguran que es una famosa hechizera, una célebre encantadora, pues convierte los hombres en bestias; y no los transforma en asnos de oro, no, sino de su necedad y pobreza. Por essa corte andan a millares, convertidos (después de divertidos) en todo género de brutos. (I, xii, 362-363)

The geographical center of Book I is Madrid, whose court represents both the evils of lasciviousness and falsehood.

Book II deals with a different set of problems. In comparison to youth, middle age is more outwardly directed, less selfish in its concerns. Thus, man's relation to intellectual culture and the socio-political complex acquires importance. This accounts for the inclusion of discussions on books, as in the "Reforma de libros" (II, i, 34-36), and the comments elicited by the visit to the palace of "Sofisbella" (II, iv), as well as the various analyses of national differences, as in the view of Europe with "Argos" (II, ii, 58-62) and the introductory "Armería de Valor" (II, viii,

247-251). A plethora of contemporary figures is mentioned, and outstanding contemporary problems are commented upon.

One important topic is war, which is bitterly criticized. According to Critilo, the age

> ... es el de bronze, que es peor, con tanto cañón y bombarda, todo ardiendo en guerras; no se oye otro que sitios, assaltos, batallas, degüellos, que hasta las mismas entrañas parece se han buelto de bronze. (II, iii, 105-106),

and the "Gran Capitán" thought of his sword that "... la mayor valentía de un hombre consistía en no empeñarse ni verse obligado a sacarla" (II, viii, 266).

Another topical subject is the religious upheaval, a subject anathematic to the author's Catholicism. "Argos" calls the palace of the King of France

> ... el Lobero (y no voi con vuestra malicia) porque aí se les ha armado siempre la trampa a los rebeldes lobos con piel de ovejas; digo, aquellas horribles fieras hugonotas. (II, ii, 61)

Salastano admires the purges of Ferdinand and Isabela and of Philip III, and regrets that comparable sovereigns did not imitate their actions in other countries:

> ... que si esso fuera, no huviera oy ateísmos donde yo sé, ni heregías donde yo callo, cismas, gentilismos, perfidias, sodomías y otros mil géneros de monstruosidades. (II, ii, 72).

In keeping with the general orientation of the book, the geographical center is the court of Ferdinand III, who represents a perfection in rulers:

> ... él es la honra de nuestro siglo, la otra columna del *non plus ultra* de la fe, trono de la justicia, vasa de la fortaleza y centro de toda virtud. Y creedme que no ai otra honra sino la que se apoya en la virtud, que en el vicio no puede aver cosa grande. (II, xii, 347-348)

Emotionally, the main passion which must be resisted is that for worldly possessions. Wealth is represented in the "Palacio del

Interés" (II, iii), which the pilgrims discover to be a "... dorada cárcel, palacio de Plutón, que toda casa de avaro es infierno en lo penoso y limbo en lo necio" (II, iii, 121). Power is represented in the antics of the "Assombrado" (II, xii). Ruling over these fallacious aspirations is the ominous figure of "Fortuna," with whom the pilgrims have a climactic meeting (II, vi). Intellectually the *psychomachia* proceeds between knowledge, represented by "Sofisbella" (II, iv), as opposed to vulgarity, or false learning, represented by the monster "Vulgacho" (II, v), and between virtue, represented by "Virtelia," and vice, or false virtue, represented by "Hipocrinda," whose evil is climaxed in the appearance of the threefold monster of "Mundo," "Carne," "Diablo" (II, ix).

In Book III the topics dealt with are once again more personal, less worldly in their orientation. The emotional content is higher than in any of the previous books because the subject is man's confrontation with death, the personification of which the pilgrims must face at the end of their journey (III, xi). Even old age is filled with temptations. The sin of gluttony, especially drunkenness, must be withstood. As stated in the introduction to *Crisi* ii, the most difficult part of man to control is

> ... el vientre, y esto en todas las edades: en la niñez por la golosina, en la mocedad por la lascivia, en la varonil edad por la voracidad, y en la vejez por la vinolencia. ... Es la embriaguez fuente de todos los males, reclamo de todo vicio, origen de toda monstruosidad, manantial de toda abominación, procediendo tan anómala, que quando todos los otros vicios caducan y se despiden en la vejez, ella entonces comiença y, sepultados ya, los aviva. ... (III, ii, 50-51)

The other sins of old age are sloth, personified in the figure of "el Ocioso," and pride, personified in the figure of "el Fantástico." The latter sin is an especially common pitfall of old age:

> Es la niñez ignorante, la mocedad desatenta, la edad varonil trabajada y la senectud jactanciosa: siempre está humeando presunciones, evaporando jactancias, cebando estimaciones y solicitando aplausos. (III, vii, 212)

Intellectually, the *psychomachia* proceeds between Truth, whose court they visit (III, iii), and Fraud, symbolized in the palace of "Caco" (III, v).

Structure of Allegorical Imagery in El Criticón

The allegory in the *Criticón* expresses the antagonistic trial between good and evil. Its basic structure is, therefore, antithetical. As stated by Fletcher:

> The tendency toward polarization may not always operate in practice, but underneath surface complications and subtleties one can always discern a subtending structure which opposes the powers of darkness to the powers of light. [51]

An actual battle is described only once in *El Criticón*, when the pilgrims struggle towards the palace of "Virtelia." The only way to reach her is "—Armándose primero mui bien, y peleando mejor después: que todo lo vence una resolución gallarda" (II, viii, 255). They are accosted by "... las horribles fieras pobladoras del monte" (II, x, 301) as well as by a giant who stands at the entrance of the palace. The pilgrims' method of offense is defense: "Dos vezes fiero les acometió un tigre en condición y en su mal modo, mas el único remedio fué no alborotarse ni inquietarse, sino esperalle mansamente: a gran cólera, gran sossiego, y a una furia, una espera" (II, x, 304).

An overt battle is unusual. Gracián prefers a "linguistic" opposition between good and evil, and by means of a careful selection of words, maneuvers the reader so as to elicit from him the desired emotional response. This is one of the advantages that conceptual allegory has over pictorial allegory. Rosemund Tuve explains:

> One advantage of the conceptual medium, for both moral allegory and the stricter kind, is that comparisons or associations convey directly, without statement, a constant stream of responses — values placed on things, the tiny movements of attraction or repulsion which we

---

[51] *Op. cit.*, p. 343.

share more in language than in sense experience. ...
Words tip the scales of our affections and we cannot
call this rhetorical, but simply a linguistic fact; it has
been provided by the long development of words as
instruments of communication.... This semantic fact
especially touches words that convey properties; they
amplify or deprave (the technical Elizabethan words for
magnify or *denigrate*) quite securely and almost without
our realizing what is happening. This is a great strength
when a poet wishes to convey through imagery some
great abstraction from large areas of human experience
toward which he expects to arouse attitudes of espousal
or rejection. [52]

Apocalyptic and Demonic Symbols

It is in the "participation" allegories where the chief encounters between the powers of lightness and the powers of darkness occur. The antithetical imagery expressing these powers may be called apocalyptic and demonic. [53] In psychological terms, apocalyptic imagery corresponds to the dream, for it presents images of desire, while demonic imagery is related to the nightmare, presenting images of repulsion. While apocalyptic imagery corresponds to man's taming of nature by reason, demonic imagery corresponds to untamed nature or the rule of passion.

In the *Criticón* antithetical symbols are found in the human, animal, vegetable, and mineral worlds.

In the category of the human world, the individual is opposed to the crowd, whose vulgarity Gracián does not cease to condemn. Crowds swarm the city of "Falimundo":

> Estava la plaça hecha un gran corral del vulgo, enjambre de moscas en el çumbir y en el assentarse en la basura de las costumbres, engordando con lo podrido y hediondo de las morales llagas. (I, vii, 235)

Among the crowd in the "Plaça Mayor" there is not one whole man:

---

[52] *Op. cit.*, p, 29.
[53] Terms for classification of imagery from Frye, *op. cit.*, pp. 141-150.

> ... todos lo eran a medias; porque el que tenía cabeça de hombre, tenía cola de serpiente, y las mugeres de pescado; al contrario, el que tenía pies no tenía cabeça. ... Todos eran hombres a remiendos, y assí, quál tenía garra de león, y quál de osso el pie. (II, v, 168-169)

In the category of the animal world, wild and tamed animals are contrasted. Dangerous animals and beasts of prey are associated with evil. Thus, leading the coach of "Proteo" are not horses, but instead: "Las pías que la tiravan, más remendadas que pías, eran dos serpientes, y el cochero una vulpeja" (I, vii, 218). The faucets of the "Fuente de los Engeños," "... en vez de grifos y leones, eran sierpes y eran canes" (I, vii, 221), and the incarnation of evil in the "Anfiteatro de Monstruosidades" is the dragon:

> Estava en el primero y último lugar una horrible serpiente, coco de la misma hidra, tan envegecida en el veneno, que la avían nacido alas y se iba convirtiendo en un dragón, inficionando con su aliento el mundo. (II, ix, 287)

In contrast to this, "Artemia" has miraculously tamed wild creatures:

> A la punta estava un león que le avía convertido en una mansíssima oveja, y un tigre en un cordero. ... Los gatos y los alanos de su casa ya no arañavan apretados ni mordían rabiosos, sino que, reconociendo leales su gran dueño, besavan sus generosas plantas. (I, viii, 248)

In the vegetable world, flower-bearing plants are opposed to fruit-bearing plants. As the protagonists approach "Falimundo's" reign, they are led

> ... por unos prados amenos donde se estava dando verdes las juventud. Caminavan a la fresca de árboles frondosos, todos ellos descoraçonados, gran señal de infrutíferos. (I, vii, 228)

In "Falsirena's" abode they find that

> Donde acabava el patio començava un Chipre tan verde, que pudiera darlo el más buen gusto, si bien todas sus

plantas eran más lozanas que frutíferas, todo flor y nada fruto. Coronávase de flores vistosamente odoríferas, parando todo en espirar humos fragantes. (I, xii, 352)

In contrast to this, the terrain of the "varonil edad" is devoid of flowers —

... y consolávale en aquella esterilidad de flores con la gran copia de frutos de que se veían cargados los árboles, pues tenían más que hojas, contando las de los libros. (II, i, 19)

Although "Artemia's" garden contains flowers, they are all transformed by her art:

Estava todo él coronado de flores en jardines, prodigios también fragantes, porque las espinas eran rosas, y las maravillas de todo el año; hasta los olmos davan peras, y ubas los espinos; de los más secos corchos sacava jugo y aun néctar; y los peros, en Aragón tan indigestos, aquí se nacían confitados. (I, viii, 247)

In the mineral world, Babylon is the city of hell. Madrid is the "gran Babilonia de España" (I, vi, 181); Satan is identified as "el monstruo coronado, príncipe de la Babilonia común" (II, ix, 296); and the pilgrims learn that the city of "Honoria" no longer merits this name: "Sabed que con el tiempo, que todo lo trastorna, fué creciendo esta ciudad, aumentándose en gente y confusión, que toda gran corte es Babilonia ..." (II, xi, 338).

Antithetical Patterns of Apocalyptic and Demonic Imagery

In addition to the symbols, antithetical patterns of imagery emerge, the connotations of which serve as data for recognizing evil or good as it appears in the narration. These patterns may be designated as (1) crookedness as opposed to straightness, (2) darkness as opposed to light, (3) depth as opposed to height, (4) instability as opposed to stability, and (5) ornateness as opposed to simplicity.

(1) *Crookedness as opposed to straightness:* An indication of "Proteo's" leading the pilgrims astray is that "Ya en esto les avía

sacado del camino derecho y metido en otro intrincado y torcido" (I, vii, 220), and then he takes them to "Falimundo's" court, where "... hallaron que lo que parecía clara por fuera, era confusa dentro; ninguna calle avía derecha ni despejada: modelo de laberintos y centro de minotauros" (I, vii, 228). When the false "Hermitaño" leads Critilo and Andrenio into the monastery: "Fuelos introduciendo por un camino encubierto y aun solapado entre arboledas y ensenadas, y al cabo de un laverinto con mil bueltas y rebueltas dieron en una gran casa ..." (II, vii, 231). Similarly, the palace of "Caco" is formless and confused: "Diéronle muchas bueltas sin poder distinguir la frente del embés; rodeáronle todo muchas vezes sin poderle hallar entrada ni salida" (III, vi, 162).

In the City of Truth, on the other hand, "... veíanse sus calles essentas, anchas y muy derechas, sin bueltas, rebueltas ni encrucijadas, y todas tenían salida" (III, iii, 113).

(2) *Darkness as opposed to light:* Evil is characterized by a lack of clarity. Of the court of "Falimundo" it is written that "No bien amaneció, (que allí aun el día nunca es claro) ..." (I, vii, 237), and in the Cave of Lust it is difficult to find Andrenio, for there is only a "confusa vislumbre de un infernal fuego" and a "confusa luz" (I, xii, 372). The convent of the "Hermitaño" is shaded and hidden from the sun: "Estava entre unos montes que la impedían el sol, coronado de árboles tan crecidos y tan espesos, que la quitavan la luz con sus verduras" (II, vii, 231). The darkness in the palace of "Caco" can be dispelled only by the "Zahorí":

> Discurrió luego en abrir algún resquicio por donde pudiesse entrar un rayo de luz, una vislumbre de verdad. Y al mismo instante, ¡o cosa rara!, comenzó a rayar la claridad, dió en tierra toda aquella máquina de confusiones: que toda artimaña, en pareciendo, desaparece. (III, vi, 176)

Goodness, on the other hand, is characterized by clarity and brilliance. Of the palace of "Sofisbella" it is written that:

> Era su arquitectura estremo del artificio y de belleza, engolfado en luzes y a todas ellas, que para recibirlas

bien, a más de ser diáfanas sus paredes y toda su materia transparente, tenía muchas claraboyas, balcones rasgados y ventanas patentes: todo era luz y todo claridad. (II, iv, 130)

In the City of Truth:

> Las casas eran de cristal, con puertas abiertas y ventanas patentes; no avía celosías traidoras, ni tejados encubridores. Hasta el cielo estava muy claro y muy sereno, sin niebes de emboscadas, y todo el emisferio muy despejado. (III, iii, 113)

(3) *Depth as opposed to height:* Any form of ascent in the *Criticón* is positive, and any form of descent is negative. This pattern begins to assert itself from the beginning of the novel. When the pilgrims enter the world, they witness the contention between Passion and Reason. Passion travels "... siempre cuesta abaxo ..." until she and her squadron "Hallávanse al fin de aquel paraje metidos en un valle profundíssimo ..." (I, v, 170). Reason saves the children and

> Quando los tuvo todos juntos, sacólos a toda priessa de aquella tan peligrosa estancia, guiándolos de la otra parte del valle el monte arriba, no parando hasta llegar a lo más alto, que es lo más seguro. (I, v, 171-172)

As they proceed on their journey, Andrenio notices that "... caminavan siempre cuesta arriba, ..." and Critilo explains that it is the path to heaven:

> —Assí es— le respondió Critilo, —porque son las sendas de la eternidad, y aunque vamos metidos en nuestra tierra, pero muy superiores a ella, señores de los otros y vezinos a las estrellas; ellas nos guíen, que ya estamos engolfados entre Scilas y Caribdis del mundo. (I, v, 181)

The ascent to the "edad varonil" is difficult for Andrenio:

> Hazíasele mui cuesta arriba a Andrenio, como a todos los que suben a la virtud, que nunca hubo altura sin cuesta. ... Subían tan altos, que les pareció señoreavan quanto contiene el mundo, mui superiores a todo. (II, i, 19)

In contrast to their new heights, the past terrain of their youth appears exceptionally low:

> ¡Quán baxo y quán vil parece todo lo que avemos andado hasta aquí! ¡Qué humildes y qué baxas se reconocen todas las cosas passadas! ¡Qué profundidad tan notable se advierte de aquí allá! (II, i, 19)

As might be expected, the approach to the palace of "Virtelia" is uphill, and the pilgrims are encouraged: "Porfiad en el ascenso, aunque sea con violencias, que de los valientes es la corona; y aunque sea áspera la subida, no desmayéis, poniendo siempre la mira en el fin premiado" (II, vii, 226).

The palaces of "Artemia," "Sofisbella," and "Virtelia" are all located on eminent peaks. Of "Artemia's" palace it is written that

> Campeava ya su artificioso palacio muy superior a todo, y con estar en puesto tan eminente, hazía subir las aguas de los ríos a dar la obediencia a su poderosa maña. ... (I, viii, 247),

and of "Sofisbella's" that "Campeava, sin poder esconderse, en una claríssima eminencia, señoreando quanto ai" (II, iv, 130). The pilgrims' arrival at the palace of "Virtelia" is described as follows:

> Llegaron ya a la superioridad de aquella dificultosa montaña, tan eminente, que les pareció estavan en los mismos azaguanes del cielo, convezinos de las estrellas. Dexóse ver bien el deseado palacio de Virtelia campeando en medio de aquella sublime corona, teatro insigne de prodigiosas felicidades. (II, x, 304)

The abode of Hypocrisy is contrasted to that of "Virtelia":

> ... éste está a los pies del monte, y aquél sobre su cabeça; aquél se empina hasta el cielo, y éste se roza con el abismo; aquél entre austeridades, y éste entre delicias. (II, ix, 283)

Furthermore, moments of *desengaño* or enhanced knowledge occur at a height. The "Sabio" exposes "Falimundo" to the deceived Andrenio from a mountain top: "Subamos a aquella eminencia, que levantados de tierra yo sé que descubriremos mucho" (I, viii, 258). Visions into the future take place on peaks. When the pilgrims cross the mountains into the "varonil edad" they foresee the experiences they are to encounter:

> Hallávanse ya en lo más eminente de aquel puerto de la varonil edad, coronada de la vida, tan superior, que pudieron señorear desde allí toda la humana: espectáculo tan importante quan agradable, porque descubrían países nunca andados, regiones nunca vistas, como la del Valor y del Saber, las dos grandes provincias de la Virtud y la Honra, los países del Tener y del Poder, con el dilatado reino de la Fortuna y el Mando. (II, ii, 54-55)

In the same way that this epic vision of space occurs on a mountain top, the epic vision of time presented by the "Cortesano" in Book III takes place at a height:

> Sacóles de casa, para más meterlos en ella, y fuélos conduciendo al más realçado de los siete collados de Roma, tan superior que no sólo pudieron señorear aquella universal corte, pero todo el mundo, con todos los siglos. (III, x, 303)

(4) *Instability as opposed to stability:* In the palace of "Sofisbella" the pilgrims

> Entraron dentro y admiraron un espacioso patio mui a lo señor, coronado de columnas tan firmes y tan eternas que les asseguró el varón halado podían sustentar el mundo, y algunas de ellas el cielo, siendo cada una un *non plus ultra* de su siglo. (II, iv, 131)

The house of "Falsirena" is quite different:

> En vez de firmes Atlantes en columnas, coronavan el atrio hermosas ninfas, por la materia y por el arte raras, assegurando sobre sus delicados ombros firmeza a un cielo alternado de serafines, pero sin estrella. (I, xii, 352)

(5) *Ornateness as opposed to simplicity:* Ornateness is associated with deception. The carriage of "Proteo" is described as: "... era tan artificiosa y de tan enteras bueltas, que atropellava

toda dificultad" (I, vii, 218). The dwelling place of "Volusia" is attractive: "Estava fabricada de unas piedras tan atractivas, que atraían a sí las manos y los pies, los ojos, las lenguas y los coraçones como si fueran de hierro ..." (I, x, 306).

The palace of "Virtelia," on the other hand, surprises the pilgrims:

> Y fué, sin duda, que quando le imaginaron fabricado de preciosos jaspes embutidos de rubíes y esmeraldas, cambiando visos y centelleando a rayos, sus puertas de zafir con clavazón de estrellas, vieron se componía de unas piedras pardas y cenicientas, nada vistosas, antes mui melancólicas. (II, x, 304-305)

"Lucindo" explains that

> Aquí todo va al rebés del mundo: si por fuera está la fealdad, por dentro la belleza; la pobreza en lo exterior, la riqueza en lo interior; lexos la tristeza, la alegría en el centro, que esso es entrar en el gozo del Señor. (II, x, 305)

Presentation of Allegorical Personifications

In the descriptions of the personified virtues and vices, the perfect human form is the standard. Man's perfection is described in physical terms, and each part of his body is symbolic of a moral quality. For instance, "Artemia" explains:

> —Fué el hombre —dixo Artemia— criado para el cielo, y assí, crece azia allá; y en essa material rectitud del cuerpo está simbolicada la del ánimo, con tal correspondencia, que al que le faltó por desgracia la primera sucede con mayor faltarle la segunda. (I, ix, 266-267)

Critilo concurs:

> —Es assí— dixo Critilo, —donde quiera que hallamos corbada la disposición rezelamos también torcida la intención; en descubriendo ensenadas en el cuerpo, tememos aya dobleces en el ánimo; el otro a quien se anubló alguno de los ojos, también suele cegarse de passión ... los coxos suelen tropeçar en el camino de la virtud, y aun echarse a rodar, coxeando la voluntad en los afectos. ... (I, ix, 267)

In keeping with the belief in the close alliance of the physical and the moral, evil is represented as being outrageously ugly, and good as being faultlessly beautiful. As pointed out by Schröder, good will be described as a human form in clear images, while evil assumes an animal body and is completely formless. [54]

"Artemia" is described objectively, in the third person:

> Tenía un rostro muy compuesto, ojos penetrantes; su hablar, aunque muy medido, muy gustoso; sobre todo, tenía estremadas manos que davan vida a todo aquello en que las ponía; todas sus facciones muy delicadas, su talle muy airoso y bien proporcionado, y en una palabra, todo ella de muy buen arte. (I, viii, 249)

"Virtelia" is described in similar terms:

> Hazía a todos buena cara, aun a sus mejores enemigos; mirava con buenos ojos, y aun divinos, oía bien y hablava mejor; y aunque siempre con boca de risa, jamás mostrava dientes. ... Tenía lindas manos, ... dispuesto talle y mui derecho, y todo su aspecto divinamente humano y humanamente divino. ... vestía armiños, que es su color de candidez, enlaçava en sus cabellos otros tantos rayos de la aurora con cinta de estrellas. Al fin, ella era todo un cielo de beldades, retrato al vivo de la hermosura de su celestial Padre, copiándole sus muchas perfecciones. (II, x, 310-311)

In these descriptions the emphasis is on the proportion and rectitude of the body, as well as the face and hands. This is explained in the "Moral anatomía del hombre" (I, ix), where the head is considered the "... alcáçar del alma, corte de sus potencias" (I, ix, 267), and the eyes are referred to as

> —Miembros divinos, que fué bien dicho, porque si bien se nota, ellos se revisten de una magestuosa divinidad que infunde veneración, obran con una cierta universalidad que parece omnipotencia, produziendo en el alma todas quantas cosas ay en imagines y especies, assisten en todas partes remedando inmensidad, señoreando en un instante todo el emisferio. (I, ix, 269-270)

---

[54] *Op. cit.*, pp. 178-181.

The hands are also of great importance, for

> ... ellas manan del coraçón, como ramas cargadas de frutos de famosos hechos, de hazañas inmortales; de sus palmas nacen los frutos vitoriosos, manantiales son del sudor precioso de los héroes y de la tinta eterna de los sabios. (I, ix, 280)

Both "Falimundo" and "Vulgacho" are, on the other hand, described as deformed animals, monsters of nightmarish dimensions. In the case of the sight of "Falimundo," the impact of the horror is increased because Andrenio describes the sight excitedly in the first person, conveying not only the visual horror but also his reaction of terror and loathing. He exclaims:

> Veo un monstruo, el más horrible que vi en mi vida, porque no tiene pies ni cabeça; ¡qué cosa tan desproporcionada, no corresponde parte a parte, ni dize uno otro en todo él; ¡qué fieras manos tiene, y cada una de su fiera, ni bien carne ni pescado, y todo lo parece! ¡qué boca tan de lobo, donde jamás se vió verdad! (I, viii, 258-259)

"Vulgacho" is presented as

> ... un monstruo, aunque raro y mui vulgar; no tenía cabeça y tenía lengua, sin braços y con ombros para la carga, no tenía *pecho* con llevar *tantos, ni mano en cosa alguna;* dedos sí, para señalar. Era su cuerpo en todo disforme, y como no tenía ojos, dava grandes caídas; era furioso en acometer, y luego se acovardava. (II, v, 195)

In this description the effect depends largely on the play with the literal and figurative meanings of words. Although "Vulgacho" is composed of "tantos (pechos)" or men, he has no "pecho" or courage, and the phrase "ni mano en cosa alguna" suggests the expression "tener buena mano" or "acierto." [55]

As can be seen, neither of these descriptions is in any way graphic or realistic, once again showing the stress on the con-

---

[55] Romera-Navarro, *C.*, II, v, p. 195, notes 190 and 191.

ceptual as opposed to the visual in Gracián's writing. Fletcher notes that:

> Allegory perhaps has a "reality" of its own, but it is certainly not of the sort that operates in our perceptions of the physical world. It has an idealizing consistency of thematic content, because, in spite of the visual absurdity of much allegorical imagery, the relations between ideas are under strong logical control. [56]

The disproportion and dismemberment, as well as the animal metaphors with which Gracián describes these incarnations of evil, inevitably produce a feeling of repulsion in the reader.

The figures of "Volusia" and "Falsirena" express a different and peculiar characteristic of evil, which is its desirability. As opposed to the other incarnations of evil, these figures are physically attractive. Their duplicity is, therefore, exposed by means of other devices.

The description of "Volusia" is characterized by word play. For instance, in the phrase "... una bellísima muger, nada villana y toda *cortesana* ..." (I, x, 303), "cortesana" is ambiguous because it means both a woman of the court as well as a prostitute. The statement that "... y las dos manos hazían un blanco de los afectos ..." (I, x, 303) could have two meanings. As explained by Romera-Navarro, "... es tanto como atraerse por su hermosura el cariño de los demás, y tanto como hacerles puntería en la bolsa a los encariñados." [57] Her good appearance is denied through juxtaposition with a bad action: "... hazía buena cara a todos y muy malas obras"; "... no mirava de mal ojo y a todos hazía dél ..."; "... y aunque tenía braço fuerte, de ordinario lo dava a torcer, equivocando el abraçar con el enlaçar" (I, x, 303-304).

In the case of "Falsirena," it is her manner of speech which is her distinguishing characteristic and the clue to her fraudulence. She is excessively enthusiastic, as seen in her exclamatory speech: "—¡O primo mío sin segundo! ¡O señor Andrenio! ... ¡qué retrato tan al vivo de vuestra hermosa madre!" (I, xii, 353). Her descriptions of his "mother" are hyperbolic:

---

[56] *Op. cit.*, p. 105.
[57] C., I, x, p. 303, note 98.

> ¡Ah qué linda era, y aun por esso tan poco venturosa! ¡O qué gran muger y qué discreta! Pero ¿qué Danae escapó de su engaño? ¿qué Elena de una fuga? ¿qué Lucrecia de una violencia y qué Europa de un robo? (I, xii, 353-354)

"Falsirena's" verbosity is also significant. Her sentences are long and complex:

> ... allí, mal embuelto entre unas martas que la servían a ella de galán abrigo, os encomendó en la cuna de la yerba el piadoso cielo, que no se hizo sordo, pues os proveyó de ama en una fiera; que no fué la primera vez, ni será la última, que sustituyeron maternas ausencias. (I, xii, 354)

The use of doublets adds to her verbal luxuriance:

> Quedó a la *sombra y tutela* de aquel gran príncipe que oy assiste en Alemania embaxador del Católico; allá passó con la Marquesa, como *parienta y encomendada*. ... Quedé yo aquí con mi madre, hermana suya, y aunque solas, muy acomodadas de *honra y hazienda*. ... (I, xii, 358)

Neither is her tale devoid of irony. Her statement that "Es la virtud mi empleo, procuro conservar la honra heredada, que deven más unas personas que otras a sus antepassados" (I, xi, 358-359) expresses a totally inappropriate pride in a "woman of ill repute."

Chapter IV

SATIRE IN *EL CRITICÓN*

Gracián views his novel as a union of "lo picante de la sátira con lo dulce de la épica" (I, "A quien leyere," 97), which implies a strong bond between the allegorical and the satirical content of *El Criticón*.

Allegory and satire are both modes of attack. Allegory constitutes a fictional mode of attack, for "Ayúdase con felicidad la crisi de las ficciones, para el censurar, porque como es odiosa la censura, pónese en un tercero, ya por alegoría, ya por fábula" (*Ag.*, XXVIII, 374). In this way allegory "... belongs ultimately to the area of epideictic rhetoric, the rhetoric of praise and ceremony, since it is most often used to praise and condemn certain lines of conduct or certain philosophical positions."[1] Satire, on the other hand, is a discursive mode of attack, and must avail itself of the conceit in order to be effective — "En el modo de censurar hay también su variedad y artificio; siempre que se junta con el reparo, es más artificiosa la crisi, porque, a más de lo juicioso, concluye lo ingenioso" (*Ag.*, XXVIII, 376). This concurs with David Worcester's opinion that "Contrary to popular belief, satire is seldom 'honest' in the sense of forthright expression of emotion or opinion. It has an aim, a preconceived purpose: to instill a given set of emotions or opinions into its readers. To succeed, it must practice the art of persuasion and become proficient with the tools of that art."[2]

---

[1] Fletcher, *op. cit.*, p. 121.
[2] *The Art of Satire* (New York: Russell & Russell, 1960), pp. 8-9.

Another common bond between allegory and satire is its didacticism. Allegory teaches by positive example, as "... praise for real or imputed virtue has the effect of arousing people to action." [3] Satire teaches by negative example. Gracián writes in *El Discreto* — "Encargaba, pues, Antístenes a sus tirones desaprender siniestros para mejor después aprender aciertos" (*D.*, XX, 130), and comments in the *Agudeza* that "Satirízase en general con la misma sutileza y gracia, y nótanse las necedades comunes, que no es la menos principal parte de la sabiduría prudente ..." (*Ag.*, XXVII, 363).

Both the allegory and the satire in *El Criticón* are, therefore, intended as didactic forms of censure. Possibly it was this implication of strong satirical attack on the "necedades comunes" which aroused hostility against the title of the *Criticón*.

The opposition to the title of *El Criticón* is attested to by Gracián's remark that "el título está ya provocando zeño ..." (I, "A quien leyere," 97). The cause of the criticism is believed to be the pejorative meaning of "pedant" which the word *crítico* had acquired, mentioned in Liñán y Verdugo's *Guía y avisos de forasteros*, where the *cultos* are ridiculed for the "... modo de hablar que han inventado, tan escabroso y obscuro, estos críticos, que apenas hay hombre que los entienda." [4]

According to Romera-Navarro, the title signifies "libro de críticas," a derivation from the word *crisi* meaning *juicio*. [5] This is evidently the significance Gracián gives to the word when he states that he has imitated the *crisis* of Boccalini (I, "A quien leyere," 98), referring to his *Avisos de Parnaso* (*I Ragguagli di Parnaso*). O. H. Green adds to the interpretation of *crisi-crítico* by quoting the definition in Gabriel de la Gasca y Espinosa's *Manual de avisos del perfecto cortesano, reducido a un político Secretario de Príncipes, embajadores ú de grandes Ministros* (Madrid, 1631):

> *Crítico* se deriva de *crisis*, que es tanto como *primor del entendimiento*, con que se discierne lo bueno de lo malo:

---

[3] Fletcher, *op. cit.*, p. 122.
[4] Romera-Navarro, *C.*, I, p. 97, note 19, as quoted from ed. Madrid, 1923, pp. 214-215.
[5] *Ibid.*

y así, términos cultos y críticos es decir que han de ser los términos *labrados y pulidos primorosamente* con *trabajoso* cuidado del entendimiento, limados con la propiedad de su viva significación, suavidad y dulzura de voces; buena y justa colocación de ellas, y de que procede la *elegancia* de las frases con que *en poco se dice mucho y bien*.[6]

There is yet another shade of meaning possible in this spectrum of definitions. Gracián suggests that *crisi* and attack are associated. In the *Agudeza* he begins his classification of *conceptos* by stating that "Es el sujeto sobre quien se discierne y pondera —ya en conceptuosa panegiri, ya en ingeniosa crisi, digo alabando o vituperando—, uno como centro ..." (*Ag.*, IV, 245), which implies a vituperative role for the *crisi*. In a chapter entitled "De la agudeza crítica y maliciosa" (*Ag.*, XXVI), Gracián praises Tacitus and Martial for their "Sutileza maliciosa, crítica, intencionada, al fin, todo superior gusto la estima, porque lastima" (*Ag.*, XXVI, 354). Even the "crisis juiciosas" are related to a satirical purpose — "El principal empleo, pues, deste modo de agudeza, es una censura extraordinaria, nacida de un relevante juicio" (*Ag.*, XXVIII, 374-375).

It seems, therefore, that even the title of the novel suggested censure. The hostile reaction to the title is explained by the fear which a satirist has traditionally evoked in his audience. According to Robert Elliott, "satire was originally magical ... the satirist was often thought to possess preternatural powers ... the power seems to reside in the words themselves, often in a special concatenation of words, rhymes and rhythm."[7] The most archaic form of this is the curse, an example of which is found in the *Criticón* in Critilo's warding off of the evil spirit of the "Quimera." His repeated repulsions of the "monstruo cortesano," all beginning with the imperative "vete" ("Vete a unos aduladores falsos. ... Vete a unos pretendientes engañados. ... Vete a unos

---

[6] *Op. cit.*, p. 101. Green quotes from Vol. III of *Ensayo de una biblioteca española de libros raros y curiosos*, ed. Gallardo, columns 35-36. (Emphasis added is Green's.)

[7] *The Power of Satire* (Princeton, N. J.: Princeton University Press, 1960), p. 30.

desdichados arbitristas, ..." etc. [III, iii, 85]), have the quality of a hypnotic incantation.

Although magic was no longer an effective force, Gracián could depend upon enough of a residual element of magic in satire to make it an effective tool in performing a sanative social function.

Presentation of Satire in El Criticón

The amount of satire incorporated in the *Criticón* augments in each book. The novel, which begins as a romance form, becomes more and more akin to a Menippean satire, which is described by Frye as follows:

> The Menippean satire deals less with people as such than with mental attitudes. Pedants, bigots, cranks, parvenus, virtuosi, enthusiasts, rapacious and incompetent professional men of all kinds, are handled in terms of their occupational approach to life as distinct from their social behavior. The Menippean satire thus resembles the confession in its ability to handle abstract ideas and theories, and differs from the novel in its characterization, which is stylized rather than naturalistic, and presents people as mouthpieces of the ideas they represent. [8]

During the course of the novel, the spectacle of humanity whirls before the reader, as one by one or group by group the morally diseased men and women cavort about in a chaos of confusion and deception.

Although the theme of the satire remains constant, Gracián's technique of satire changes from the first to the last books. In general, the development is from a discursive to a dramatic presentation, and from a static to a dynamic mode.

In the beginning the format for presenting the satire maintains a strict separation between the satirist, the "eiron" figure, and the satirized, the "alazons." The abnormal behavior of the fools is first noticed by Andrenio, and then interpreted by Critilo and the guide. As explained by Robert D. F. Pring-Mill, the process

---

[8] *Op. cit.*, p. 309.

... embodies a very strict process of developing discernment, moving from perception towards the fullest intellection of the image: Andrenio is charged both with the initial observation and with the first naive reaction to its incongruities, whilst Critilo and their allegorical guide share the illustrative-cum-analytical expansion and the synthetic conclusion between them. [9]

For example, in Book I "Quirón" leads Critilo and Andrenio through the "Plaça Mayor." The pilgrims see people walking upside down, which "Quirón" explains as

> Advertid que los que avían de ser cabeças por su prudencia y saber, éssos andan por el suelo; al contrario, los que avían de ser pies por no saber las cosas ... éssos mandan. (I, vi, 193)

When they see others walking backwards, "Quirón" clarifies their symbolic significance:

> —Advertid— dixo Quirón, que los más de los mortales, en vez de ir adelante en la virtud ... buelven atrás. (I, vi, 194)

This form of explanation is followed by a rapid succession of particular types specifically pointed out from the crowd, such as "¿No veis aquella muger lo que forceja, cejando en la vida?," or "Mas ¡cómo estira dellas aquel vejezuelo coxo y la fuerça que tiene!" (I, vi, 194), or "Repara en aquel otro príncipe qué haze de engullir mentiras ..." (I, vi, 198) and "... mira aquellos muy sanos de coraçón tendidos en el suelo, y aquellos otros tan malos muy en pie" (I, vi, 199).

As the novel progresses, the satirical scenes become more dramatic because the mode of presentation is through dialogue rather than through description by the observer.

For instance, in the "Palacio del Interés," Andrenio and Critilo converse directly with its inhabitants, who themselves explain the intellectual significance of an absurd action or visual

---

[9] "Some Techniques of Representation in the *Sueños* and the *Criticón*," *BHS*, XLV (1968), 282.

image. Upon asking one why he surrounds himself with cats, he responds that their voices are pleasing:

> Aquel dezir *mío, mío* y todo es *mío* y siempre *mío*, y nada para vos; éssa es la voz más dulce para mí de quantas ai. (II, iii, 117)

In the "Anfiteatro de Monstruosidades" Satan turns to the pilgrims and addresses them directly:

> Veamos aora en qué pecan estos dos peregrinos de la vida— dixo señalando a Critilo y Andrenio—, para que rindan vassallage de monstruosidad; que ni ai bestia sin tacha, ni hombre sin crimen. (II, ix, 297)

The resistance to aging in the Palace of "Vejecia," instead of being narrated, is expressed in a symmetrical question and answer series of the victims themselves:

> —¿Que estoy muy viejo? Esso niego.
> ... ...
> —¿Que me muero? No ay tal.
> ... ...
> —¿Que os entregue la hazienda? Aun es presto. (III, i, 39)

When the "Descifrador" is describing human beings in grammatical terms, he enlivens his explanation by means of imitating the dialogue of the fools:

> "—Y aquella otra ¿quién es? —Qué, ¿no la conocéis? Aquélla es la que &c. —Sí, sí ya doy en la cuenta. —Aquél es cuya hermana &c. —No digáis más, que ya estoy al cabo." (III, iv, 125)

Because the *ociosos* speak for themselves, Gracián is able to add to his satirical repertoire a phonic imitation of Italian. Critilo and Andrenio are told that in the House of Pleasure "... todo al cabo viene a parar en *placheri* y *placheri* y más *placheri*" (III, ii, 63). In the reign of "Ociosidad" they hear the following recommendations: "—*Pian piano* —dezían los italianos" (III, viii, 250), and "—¡*Placheri, placheri* y más *placheri!* —dezía un italiano" (III, viii, 251).

One of the most vivid scenes is the servant's recounting of his first experience with undressing his master, whose hair, teeth, and eyes are all false. He recalls the conversation between them and his own growing fear:

> "¿Eres amo o eres fantasma? ¿qué diablo eres?" Sentóse en esto para que le descalçasse, y aviendo desatado unos correones: "Estira, le dixo, de essa bota." Y fué de modo que se salió con bota y pierna, quedando de todo punto perdido viendo su amo tan acabado. Mas éste, que devía tener mejor humor que humores, viéndole assí turbado: "De poco te espantas, le dixo. Dexa essa pierna y ase de essa cabeça." Y al mismo punto, como si fuera de tornillo, amagó con ambas manos a retorcer y a tirársela. El moço, no bastándole ya el ánimo, echó a huir con tal espanto, creyendo que venía rodando la cabeça de su amo tras él, que no paró en toda la casa ni en quatro calles al rededor. (III, i, 30)

The combination of visual description and dialogue approximates this scene to a staged comedy.

Content of Satire in El Criticón

The seriousness of Gracián's satire, as of Quevedo's, has been questioned. Karl Vossler writes of Gracián that "Para él los males de la vida son, más bien que un problema filosófico, un tema literario, y los abusos de su pueblo y sociedad contemporánea son, más bien que un objeto y asunto de reforma, una muy bien venida ocasión de esparcir sales, conceptos y parábolas," [10] and concludes that "Así la sátira del fin del Siglo de Oro, por su falta de radicalismo religioso, ético y político, se va perdiendo en pequeñeces y futilidades." [11]

But Gracián is a moralist, not a sociologist. He does not question the institutions or structure of society, but rather man's excesses and abuses within the given order. He is not a revolutionist who believes that society is degrated, but a conformist who

---

[10] *Introducción a la literatura española del Siglo de Oro* (Madrid: Cruz y Raya, 1934), p. 119.

[11] *Ibid.*, p. 123.

judges man responsible for his own degradation, as well as for society's chaos:

> Y es cosa de notar que, siendo el hombre persona de razón, lo primero que executa es hazerla a ella esclava del apetito bestial. Deste principio se originan todas las demás monstruosidades, todo va al rebés en conseqüencia de aquel desorden capital: la virtud es perseguida, el vicio aplaudido. (I, vi, 211)

The objects of Gracián's satire are the flaws and foolishness of men, as he reveals "the nature and workings of dullness." [12] This is not a trivial subject. The satire is, in fact, so serious that "... even common sense and the reality of immediate perceptions ... are called into doubt. Man and his world, which the dunces take as sure and certain, are fragmented and shown in grotesque, strange and frightening shapes." [13]

The crowd is the demonic symbol throughout *El Criticón*. Its vulgarity and stupidity are expressed by its inability to distinguish between illusion and reality. Crowd scenes are, therefore, where the chief satirical attacks of the author are consummated and where the theme of *ser — parecer* acquires its maximum expression. The masses follow "Mentira" and oppose "Verdad" — "Todo el mundo la iba en contra, no sólo el vulgo, sino los más principales, y aun ..." (I, vi, 202); they populate the reign of "Falimundo" — "Estava la plaça hecha un gran corral del vulgo, enjambre de moscas en el çumbir y en el assentarse en la basura de las costumbres, engordando con lo podrido y hediondo de las mortales llagas" (I, vii, 235), and it is the "Villanía" who opposes "Artemia." They are easily beguiled by the "Chartalán" (III, iv), and Critilo y Andrenio cannot approach the reign of Truth for "Estorvóles el proseguir un confuso tropel de gentes que, a todo correr, venían haziendo por aquellos caminos, harto descaminados, al derecho y al través, atropellándose unos a otros, y todos desalentados" (III, iii, 100). The masses flee from Truth as though she were a dangerous beast.

---

[12] Alan B. Kernan, *The Plot of Satire* (New Haven, Conn.: Yale University Press, 1965), p. 5.
[13] *Ibid.*, p. 15.

Gracián's deprecating attitude toward the crowd is expressed by means of paradox — "Donde quiera que se volvían topavan, o locos o mentecatos, todo el mundo lleno de vacío" (II, xiii, 380), or by the frequent semantic distinction between *hombre* and *persona* — "Entraron ya en la plaça mayor del universo, pero nada capaz, llena de gentes pero sin persona" (II, v, 168) and "Toparon una gran muela de gentes, y no personas ..." (III, viii, 251). Word play is also used. In the statement "Acudía tanta gente, que no cabía de pies, aunque sí de cabeças" (I, xiii, 391), the smallness of the head refers to a lack of intelligence.

The mob is associated with acts of physical as well as moral violence. They attack the pilgrims, looking for victims of their fury — "... se enferecieron todos y arremetieron contra ellos de todas partes y naciones ... (II, xiii, 381). Their repulsiveness is emphasized by actions of physical deterioration and moral defilement. "Vinolencia" vomits, and although it has an allegorical significance, it is nevertheless described in emphatic physiological terms:

> Pero ¡qué cosa, aunque no rara, sí espantosa! Aquella embriagada reyna, anegada en abismos de horrores, començó a arrojar de aquella ferviente cuba de su vientre tal tempestad de regüeldos, que inundó toda la bacanal estancia de monstruosidades; porque, bien notado, no eran otro sus bostezos que reclamos de otros tantos monstruos de abominables vicios. Bolvía el feroz aspecto a una y otra parte, y, en arrojando un regüeldo, saltava al punto de aquel turbulento estanque del vino una horrible fiera, un infame acroceraunio que aterrava a todo varón cuerdo. (III, ii, 80)

The aberrations of the mob reach a climax in a scene of cannibalism, in which moral carnage is represented physically:

> Iban dando la buelta y viendo portentosas fealdades. Fuélo harto ver una muger que de dos ángeles hazía dos demonios, digo, dos rapazas endiabladas; y teniéndolas desolladas, las metío a assar a un gran fuego, y començó a comer dellas sin ningún horror, tragando mui buenos bocados. (II, ix, 288)

The pilgrims learn that it is a mother devouring her daughters:

> Esta es la que teniendo dos hijas tan hermosas como viste, las mete en el fuego de su lascivia; dellas come y traga los buenos bocados. (II, ix, 288)

The evil of the crowd is contrasted to the ideal of the individual in the form of examples of illustrious personages. The mob is nameless and faceless; its opposite, the outstanding individual, is identified by name and usually by deed. The polarity is frequently expressed by opposing past fame to present degeneration. As Andrenio and Critilo search for *hombres* in the "Plaça Mayor," "Quirón" is not surprised that they do not encounter any:

> —No me espanto— dixo él, que no es éste siglo de hombres: digo, aquellos famosos de otros tiempos. Qué, ¿pensavais hallar aora un don Alonso el Magnánimo en Italia, un Gran Capitán en España, un Enrico Quarto en Francia haziendo corona de su espada y de sus guarniciones lises? Ya no ay tales héroes en el mundo, ni aun memoria dellos. (I, vi, 185-186)

At the "Rueda del Tiempo" the present ineptitude of the multitude is contrasted to the past efficacy of one man:

> Sale una vez un Gran Capitán y bullen después cien capitanejos, con que se ha de mudar cada año un gefe. He aquí que para conquistar a todo Nápoles, bastó el gran Gonçalo Fernández, y para Portugal un Duque de Alva, para la una India Fernando Cortés, y para la otra Alburquerque; y oy para restaurar un palmo de tierra, no han sido bastantes doze cabos. (III, x, 332)

This is also expressed by means of word play: "—Tras de una reyna doña Blanca —proseguía el Cortesano—, salen cien negras" (III, x, 333).

Another method of contrast is the juxtaposition of the examples of the illustrious personages to the sights of the common mob. In the "Plaça del populacho y corral del Vulgo" Andrenio, seeing a group of men fighting, inquires: "—¿Quién son éstos —preguntó Andrenio— que tan vizarramente pelean? ¿Si estaría aquí el bravo Picolomini? ¿Es por ventura aquél el Conde de Fuensaldaña, y aquel otro Totavila?," and to his surprise learns that they are "quatro villanos de una aldea" (II, v, 170-171). They see "... un valiente hombre que pudiera competir con el mismo Pablo de Parada" (I, vi, 205), and subsequently realize the falseness of his appearance. Such juxtapositions serve to emphasize the disparity between the ideal possibility and the mediocre reality.

In some examples, the order of the contrast is reversed. After a misogynic condemnation of women, the comparison is presented: "Pero sean excepción de mugeres las que son más que hombres: La gran Princesa de Rosano y la excelentíssima señora Marquesa de Valdueza" (I, vi, 196). After describing the omnipresence of hypocrisy, examples are given of men of integrity, who are so rare that

> ... oymoslos nombrar como al unicornio en la Arabia y la fénix en su Oriente. Con todo, si queréis ver alguno, buscad un Cardenal Sandoval en Toledo, un Conde de Lemos governando Aragón, un Archiduque Leopoldo en Flandes. Y si queréis ver la integridad, la rectitud, la verdad y todo lo bueno en uno, buscad un Don Luis de Haro en el centro que merece. (I, vi, 208-209)

As L. Spitzer has pointed out, the proper names are in many instances used as appelatives.[14] The names are paradigms representing certain desirable qualities, and as such acquire metonymic force.

The Patterns of Satire

The movement of the allegorical journey is steadfastly upward and forward, as vice is conquered and its corresponding virtue appreciated. The intentionality of the allegorical dialectic contrasts sharply with the haphazardness of the satirical movement. The victim of satirical wrath lacks purpose or direction, with the result that "Whatever particular form dullness may take in a given satire, it moves always toward the creation of messes, discordances, mobs, on all levels and in all areas of life, chaos and uncreation."[15]

---

[14] *Op. cit.*, pp. 177-178.
[15] Kernan, *op. cit.*, p. 68.

The self-defeating patterns of movement in the satire of *El Criticón* may be described as (1) the rise which becomes a fall, (2) the forward motion which becomes backward, (3) progress which becomes a *circulus vitiosus,* and (4) motivation which becomes inertia. These will be discussed separately and examples given of each.

(1) *The rise becomes a fall:* Men raise themselves to false elevations and suffer an inevitable fall. Man, as an earthbound being, has a predestined location, as stated by Critilo:

> ¿No es la tierra su logar propio del hombre, su principio y su fin? ¿No les fuera mejor conservarse en este medio y no querer encaramarse con tan evidente riesgo? (I, vi, 188)

Most men's lack of contact with reality is then expressed by describing literal physical location which has a figurative meaning: "... se han fabricado castillos, en el ayre" (I, vi, 187); "... se han subido a las nubes ... pero la mayor parte hallaréis acullá sobre el cuerno de la luna, y aun pretenden subir más alto, si pudieran" (I, vi, 188). Andrenio dramatizes the scene by visualizing it:

> ¡... acullá están, allá los veo! Y aun allí andan empinándose, tropezando unos y cayendo otros, según las mudanças suyas y de aquel planeta, que ya les haze una cara; ya otra, y aun ellos también no cessan entre sí de armarse çancadillas, cayendo todos con más daño que escarmiento. (I, vi, 188)

Even those who are able to see choose to follow a blind man, falling when he falls, which Andrenio cannot comprehend:

> ... mas ellos, que ven y advierten el peligro común, que con todo esso le quieran seguir, tropeçando a cada punto y dando de ojos a cada passo hasta despeñarse en un abismo de infelicidades, éssa es una increíble necedad y una monstruosa locura. (I, vi, 200)

Other images of falling are found in the allegorical ball game, where a man's head is played with, until "... cayó en tierra rebentada, donde la pisaron," although at one stage "... estava tan alta que se perdía de vista" (I, viii, 256-257), as well as in the scene of the "Cueva de la Nada," where all false pretenders are doomed, "... y nunca se llenava la infeliz sima de las honras y de las haziendas" (III, viii, 263). The precarious position of the trapeze artist is used as a warning against falling:

> De esto sí que devrían andar atónitos, aquí sí que se les avían de erizar los cabellos, y más reconociendo el abismo de infelicidades donde los despeña el grave peso de sus muchos yerros. (III, xi, 340)

(2) *Forward motion becomes backward:* Man's inherent motion ought to be forward, for

> —¿No nos puso— ponderó Critilo —la próvida naturaleza los ojos y los pies azia delante para ver por donde andamos y andar por donde vemos con seguridad y firmeza? (I, vi, 193-194)

Even man's appearance symbolizes progress forward, but he fails to live up to this:

> —Advertid— dixo Quirón —que los más de los mortales, en vez de ir adelante en la virtud, en la honra, en el saber, en la prudencia y en todo, buelven atrás: Y assí muy pocos son los que llegan a ser personas. (I, vi, 194)

Instead, they resist their natural course, as "Quirón" points out:

> ¿No véis aquella muger lo que forceja, cejando a la vida? No quería passar de los veinte, ni aquella otra de los treinta, y en llegando a un cero se hunden allí, como en trampa de los años, sin querer passar adelante; aun mugeres no quieren ser: siempre niñas. (I, vi, 194)

The dunces never move in an upright and forward direction. They are found upside down:

> Assomavan ya por un cabo de la plaça ciertos personajes que caminavan, de tan graves, con las cabeças azia baxo por el suelo, poniéndose del lodo, y los pies para arriba muy empinados, echando piernas al ayre sin acertar a dar un passo: antes, a cada uno caían y aunque se maltratavan harto, porfiavan en querer ir de aquel modo tan ridículo como peligroso. (I, vi, 192)

Very frequently they move backwards:

> Caminavan azia atrás, y a este modo todas sus acciones las hazían al rebés. (I, vi, 193)

They also see an *estadista:*

> Más admiración les causó uno que, yendo a cavallo en una vulpeja, caminava azia atrás, nunca seguido, sino torciendo y rebolviendo a todas partes; y todos los del séquito, que no eran pocos, procedían del mismo modo, hasta un perro viejo que de ordinario le acompañava. (I, vi, 196)

Furthermore, the dunces are incapable of choosing a correct path. At the crossroads the pilgrims wisely choose the road of moderation. The fools, on the other hand, inevitably go astray:

> Mas ya en esto se avía juntado mucha gente en pocas personas, porque los más, sin consultar otro numen que su gusto, davan por aquellos estremos llevados de su antojo y su deleite. (I, v, 178);

> ... No era menos calificada la de otros que todo el día andavan al rededor, moliéndose y moliendo, sin passar adelante ni llegar jamás al centro. No hallavan el camino otros: todo se les iba en començar a caminar, nunca acabavan, y luego paravan, no acertando a dar un passo, con las manos en el seno, y si pudieran aun metieran los pies: éstos jamás llegavan al cabo con cosa. (I, v, 180)

This perpetual confusion is blamed on "Engaño," who

> A todos les venda los ojos, jugando con ellos a la gallina ciega, que no ay oy juego más introducido. Todos andan desatinados, dando de ojos de vicio en vicio; unos ciegos de amor, otros de codicia, éste de vengança, aquél de su ambición, y todos de sus antojos, hasta que llegan a la vejez, donde topan con el Desengaño. (III, v, 152-153)

(3) *Progress becomes a "circulus vitiosus":* The fools' stupidity prevents their perceiving the attitudes and actions of others, with the result that their mockery of others is circular, for they themselves are simultaneously being ridiculed.

Their whole life is a vicious circle. Guided by Proteus, Andrenio and Critilo enter the city, in which they learn that

> —Este lado del mundo embaraçan los engañados— ... aquel otro lo ocupan los engañadores: aquéllos se ríen de éstos, y éstos de aquéllos, que al cabo del año ninguno queda deudor. (I, vii, 231)

Their enjoyment at seeing another person ridiculed is self-defeating:

> Y todo esto, con gran risa y entretenimiento de los presentes, que todos gustan de ver el ageno engaño. Faltándoles el conocimiento para el propio, ni advertían que mientras estavan embelesados mirando lo que al otro le passava, les saqueavan a ellos las faldriqueras y tal vez las mismas capas. De suerte que al cabo, el mirado y los que miravan todos quedavan iguales, pues desnudos en la calle y aun en tierra. (I, vii, 238)

The gossip is such in the reign of "Honoria" that

> Desta suerte andava el juego y la risa de todo el mundo, que siempre la mitad se está riendo de la otra, burlándose unos de otros, y todos mascarados; éstos se fisgavan de aquéllos y aquéllos déstos, y todo era risa, ignorancia, murmuración, desprecio, presunción y necedad, y triunfava el ruincillo. (II, xi, 329-330)

In the "Jaula de Todos" each is unable to recognize his own absurdity:

> A todos los otros imaginavan sus antípodas y que andavan al revés, persuadiéndose cada uno que él iba derecho y el otro cabeça abaxo, dando de colodrillo por essos cielos, él mui tieso y los otros rodando. ... Todos se burlavan, unos de otros: el avaro del deshonesto y éste de aquél, el español del francés y el francés del español. (II, xiii, 372)

Even greed degenerates into a vicious cycle. Critilo and Andrenio, trapped in the "Palacio del Interés," describe what they see:

Aquí vieron executada aquella exagerada crueldad que cuentan de las víboras (cómo la hembra al concebir corta la cabeça al macho, y después los hijuelos vengan la muerte de su padre agujerándola el vientre y rasgándola las entrañas por salir y campear) quando vieron que la muger, por quedar rica y desahogada, ahoga al marido; luego el heredero, pareciéndole vive sobrado la madre y él no vive sobrado, la mata a pesares; a él, por heredarle, su otro hermano segundo le despacha. De suerte que unos a otros como víboras crueles se emponçoñan y se matan. (II, iii, 119)

(4) *Motivation becomes inertia:* The almost obsessive motivation of the allegorical characters to reach their goal provides a startling contrast to the passivity and inertia of the dunces. When Critilo and Andrenio approach the crossroads, seeing

... entre ellos algunos personajes de harta importancia, preguntáronles cómo iban por allí, y respondieron que ellos no iban, sino que los llevavan. (I, v, 180)

As the pilgrims pass through the "Aduana de la Vida," it is evident to them that

... los más no saben dar razón de sí mismos. Y assí, preguntándole a uno dónde caminava, respondió que adonde le llevava el tiempo, sin cuidarse más que de passar y hazer tiempo. ... Respondió otro que él passava adelante por no poder bolver atrás. Los más dezían que porque los avían echado, con harto dolor de su coraçón, de los floridos países de su mocedad; que si esso no fuera, toda la vida se estuvieran con gusto dándose verdes de mocedades. (II, i, 33)

The life of the allegorical characters is defined by their goal. The lifelessness of the fools in the reign of "Ociosidad" is defined by their lack of a goal other than eating:

—Esso es dezir que están muertos desde que nacieron y passan plaça de finados, pues ya llegaron al fin de el ser personas; que si la definición de la vida es el moverse, éstos no tienen acción propia ni obran cosa que valga: ¿qué más muertos los quieres? (III, viii, 259)

The Rhetoric of Satire

The final impression of the reader upon terminating the *Criticón* is that of a nightmarish world populated by monsters from which the only release is death. In accordance with Frye's classification, the *Criticón* is a satire of the low norm, in which;

> Once we have finished with it, deserts of futility open up on all sides, and we have, in spite of the humor, a sense of nightmare and a close proximity to something demonic.
>
> ... ...
>
> ... It takes for granted a world which is full of anomalies, injustices, follies and crimes, and yet is permanent and undisplaceable. Its principle is that anyone who wishes to keep his balance in such a world must learn first of all to keep his eyes open and his mouth shut. ... What is recommended is conventional life at its best: a clairvoyant knowledge of human nature in oneself and others, an avoidance of all illusion and compulsive behavior, a reliance on observation and timing rather than aggressiveness. [16]

Most important in creating this demonic impression are the rhetorical devices which Gracián employs to persuade the reader of the iniquity of the ways of the world. Gracián's satire is centripetal,[17] concentrating on the central evil, the dunces' illusion which is illustrated and increasingly defined as the novel progresses. The rhetorical devices will, therefore, aim at stripping the illusion from the fools, thereby exposing their follies to the reader.

The rhetorical devices which Gracián utilizes are discussed as (1) technique of low burlesque, (2) technique of high burlesque, (3) technique of irony, and (4) technique of transformation. Each of these is described and illustrated separately.

(1) *Technique of low burlesque:* According to Worcester, this method "creates a standard below its victim and makes the reader measure him against that standard.[18] This form of denigration

---

[16] *Op. cit.*, p. 226.
[17] Paulson, *op. cit.*, uses the terms "centripetal" and "centrifugal" to describe satire, p. 44.
[18] *Op. cit.*, p. 44.

is used by Gracián in various ways, which may be called "animalization," "mechanization," "diminutivization," and "deformation." All of these methods reduce men from a human to a subhuman level.

a) *Animalization* — This consists of a metaphoric comparison of men to animals. In Gracián's terminology, it can be considered a *metamorfosis* in which

> Consiste su artificio en la semejanza de lo natural con lo moral, explicada por transformación o conversión fingida del sujeto en el término asimilado, de donde es que cualquiera símile se pudiera convertir en metamorfosi. ... Sea ejemplo El asno de oro. ... Describe en ella el ingenioso africano la semejanza de un hombre vicioso, y por el consiguiente necio, con el más vil de los irracionales, y que si sus apetitos bestiales y sus pasiones le transformaron en bruto, la sabiduría y el silencio simbolizado en la rosa que comió, que por eso daban los antigos rosas al principio del convite, le vuelven a rehacer hombre. (Ag., LVI, 478)

This device is initially used for didactic purposes by Critilo to warn Andrenio of man's dangerous cruelty — "Dichoso tú que te criaste entre las fieras, y ¡ay de mí!, que entre los hombres, pues cada uno es un lobo para el otro, si ya no es peor el ser hombre" (I, iv, 148), which he proceeds to emphasize by exaggerating the comparison — "... que si los hombres no son fieras es porque son más fieros, que de su crueldad aprendieron muchas vezes ellas" (I, iv, 150). He follows this with an exclamatory synonymic enumeration of the evils: "—¡Qué de engaños, qué de enredos, traiciones, hurtos, homicidios, adulterios, invidias, injurias, detracciones, y falsedades que experimentarás entre ellos! Todo lo qual no se halla ni se conoce entre las fieras. Créeme que no ay lobo, no ay león, no ay tigre, no ay basilisco, que llegue al hombre: a todos excede en fiereza" (I, iv, 152), and concludes with a relevant tale of a man killed not, as one might expect, by a wild animal, but rather by a fellow being. This "example" illustrating a doctrinal statement constitutes a technique applauded in the *Agudeza:*

> Por cuentos y por chistes, han intentado algunos sabios el introducir la moral filosofía y comunicar sus desenga-

ños a la razón; es de gran artificio, porque con la añagaza de la dulzura de la narración, se va entrando la sagacidad y la enseñanza prudente. (*Ag.*, LVII, 484)

This tale is especially appealing because of "... la ingeniosa y pronta salida" (*Ag.*, LVII, 485).

Such a doctrinal statement does not reoccur. Once the simile has been established that man is like a beast, the theory is put into practice, and men metaphorically become beasts. Needless to add, all the animals mentioned have a symbolic value. As stated by Francisco Yndurain:

> El bestiario de la obra gracianesca, sean animales reales o fantásticos, es también un buen ejemplo de solicitación hacia su sentido simbólico, siempre de orden moral: "El león de un poderoso, el tigre de un matador, el lobo de un ricazo, la vulpeja de un fingido, la víbora de una ramera ..." (*Criticón*, I, vi) no están "vistos," sino entendidos como ejemplos de caracterizaciones morales. [19]

Once the pilgrims enter the world, the bestiality of man becomes more vividly portrayed. Initially, the metaphoric process proceeds in two stages. The animal is first described, and then its symbolic significance is given.

As they enter the "Plaça Mayor," the pilgrims see that the square is filled with beasts:

> Avía leones, tigres, leopardos, lobos, toros, panteras, muchas vulpexas; ni faltavan sierpes, dragones y basiliscos. (I, vi, 190)

"Quirón" proceeds to interpret these symbols:

> El león de un poderoso, con quien no ay poderse averiguar, el tigre de un matador, el lobo de un ricazo, la vulpeja de un fingido, la víbora de una ramera. ... (I, vi, 190)

Similarly in the city of "Falimundo," the officials are described as "... cuervos muy domésticos y muy hallados con sus amos." The "ground" of the metaphor is explained later, and is based on

---

[19] *Op. cit.*, p. 183.

onomatopeic similarity of the cry of the bird, "cras," and the latin word for "tomorrow," for

> ... las almas de los oficiales, ... las dava a cuervos; y como siempre avían mentido diziendo: "Mañana, señor, estará acabado: para mañana sin falta," aora, prosiguiendo en su misma canción, van repitiendo por castigo y por costumbre aquel su ¡*cras, cras!* que nunca llega. (I, vii, 229)

Another example of this double step occurs in the search for Andrenio. He has become the victim of "Falsirena," who is able, like Circe, to convert men into beasts. They look for him in the "vulgares plaças," and see "... unas grandes azémilas atadas unas a otras, ..." which are interpreted by "Egenio" as being

> ... grandes hombres, gente de cargo y de carga, y aunque los ves tan vizarros, en quitándoles aquellos ricos jaezes parecen llenos de feíssimas llagas de sus grandes vicios. ... (I, xii, 366-367)

As can be seen, there is little visual description, although there are a few examples where the verbs describing animal gestures are pictorially vivid, such as "—¿Y aquel perro viejo que está allí ladrando?," or "—Sé que no sería aquel gimio que nos está haziendo gestos en aquel balcón" (I, xii, 368).

As the *Criticón* progresses, the satirical scenes of animalization become more elliptical and more is expected of the reader.

For instance, as Critilo and Andrenio enter the "Plaça del Populacho," they see that

> Todos eran hombres a remiendos, y assí, quál tenía garra de león, y quál de osso el pie; hablava uno por boca de ganso, y otro murmurava con ozico de puerco; éste tenía pies de cabra, y aquél orejas de Midas; algunos tenían ojos de lechuza y los más de topo; risa de perro quien yo sé, mostrando entonces los dientes. (II, v, 169)

In this brief description there are two allusions to proverbial statements — "hablar por boca de ganso," meaning to speak incorrectly, and the "risa de perro" which is based on the expression "risa de conejo," meaning a forced laugh. Furthermore, the "orejas de Midas" necessitates a knowledge of Ovid's *Metamorphosis*, where Midas' ears are described as those of an ass. [20]

Throughout the *Criticón*, for satirical purposes men are associated with the most repulsive beasts. These include birds of prey, in the comment that "Chupa la sangre del pobrecillo el ricazo de rapiña ..." (I, xi, 331), where the phrase "ave de rapiña" has been converted into "ricazo de rapiña," as well as flies:

> Estava la plaça hecha un gran corral del vulgo, enjambre de moscas en el çumbir y en el assentarse en la basura de las costumbres, engordando con lo podrido y hediondo de las morales llagas. (I, vii, 235)

Reptiles prompt a reaction of disgust. Snakes are mentioned when their familial cruelty is compared to man's —

> ... (cómo la hembra al concebir corta la cabeça al macho, y después los hijuelos vengan la muerte de su padre agujerándola el vientre y rasgándola las entrañas por salir y campear). ... De suerte que unos a otros como víboras crueles se emponçoñan y se matan. (II, iii, 119) —

and the "sabandija" is referred to in the statement that some men

> Tienen reconcentrada la malicia, y assí tienen malas entrañuelas; son de casta de sabandijas pequeñas, que todas pican que matan. (III, iv, 130)

Any form of degradation is described as a capitulation to bestiality. In the "Anfiteatro de Monstruosidades,"

> Lo primero que encontraron en el mismo atrio fué un establo, nada estable, aunque lleno de gente lucida, hombres de mucho porte y más cuenta, mui hallados todos con los brutos; sin asquear el mal olor de tan inmunda estancia. ... No se sentía otro dentro que malas vozes y bramidos de fieras, ni se oían sino monstruosidades. Era introlerable la hediondez que despedía. (II, ix, 283-284)

The inebriated men in the "Casa de Alegría" are reduced to vile beasts, who

---

[20] Romera-Navarro, *C.*, II, p. 169, notes 16, 18, and 19.

> ... en tropa de brutos se metían muy adentro, no parando hasta encontrar con el mayor estanque, y assí se arrojavan de bruzes. (III, ii, 71)

Critilo soon discovers that the palace of "Vinolencia" is not fit for human habitation:

> Halló lo primero que la bacanal estancia no se componía de doradas salas, sino de ahumadas çaurdas. (III, ii, 72)

In the same way that the common crowd is opposed to the unique individual, the standard of comparison for the prevalent, ignoble beast is the rare and valuable animal. "Quirón" explains that illustrious men are hard to find, for

> Hállanse pocos, y éstos están muy retirados: oymoslos nombrar como al unicornio en la Arabia y la fénix en su Oriente. (I, vi, 208-209)

(b) *Mechanization:* In this method the degrading comparison is made not to an animal but to an inanimate object. Such a detached view of man reflects an advanced stage of disilusionment. It is a form of "cosmic irony" which, in the words of David Worcester,

> ... is the satire of frustration, uttered by men who believe that however high man's aspirations and calculations may reach, there is always a still higher, unattainable level of knowledge, in the light of which those aspirations and calculations must become stultified and abortive. [21]

Paul Ilie states that "It is in this symbolic representation of the lack of human substance that Gracián's grotesque draws closest to the modern age." [22]

The most extreme form of the negation of life occurs in the discussion of the *ociosos,* whose only sign of life is their intake of food. These Gracián condemns to living death:

---

[21] *Op. cit.,* p. 129.
[22] "Gracián and the Moral Grotesque," HR, XXXIX (1971), 44.

> Esso es dezir que están muertos desde que nacieron y passan plaça de finados, pues ya llegaron al fin de el ser personas; que si la definición de la vida es el moverse, éstos no tienen acción propia ni otra cosa que valga: ¿qué más muertos los quieres? (III, viii, 259)

More frequent is a form of decomposition from flesh and blood to mineral substances. In the "Fuente de los Engaños," the fools' lack of substance is exposed:

> Los coraçones se les bolvieron de corcho, sin jugo de humanidad ni valor de personas, las entrañas se les endurecieron más que de pedernales, los sesos de algodón, sin fondo de juizio, la sangre agua, sin color ni calor, el pecho de cera, no ya de azero, los nervios de estopa, sin bríos, los pies de plomo para lo bueno y de pluma para lo malo, ... las lenguas de borra, los ojos de papel: y todos ellos, engaño de engaños y todo vanidad. (I, vii, 226-227)

There are examples of a metallic composition, when the restlessness of the idiots is considered of a mercurial nature:

> ... moviéndose todos, que ni paran ni dexan parar, amassados con azogue, que todos se mueven, hechos de goznes, gente de polvorín, picantes granos. (III, iv, 129)

Others are reduced to food substances:

> Los indoctos afectados son buñuelos sin miel, y los podridos, vizcochos de galera. (III, iv, 123)

Men are also diminished to puppets and toys. "Argos" prognosticates a continual diminuition in size: [23]

> Sin duda que assí como dizen que van degenerando los hombres y siendo más pequeños quanto más va (de suerte que cada siglo merman un dedo, y a este passo vendrán a parar en títeres y figurillas, que ya poco les falta a algunos). (II, ii, 57)

---

[23] This sign of human degeneration is related to the Legend of the Ages. Pliny mentions the decrease in stature in his *Natural History*. See Lovejoy and Boas, *op. cit.*, pp. 101-102.

The "Cortesano" describes men as puppets dangling on strings which are liable to be cut at any instant:

> Era mucho de ver quáles andavan los hombres rodando y saltando como si fueran otros tantos ovillos, sin parar un instante, al passo que las celestiales esferas les iban sacando la sustancia y consumiendo la vida hasta dexarlos de todo punto apurados y deshechos, de tal suerte, que no venía a quedar en cada uno sino un pedaço de trapo de una pobre mortaja, que en esto viene a parar todo. (III, x, 334)

In Book III, such belittling comparisons are enriched by a series of grammatical metaphors. There are sporadic examples of these terms used as descriptive metaphors, [24] such as "paréntesis de mi vida" (I, ii, 118) and "¿Qué dipthongo de estancia es ésta?" (III, v, 161), but it is during the pilgrims' encounter with the "Descifrador" that the technique is developed as a satirical one. It is this guide who deciphers the masks of men in terms of the "dipthongo" (III, iv, 122-124), the "etcéteras" (III, iv, 125-126), and the lowest form possible, the "puntillos de íes y tildes de enes" (III, iv, 129-130). The reader's expectation is aroused because the peculiar metaphor is first stated, and only later explained by means of examples, as in

> Dipthongo es un hombre con voz de muger, y una muger con habla de hombre; dipthongo es un marido con melindres, y la muger con calçones. ... (III, iv, 122)

Furthermore, the explanations are enlivened by satirical imitations of foolish conversations, as in the explanations of the "etcéteras" —

> "—Y aquella otra, ¿quién es?— ¿Qué, no la conocéis? Aquélla es la que &c. ..." (III, iv, 125)

or by dramatically indicating a living example of a disorder —

---

[24] Curtius, *op. cit.*, discusses grammatical terms employed as metaphors and their use in Spanish Mannerism. See "Grammatical and Rhetorical Technical Terms as Metaphors," pp. 414-416.

> Reparad en aquel monstruo casado con aquel ángel. ¿Pensaréis que es su marido? / —¿Pues qué avía de ser? / ... —No se puede dezir: es ¡un &c! (III, iv, 125)

Even the grammatical terms can serve as the basis of a word play, such as the phrase "puntillos de íes y tildes de enes," where the technical term "puntillo" is connected with the phrase "andar de puntillas" —

> Por esso es menester guardarles los ayres, que siempre andan en puntillos y de puntillas. ... (III, iv, 129)

(c) *Diminutivization:* One of Gracián's favorite methods of denigration is the conversion of nouns into their diminutive forms, usually by means of the addition of the suffix *-illo*. It seems that the author became increasingly aware of the efficacy of such a method, for though there are few examples of satirical diminutives in the First Book, their frequency increases in each subsequent part.

Man's inanity is expressed by emphasizing the triviality of his concerns. The "boquirrubio" loses his reason over a woman, whose "ayrecillo" he likes; one man kills another because of a "palabrilla" he uttered, and although not offensive in itself, "... el ayrecillo con que la dixo me ofendió mucho" (I, xiii, 399). In spite of his noisiness, nothing that the dunce says is of importance, which causes Andrenio to exclaim — "—¡Prodigiosa cosa —dixo Andrenio— que con meter tanto ruido, no tengan habla!," for "... todas son hablillas y todas falsas" (II, v, 184).

The insignificance of most men is expressed by means of diminutives. At the entrance of the "Anfiteatro de Monstruosidades," they are greeted by an "hombrecillo de media" (II, ix, 283), and the women are described as a "donzellita" or a "loquilla" (II, ix, 284-285). Andrenio disdains the "... ruincillos ... aquéllos que hazen del hombre porque no lo son, ..." as well as "... el otro gravecillo que afecta el ser persona y nunca sale de personilla ..." (III, iv, 129). The "puntillos de íes y tildes de enes" are nothing, for "Son chiquitos y poquitos y menuditos y assí dize el catalán: *Poca cosa para forsa*" (III, iv, 130). The false vanity which Andrenio witnesses in the House of Pride irritates him:

> —Señores— ponderava Andrenio, —que a los grandes hombres no les pese de aver nacido, que los entendidos quieran ser conocidos, súfraseles. Pero que el nadilla y el nonadilla quieran parecer algo, y mucho, ... que el ruincillo se estire, ... ¿cómo nos ha de bastar la paciencia? (III, vii, 238-239)

In the "Cueva de la Nada," the most extreme forms of dwarfing are the

> Nonadillas, que aun de la nada no se hartan, y assí les llaman cosillas y figurillas, y ruincillos y nonadillas. (III, ix, 276)

There are passages in which the use of the diminutive reveals the latent irony of the statement. An example of the importance of context is the self-defense of vanity, who insists that

> No ai aura más fragante ni que más vivifique que la fama, que tan bien alienta el alma como el cuerpo, y es su puríssimo elemento el airecillo de la honrilla. (II, xi, 319)

Another example is the "Premática de Vejecia," where the use of the diminutive discloses the comedy of the mock serious proclamation. Included is the following prohibition:

> Ni por esso han de andar vestidos de figura con monterillas o sombrerillos chiquitos y puntiagudos, ni con lechuguillas y calças afolladas haziendo los matachines. (III, ii, 55-56)

(d) *Deformation:* The moral chaos that man has created is symbolized in physical displacements and distortions of his bodily functions.

One form of this is the case of the "Assombrado" who is merely a "... sombra de hombre, rara visión y al cabo nada," whose intent it is to go "... en busca de algún gran hombre para ser sombra suya y poder mandar el mundo" (II, xii, 347). He begins to accumulate others' discarded extremeties:

> ... vieron caer a los pies de la Sombra unas espaldas de hombre, y mui hombre, fuertes ombros y travadas cos-

tillas. ... Y cayeron dos manos con sus braços tan rollizos, que parecía cada uno un braço de hierro. Desta suerte fueron cayendo todas las prendas de un varón grande. Estavan los circunstantes atónitos de ver el suelo poblado de humanos miembros, mas la Sombra los fué recogiendo todos y rebistiéndoselos de uno en uno, con que quedó mui persona, hombre de poder y valer. (II, xii, 351-352)

This is followed by a summary in which the author makes use of proverbial statements involving parts of the body in order to play with their literal and figurative senses: "De modo que uno le hizo espaldas [to favor], otro la barba [to be of aid], no faltó quien le dió la mano [to help], ni quien le fuesse pies [to help], con que pudo hazer piernas y hombrear [to be firm and resolute] (II, xii, 352)." [25]

The opposite form of this is the case of the individual whose limbs are all removable. The servant, helping his master undress, finds that the "cabellera" becomes a "calavera," and the "dientes" turn into a "páramo." The climax of this reduction to nothingness occurs when the master says:

"De poco te espantas, le dixo. Dexa essa pierna y ase de essa cabeça." Y al mismo punto, como si fuera de tornillo, amagó con ambas manos a retorcer y a tirársela. (III, i, 30)

There may also be a deformation in bodily functions. For instance — "Observó de buena nota Andrenio que los más hablavan a la boca, y no al oydo," which is clearly an abuse of the normal procedure, for "Las palabras se oyen, que no se comen ni se beben, y éstos todo se lo tragan" (I, vi, 197). This is subsequently explained through the use of concrete verbs of physical action to clarify abstract moral concepts, when "Quirón" points out:

¿No adviertes, ¡o Andrenio!, aquel señor cómo se está saboreando con las lisonjas de azúcar? ¡Qué hartazgos se da de adulación! ... Repara en aquel otro príncipe qué haze de engullir mentiras. ... (I, vi, 198)

---

[25] Parenthetical comments are mine. For explanation of the *refranes*, see Romera-Navarro, *C.*, II, xii, p. 352, notes 69-72.

The corruption of man, his debasement from the ideal standard of wholeness, is also accomplished by turning men into hybrids of man and beast. In the "Plaça del Vulgo," in the manner of Diogenes, they cannot find a whole man:

> ... todos lo eran a medias: porque el que tenía cabeça de hombre, tenía cola de serpiente, y las mugeres de pescado; al contrario el que tenía pies no tenía cabeza. ... Todos eran hombres a remiendos. (II, v, 168-169)

Height can also be a decisive factor, because smallness of body is indicative of moral exiguity. The term "medio hombre" is found frequently to describe the dunces, as in the Wheel of Fortune, where present men are seen to be "Sombras de aquéllos que van delante: medio hombres, pues no tienen entereza" (III, x, 318). According to "Argos":

> ... van degenerando los hombres y siendo más pequeños quanto más va (de suerte que cada siglo merman un dedo, y a este passo vendrán a parar en títeres y figurillas, que ya poco les falta a algunos), sospecho que también los coraçones se les van achichando. (II, ii, 57)

In order to pass into honored old age across the Alps, they must be measured, and most do not pass the test:

> Y era cosa rara que, llegando cada instante unos y otros a medirse, ninguno se ajustava de todo punto. Unos se quedavan mui cortos, a tres o quatro dedos de necios, ya por esto, ya por lo otro. ... Al contrario, otros passavan del coto y eran bachilleres, resabidos, sabiondos, y aun casi locos: ... Assí, que unos por cortos, otros por largos, unos por carta de más, otros de menos, todos perdían: a unos les faltava un pedazo de entendimiento, y a otros les sobrava. (II, xiii, 369.)

(2) *Technique of high burlesque:* Certain types of satire may be classified as treating "... a trivial subject in an elevated manner." [26]

---

[26] Worcester, *op. cit.*, p. 47.

One form of this is the mock heroic, in which the disparity between the lowly subject and his inflated pretensions serves to expose his triviality. One example of this in the *Criticón* are the tradesmen who make a pretense at having a patron god, and fight among each other as to who is most important:

> —Sí —repitieron los herreros—, que no tenéis un dios sastre, como nosotros un herrero, y quando todos le tienen, los taberneros a Baco, aunque anda en zelos con Tetis, los mercaderes a Mercurio, de quien tomaron las trampas con el nombre, los panaderos a Ceres, los soldados a Marte, los boticarios a Esculapio. ¡Mirá qué tales sois vosotros, que ningún dios os quiere! (II, v, 183)

Another example occurs when the dunces become involved in ridiculous arguments, and the pilgrims' guide asks

> —¿Qué te parece? —dixo el Cécrope—. ¿Pudieran discurrir mejor los siete sabios de Grecia? Pues advierte que todos son mecánicos, y los más sastres. (II, v, 172)

In the same disdainful tone, the presiding tribunal of the "Plaça del Populacho" is compared to the Athenian tribunal:

> —Este es —dixo— el Areópago; aquí se tiene el Consejo de Estado de todo el mundo. (II, v, 172)

In another scene the "Charlatán" entices his spectators by means of a hyperbolic comparison of his exhibition to the personages of classical mythology: "—¡Agora sí —dezía— que os propongo no menos que un famoso gigante, un prodigio de la fama! ¡Fueron sombra con él Encelado y Tifeo!," but the supposed giant he introduces is nothing but "... un nonada, pigmeo en todo, en el ser y en el proceder" (III, iv, 142). The same showman introduces a mirror, in reality nonexistent, but which is glorified by hyperbolic comparison —"¿Qué tenía que ver con éste el del Faro?" (III, iv, 144), and which merits being placed beside the anvil of Vulcan (III, iv, 145).

Another type of mock heroism involves the assignation of titles and absurd names which express the vanity of the fools' pretenses.

Among the overly innocent, they meet a "don Fulano de Maçapán" and the "canónigo Blandura" (III, vi, 186), as well as "don Fulano de Todos" and "don Fulano del Sí" (III, vi, 187). In the Palace of Pride, the author takes advantage of certain proper names to undermine his victims, in keeping with what he had written in the *Agudeza* —"Siempre el nombre fué origen de grandes conceptos," for it can be made use of for an "agudeza" "... exprimiendo sus dos afectos" (Ag., X, 283). The descent of one from a "Conde Claros," a name appearing in romances,[27] is corrected to "Conde Obscuros" (III, vii, 225). Another vain individual claims "don Pelayo" as his predecessor, which Andrenio reinterprets — "... que los más linajudos suelen venir de Pelayo en lo pelón, de Layn en lo calvo y de Rasura en lo raído" (III, vii, 226), referring to Nuño Rasura and Laín Calvo, ancient Castilian names.[28]

The reaction to the woman who traces her lineage to the "infanta Doña Toda" (a figure from the ninth century)[29] is that "—Poco le aprovecha esso, señora doña Calabaça, si vuestra señoría es doña Nada" (III, vii, 227). In this example, the name of "Todo" is converted into its opposite, "Nada," in accordance with the principle that "No arguye menos sutileza describir la primorosa improporción y repugnancia entre el nombre y los efectos o contingencias del sujeto denominado" (Ag., XXXI, 389). Furthermore, the second appellation, "Calabaça," is appropriate because of its degrading comparison to a pumpkin, and because it contains an allusion to the expression "Tener cascos de calabaza," meaning to be silly or stupid.

Falsified names of the aristocracy are also ridiculed:

> —¿No notáis —dezía el Poltrón— las colas que añaden todos a sus apellidos, González de Tal, Rodríguez de Quál, Pérez de Allá y Fernández de Acullá? ¿Es possible que ninguno quiere ser de acá? (III, vii, 229)

The complete lack of individuality of the dunces is shown by naming them according to traditional types, such as "Juan de Buen Alma" (III, vi, 184), or as personifications of traditional

---

[27] Romera-Navarro, *C.*, III, vii, p. 225, note 93.
[28] *Ibid.*, p. 226, note 98.
[29] *Ibid.*, p. 226, note 99.

expressions, such as *Tal sea mi vida* or *Mi alma con la suya* (III, vi, 185). Contemptuous adjectives also become personified into "el Bobico," "el Dropo," and "el Zaino" (III, vi, 181).

(3) *Technique of irony:* The ironic mode would understandably be appealing to Gracián's intellectualism, for "In literature the percipients of irony always feel themselves to be members of a small, select, secret society headed by the author. The victims, by implication, are legion. Satire enters when the few convict the many of stupidity. ... The ironist appeals to an aristocracy of brains." [30]

The examples of ironic usage in the *Criticón* require close attention to context. It is the context in which they are used which causes the inversion of meaning in the truisms which are uttered. For instance, throughout the novel the past is praised and the present criticized. This *topos,* however, acquires an ironic sense when uttered by "Villanía" against "Artemia":

> —Advertid que después que esta fingida reyna se ha introduzido en el mundo, no ay verdad, todo está adulterado y fingido, nada es lo que parece. ... De aquí es que los hombres no son ya los que solían, hechos al buen tiempo y a lo antiguo, que fué siempre lo mejor. (I, ix, 285-286)

Although man's aspiration toward self-improvement is the basic theme of the novel, when the concept is expressed by Vanity, its meaning is perverted:

> No vive —dezía— la vida material quien no respira, ni la formal quien no aspira. No ai aura más fragante ni que más vivifique que la fama, que tan bien alienta el alma como el cuerpo, y es su puríssimo elemento el airecillo de la honrilla. (II, xi, 319)

In the case of "Artemia," art does indeed perfect and better nature:

> Préciase de aver añadido un otro mundo artificial al primero, suple de ordinario los descuydos de la naturaleza,

---

[30] Worcester, *op. cit.*, p. 77.

perficionándola en todo: que sin este socorro del artificio, quedara inculta y grosera. (I, viii, 243)

When, however, the "colgaduras naturales" at the "Casa de Alegría" are hyperbolically praised over Flemish tapestries and Rubens' drawings, the statement that "Creedme que todo lo artificial es sombra con lo natural, y no más de un remedo" (III, ii, 68), is obviously false.

There is also a parody of the *topos* of the *carpe diem*, which acquires an evil connotation when it is enunciated by Satan:

> —¡Ea, acabá, dexáos de pesares! Venid, holguémonos, logremos la vida, gozemos de sus gustos, de los olores y ungüentos preciosos, de los banquetes y comidas, de los lascivos deleites. Mirá que se nos passa la flor de la edad; passemos la edad en flor, comamos y bevamos, que mañana moriremos; andémonos de prado en prado, dando verdes a nuestros apetitos. (II, ix, 296)

The parody of the *beatus ille topos* is one of the most effective examples of inversion of meaning. What is apparently praise of "Falsirena" is converted into condemnation:

> —Mi señora —decía el rapaz— la honestíssima Falsirena, vive muy fuera del mundo, agena del bullicio cortesano, ya por natural recato, haziendo desierto de la corte, ya por poder gozar de la campaña en sus alegres jardines. (I, xii, 351)

The reader's knowledge of "Falsirena's" occupation converts the positive connotation of the *beautus ille* theme into a completely negative one.

(4) *Technique of transformation:* This is what Gracián terms "ingeniosas transposiciones" in the *Agudeza*, adding that

> Esta especie de conceptos es una de las más agradables que se observan. Consiste su artificio en transformar el objeto y convertirlo en lo contrario de lo que parece: obra grave la inventiva y una pronta tropelia del ingenio. (*Ag.*, XVII, 311)

It can be used to replace the simile:

> La semejanza tercia mucho para la transposición, y lo que otro exprimiera por un símile, el ingenioso lo pondera por esta sutil transformación. El juicioso Alciato dice que el palacio no lo es aunque lo parece, sino verdadera cárcel; las cadenas de oro de los aúlicos no son adornos, sino prisiones; y las riquezas, grillos. (Ag., XVII, 312)

This is perhaps one of the most characteristic means of Gracián to expose the disparity between the dunces' illusion of themselves and the reality of their mediocrity. Spitzer considers this a typical Baroque technique, in which

> ... l'imagination du lecteur est tiraillée entre le sommet et l'abîme, dynamisme propre du desengaño de Gracián.
> ... ...
> ... On pourrait même trouver que ces sortes de phrases antithétiques sont les reflets d'un "sentimiento de la vida antitético," d'une conception "baroque" du monde comme antinomie irréductible, basée sur le contraste: apparence trompeuse, vérité décevante. [31]

This antithesis is expressed in the sentence structure as well as in the word play.

One method of presenting the dichotomy between appearance and reality is by means of antithetical sentences, in which the second part of the sentence, introduced by the conjunction *mas* or *pero* (whether it be stated or implied), undermines the first part of the sentence. The dunce is thus stripped and exposed in his naked reality.

The falseness of the soldier is revealed in such a way:

> Venía armado de un temido peto conjugado por todos tiempos, números y personas; traía dos pistolas, pero muy dormidas en sus fundas, a lo descansado; cavallo desorejado, y no por culpas suyas; dorado espadín en sólo el nombre, hembra en los hechos, nunca desnuda por lo recatada; coronávase de plumas, avechucho de la vizarría, que no del valor. (I, vi, 205)

The most extended example of such a sentence structure occurs in the scene of the "Puente de los peros," in which the bifurcation

---

[31] *Op. cit.*, p. 175.

between illusion and reality is expressed in concentrated juxtaposition:

> ¡Qué valiente soldado!, pero gran ladrón; ... Diligente ministro, pero no es inteligente. ... ¡Qué gran muger aquélla!, sino que se descuida; ¡qué hermosa dama!, si no fuera necia. ... Lindo ingenio, pero sin juizio: no tiene sindéresis. (II, xi, 322)

When the positive aspect is stated in the exclamatory form, the antithesis is extremely effective because the negative aspect appears even more devastating.

Another means of demonstrating the divergence between the *ser* and the *parecer* more closely resembles a cause and effect structure. The antithetical sentence remains the basis, but the second part shows the consequences of man's fall from the ideal standard. The second part of the sentence constitutes, as it were, a punishment for the evil expressed in the first part of the sentence. As Paulson comments, "... in this sense, punishment is a vestige of satire's origin in ritual and magic." [32]

In Gracián's world, the wages of sin are brutal and fast, allowing no time for repentence:

> El farsante para en charlatán y saltimbanco; el acuchillador, en maestro de esgrima; el murmurador, quando viejo, en testigo falso; el holgazán, en escudero; el malsín, en catedrático del duelo; el infame, en libro verde; y el bevedor, en tabernero, aguándoles el vino a los otros. (II, ix, 287-288)

Similarly, the prognostications of the "Acertador" prove to be correct:

> A cada uno le adevinava su paradero como si lo viera, sin discrepar un tilde: a los liberales, el hospital; a los interessados, el infierno; a los inquietos, la cárcel, y a los reboltosos, el rollo; a los maldicientes, palos, y a los descarados, redomas, a los capeadores, jubones ... a los perdidos, pregones; a los entremetidos, desprecios. ... (III, iii, 95)

---

[32] *Op. cit.*, p. 12.

The rapidity of the enumeration and the elision of the verb serve to accentuate the relentless speed with which the sinner is doomed to fall.

Most of the *transposicones* in the *Criticón* depend largely on word play for their effect, for, as is stated in the *Agudeza*: "Es más fundada la transmutación cuando el término transformado tiene algo de equivocación con el otro en que se transforma, y está como a dos luces, dos vertientes" (Ag., XVII, 312).

Examples of word play are ubiquitous. For instance, there is a magic stone which reveals the truth of men:

> Y assí, al juez que le hallamos las manos untadas, luego le condenamos de oydor a tocador; el prelado que atesora los cinquenta mil pesos de renta, por bien que lo hable, no será el boca de oro, sino el bolsa de oro. (I, xiii, 382-383)

Once honor was destroyed,

> ... la matrona dió en matrera, la donzella de vestal en bestial, el mercader a escuras para dexar a ciegas, el juez se hizo parte con el que parte, los sabios con resabios, el soldado quebrado, hasta el espejo universal se hizo común. (II, xi, 338-339)

When the "Palacio de Interés" collapses

> Y fué un espectáculo bien horrible ver los que antes eran estimados por reyes, aora fueron reídos; los monarcas arrastrando púrpuras, las reinas y las damas rozando galas, los señores recamados, todos se quedaron en blanco, y no por aver dado en él, no ya ocupavan tronos de marfil, sino tumbas de luto; de sus joyas sólo quedó el eco en hoyas y sepulcros, las sedas y damascos fueron ascos, las piedras finas se trocaron en losas frías, las sartas de perlas en lágrimas, los cabellos tan rizados ya erizados, los olores hedores, los perfumes humos. Todo aquel encanto paró en canto y en responso, y los ecos de la vida en huecos de la muerte, las alegrías fueron pésames. ... (II, iv, 126-127)

In many cases a simple consonantal change varies the significance: "Múdase la significación con mudar alguna letra, y cuando es con propiedad grande y muy conveniente al sujeto, es sublime el concepto" (*Ag.*, XXXII, 391). Thus "oydor" becomes "tocador," the "virgen vestal" becomes "bestial," and the "joyas" turn into "hoyas." Another technique is that of a polysemous play, such as in the description of the judge who "se hizo parte con el que parte," in which the second usage refers to the sense of "repartir," and in the phrase "el soldado quebrado," which is based on the use of "soldado" as a noun and as a past participle of the verb "soldar." [33] In some instances a word is divided into significant parts —"Pártese algunas veces todo el vocablo, quedando con significación ambas partes" (*Ag.*, XXXII, 392). Thus "encanto" becomes "en canto." A prefix may also be added —"Añádensele al vocablo otras veces, ya sílabas, ya dicción entera" (*Ag.*, XXXII, 393). Thus "sabios" is changed to "resabios" and the "cabellos rizados" become "erizados."

The amount of word play and play with proverbial expressions reaches such overwhelming proportions in the *Criticón* that it raises the general question of the relation of "wit" to satire.

On a personal level, Gracián's interest in the "deslexicalización," [34] or breaking the form of a set phrase, can be accounted for by his desire for novelty, his disdain for the trite and common. This is especially apparent in the "crítica reforma de los comunes refranes" (III, vi, 200-211), which is reminiscent of Quevedo's *Cuento de cuentos.*

On a psychological level, the use of with in satire can be explained as a form of sublimation. The hostility latent in all satire accounts for its being such a highly rhetorical mode. Sigmund Freud, writing on *Wit and Its Relation to the Unconscious*, believes that satire provides a means for sublimating hostile feelings: "Violent hostility, no longer tolerated by law, has been replaced by verbal invectives.... By belittling and humbling our enemy, by scorning and ridiculing him, we indirectly obtain the pleasure of his defeat by the laughter of the third person, the inactive spectator." [35] He adds that "The pleasure in tendency

---

[33] Romera Navarro, *C.*, II, p. 338, notes 141 and 143.
[34] Term used by Gili Gaya, *op. cit.*, p. 93.
[35] Trans. by A. A. Brill (London: Kegan Paul, Trench, Trubner and Co., 1922), pp. 149-150.

wit results from the fact that a tendency, whose gratification would otherwise remain unfulfilled, is actually gratified." [36] The close alliance between wit and satire also performs another psychological function. Both author and reader are thus permitted the pleasure of the "play" of the paronomasia by justifying it through the senseful connection associating the words — "We are apt to attribute to the thought the pleasure derived from the witty form, and we are not inclined to consider improper what has given us pleasure, and in this way deprive ourselves of a source of pleasure." [37]

On a metaphysical level, the *agudeza* can function as an instrument of truth, which is enlivened by the beauty of the conceit, for "No se contenta el ingenio con sola la verdad, como el juicio, sino que aspira a la hermosura" (*Ag.*, II, 239). Words can be used to discover hidden meanings. They are not static and permanent entities, but grow and change constantly through new associations, by that "... acto de entendimiento que exprime la correspondencia que se halla entre los objetos" (*Ag.*, II, 240).

An indication of the "truth" inherent in words is found in the many etymological plays in the *Criticón*, although most of them do not correspond to the historical reality of the derivation. They are related to what Leo Spitzer, in his analysis of the *Quijote*, describes as

> ... direct relationships established between words vaguely associated because of their homonymic ring — not the relationships established by "historical grammar" or those obtained by decomposition of the word into its morphological elements. In other words, we are offered edifying ideal possibilities, not deterministic historical realities. [38]

It is in this sense that Critilo utilizes etymologies in order to instruct Andrenio. He explains the importance of the sun to his pupil by saying

---

[36] *Ibid.*, p. 177.
[37] *Ibid.*, p. 202.
[38] "Linguistic Perspectivism in the *Don Quijote*," *Linguistics and Literary History. Essays in Stylistics* (Princeton, N. J.: Princeton University Press, 1948), p. 48.

> Llámase *sol* porque en su presencia todas las demás lumbreras se retiran y solo él campea. (I, ii, 121)

The significance of the "coraçón" is seen in its name:

> Llámase assí de la palabra latina *cura* que significa cuydado, que el que rige y manda siempre fué centro dellos. (I, ix, 283)

Andrenio is puzzled by the word "manos":

> —¿Porqué se llaman assí? —preguntó Andrenio—, que según tú me has enseñado viene del verbo latino *maneo,* que significa quietud, siendo tan al contrario, que ellas nunca han de parar. (I, ix, 280)

Critilo replies that

> —Llamáronlas assí —respondió Critilo—, no porque ayan de estar quietas, sino porque sus obras han de permanecer o porque de ellas ha de manar todo el bien. (I, ix, 280)

Plato had suggested in the *Cratylus* that a name is not simply a matter of convention but has by nature a truth.[39] Gracián abides by this dictum in his creation of names. The author states of "Egenio" that "éste era su nombre, ya definición" (I, xii, 366). Some personages "fulfill" their names, such as "Artemia," of whom it is assured that "Llamávase aquélla, que no niega su nombre ni sus hechos, la sabia y discreta Artemia ..." (I, viii, 244). Even the names of countries contain some meaning. The pilgrims conclude that the name of Germany is justified:

> Sin duda que su nombre fué su definición, llamándose Germania, *a germinando,* la que todo lo produze y engendra, siendo fecunda madre de vivientes y de víveres y de todo quanto se puede imaginar para la vida humana. (III, iii, 97)

If it is true that Gracián, as F. Yndurain writes, "En algún modo parece seguir la teoría de que *nomina sunt consequentia*

---

[39] *The Dialogues of Plato,* trans. by B. Jowett (3 vols.; New York: Scribner, 1887), I, 629.

rerum, ..."[40] then etymological significance can be used for satirical purposes. Inherent in a name is its ideal being, with the result that when it falls from this ideal, it literally does not "live up to its name." For instance, the present corruption is criticized by pointing out that

> Quien oye dezir mundo concibe un compuesto de todo lo criado muy concertado y perfecto, y con razón, pues toma el nombre de su misma belleza: mundo quiere dezir lindo y limpio. ... Assí avía de ser, como el mismo nombre lo blasona, su principio lo afiança y su fin lo assegura; pero quán al contrario sea esto y quál le aya parado el mismo hombre, quánto desmiente el hecho y dicho, pondérelo Critilo. ... (I, vi, 184)

Later Andrenio concurs:

> —¡Que a éste llamen mundo! —ponderava Andrenio—. Hasta el nombre miente, calçóselo al rebés: llámase inmundo y de todas maneras disparatado. (I, vi, 210)

In the final scene, "Muerte" chastises "Guerra," justifying her complaint through etymology:

> Pero quítateme de delante, anda de ay, Guerra mal nacida y peor exercitada, pues sin pelear, quando el exército se denominó del exercicio. (III, xi, 353)

Words correspond to a reality, and in order to know the reality one must know its correct name. The dunces, however, cannot see or understand anything, and they live constantly deceived. They call the keeper of the gate of the false monastery "Sosiego," but in reality his name should be "Pereça" (II, vii, 231).

In the Agudeza Gracián had belittled the equívocos as being "... poco graves ... y así más aptos para sátiras y cosas burlescas que para lo serio y prudente" (Ag., XXXIII, 399) and the retruécano as being "... la popular de las agudezas, y en que todos se rozan antes por lo fácil que por lo sutil ..." (Ag., XXXII, 391). It is evident, however, that by the time of the writing of the

---

[40] Op. cit., p. 177.

Criticón he realized that word transformation was an effective means of exposing the truth. He had to make use of rhetorical means to destroy the enemy. As stated by Pablo González Casanova:

> Y su consideración preferente del problema de la verdad como problema ético, como un problema de engaño más que de error, no hace sino reforzar su idea de que es necesario emplear los recursos retóricos para descubrir la verdad, lo que le planta de nuevo en el terreno de la agudeza, de la erudición, de la elección de todas las demás estratagemas que es necesario emplear para convencer, para destruir un enemigo engañoso, que se sabe engañoso, y para desengañar y desengañarse, más que para enseñar o aprender. [41]

This plethora of word play, as well as play with idiomatic and proverbial expressions, is such a condensed form of satire that much is required of the reader. At the same time, it is also a most effective tool against deception. Various methods are used.

Illusion and reality are juxtaposed in such phrases as "Acercósele un monstruo o ministro ..." (II, xii, 358); "—¿Qué estancia o qué estanque es éste? preguntó Andrenio" (II, v, 172); "... razones, no de Estado, sino de establo" (I, vii, 236); "La fiesta era una farsa ..." (I, vii, 237); "Falimundo's" palace is described as "Aquí vivía, o aquí yacía, aquel tan grande como escondido monarca ..." (I, vii, 235).

Parenthetical comments by the author serve to rectify false impressions. The danger of "Volusia" is clear when the "Sabio" explains that "Esta los cautiva, los aloja (o los aleja), unos en el quarto más alto ..." (I, xi, 320). As Andrenio and Critilo are being trapped by "Falsirena" in her palace, the author writes that "Fueron subiendo por unas gradas de pórfidos (ya pérfidos, que al baxar serían ágatas) a la esfera del sol ..." (I, xii, 355), which includes the word play with the stone, "ágata," and the expression "andar a gatas." Sometimes the comments rectify idiomatic expressions, as in "... andávase todo el día (y no santo) tirando peros y piedras ..." (II, xi, 328), which disrupts the expression, "todo

---

[41] "Verdad y agudeza en Gracián," *CA*, XII (1953), 158.

el santo día," or "... conoció que no era la corte para ella, tomóse la honra (por mejor quitarla) y desterróse voluntariamente" (I, ix, 284).

Division of a word into two meaningful parts forms the basis for the following exposures: "... todo es predicar ayuno, y no miente, que en aviéndose comido un capón, con verdad dize: 'Ay uno'" (II, vii, 235); when one says "—Y tras toda esta austeridad que usa consigo, es mui suave," the reply is "—Assí lo entiendo, suave de día y suave de noche" (II, vii, 235), which could be written "su-ave," as in the previous example. The play with "devota" and "de bota" (wine bag) is common, as in the reference to "... aquellos otros, los que en siendo de voto son de bota" (II, v, 174), and in the "Hermitaño's" invitation to the pilgrims in the false monastery that "Pero entremos en su celda, que es mui devota" (II, vii, 236).

The changes in aphorisms are also intended to tell the truth more aptly. Gracián admires Quevedo's "equívocos continuados" and calls the change of idiomatic expression "corrección irónica" (Ag., XXXIII, 399). Some expressions acquire a second ironic meaning simply because of the situation, as in the case of "Ibanse encaramando por aquellas alturas y subidas con buen aire y mucho aliento ..." (III, vii, 221), where the expression "con buen aire," which means "good breeding," because they are approaching the Palace of Pride, acquires a second meaning of "vanity." The expression "vale más estar solo que mal acompañado" is corrected to "vale más estar solo que mal aconsejado" (I, ix, 271) to criticize bad court advisors. In the description of the palace of "Volusia" — "... escurecía tanto el palacio de Eliogávalo, que lo dexó a malas noches" (I, x, 307), there is a "corrección irónica" of the expression "dejar a buenas noches."

In Gracián's view, neither words nor expressions are permanent. They must be modified in order to express the truth that they are supposed to represent. His use of puns is an attempt to arrive at this reality. In the words of Kernan:

> Satire expresses no particular joy in the way of the world, but it does assume that the nature of reality can be known by reason and that life can therefore be lived in reasonable conformity with what is, even if the

majority of men are too senseless to accept the given existence. [42]

In the words of Gracián, "... no ay mayor enemigo de la verdad que la verisimilitud" (III, iv, 124), but the fools are forever deceived.

---

[42] *Op. cit.*, p. 212.

CONCLUSION

Gracián, in the section on the compound conceit of his *Agudeza y arte de ingenio* (1642 and 1648), expresses his awareness of the difficulties inherent in didactic literature, and stresses the need to entertain the reader in order to instruct him in moral truths. He considers variety and novelty the chief inducements to a reader's enjoyment, and because he believes that these cannot be achieved in the content, they must be achieved in the style. These theories concerning variety and novelty were first put into practice in *El Discreto* (1646). In this work Gracián varies the forms of narration as well as their methods of internal organization, and employs a wealth of rhetorical devices to enhance the appeal of the doctrinal material and enliven the as yet imperfectly realized modes of dialogue, allegory, and satire.

From the simple, fragmented form of *El Discreto* developed the complex, unified *El Criticón* (1651, 1653, 1657). The unity is achieved thematically in the conflict between illusion and reality which results in *desengaño,* and structurally in the pilgrimage of Andrenio and Critilo as they search in vain for "Felisinda," or Happiness. Although the spatial structure is circular, moving from the island of St. Helena to the "Isla de Inmortalidad," it symbolizes spiritual progression, because the culmination of the terrestrial journey is Rome, the center of the Christian world and the summit of human perfectability. The temporal structure is determined by the division of the novel into the four ages of man ("niñez," "juventud," "varonil edad," and "vejez"), a pattern which is reiterated in the cyclical rhythm of nature and the rising and falling movement of civilization. Although the linear downward direction of the *memento mori* theme is stressed in the first two books, the cyclical pattern of return asserts itself in the final book. In addition to maintaining a thematic and structural unity, the author employs novelistic narrative devices to heighten the interest and suspense of the reader.

Within the genre of the novel, *El Criticón* may be defined as a satiric allegory. Both allegory and satire are useful for didactic purposes. They can delight while they teach because each has a double level of meaning. Allegory has a primary, or literal level, as well as a secondary, or abstract significance, and satire is metonymic in that a larger truth is conveyed by the individual presented. The secondary level of moralistic intention depends for its clarity and persuasiveness on the excellence of the presentation of the primary level of narration. It is evident that Gracián realized that in order for the content to be appreciated, the form had to be enticing, and took care to animate the ethical framework of *El Criticón* with a linguistic and structural dynamism.

The allegory in *El Criticón* is diversified. There is variation both in the types of allegory and in their method of incorporation in the text. There are two basic types of allegory used. The protagonists are "symbol-allegories." Because they have two levels of meaning, their significance and relationship are capable of change during the course of the novel, and it is found that while the literal level predominates in the First Book, the figurative level takes precedence thereafter. In contrast to the "symbol-allegories," the "personification-allegories" have only one level of meaning. Their role is to define the conceptual movement of the novel.

The "personification-allegories" may be classified according to their function within the text as "generalization," "spectator," and "participation" allegories. The "generalization" allegories constitute a thematic definition of a *crisi*, and usually precede the main narration or occur as a story. The "spectator" allegories are those which the protagonists witness, but in which they do not participate. These secondary forms of the "personification-allegory" decrease in number from the First to the Third Book, as the author concentrates less on variety and more on the unity and cohesion of the text.

The primary form of the "personification-allegory" is the "participation" allegory, in which the protagonists actually encounter personified figures. These illustrate the thematic structure of the novel. The fundamental theme is that of temptation, as the protagonists move from the order of nature to the apocalyptic world above, from the terrestrial to the celestial, in their struggle against vice. Each victorious step in the liberation from the tyranny of passion is accompanied by an "epiphany" of increased self-awareness. The *psychomachia* between evil and good represented by the personifications is also expressed in an antithetical pattern of demonic and apocalyptic symbols and images.

The satire in the novel is also functional in defining basic themes. It shows man's deviation from his natural harmony and purpose, caused by his moral aberrations. The subject of Gracián's satire is man's resistance to truth, and the symbol of this self-deception is the crowd. The satire increases as the novel progresses, becoming more vividly and dramatically portrayed, and receives elaborate formal expression. The intensity of the censure is conveyed by means of rhetorical devices in which word play is a basic tool.

There is an inherent tension in the main patterns of movement in the novel, for the steady upward progression of the allegory is opposed to the haphazard chaos of the satire. This opposition provides a dynamic contrast and has a thematic importance. Allegory focuses on the perception of the privileged few; satire condemns the deception of the majority. Allegory mirrors man's ideology; satire reflects his degradation.

El Criticón is a monument to man's ideals. The seriousness of this subject might well cause the structure to become weighty and archaic. The contrasting patterns and imagery of the allegory and satire, as well as their careful rhetorical elaboration, eliminate this problem by creating tension and vitality in the novel.

INDEX OF RHETORICAL FIGURES *

Agnominatio (or paronomasia). (Play on sounds of words or repetition of the same word in different senses.) Many examples of this are quoted, only a few of which are included here: "Autor. —¿De modo que se hace un rey? / Canónigo. —Sí que no se nace hecho ..." (*D.*, XVII, 123); "Acercósele un monstruo o ministro ..." (II, xii, 358); "—¿Qué estancia o qué estanque es éste? preguntó Andrenio" (II, v, 172); "... razones, no de Estado, sino de establo" (I, vii, 236); "La fiesta era una farsa ..." (I, vii, 237); "Aquí vivía, o aquí yacía, aquel tan grande como escondido monarca ..." (I, vii, 235); "Esta los cautiva, los aloja (o los aleja), unos en el quarto más alto ..." (I, xi, 320); "... la matrona dió en matrera, la donzella de vestal en bestial, el mercader a escuras para dexar a ciegas, el juez se hizo parte con el que parte, los sabios con resabios, el soldado quebrado, hasta el espejo universal se hizo común" "II, xi, 338-339); "—No dezís cosa —replicó el francés—. Asseguroos que no es sino el siglo de oro. ... —Sólo el oro es el estimado, el buscado, el adorado y querido. No se haze caso de otro, todo va a parar en él y por él ..." (*C.*, II, iii, 106).

Alliteration. (Repetition of initial consonants in two or more adjacent words): "... bramava el furioso *v*iento *v*omitando en tempestades por la boca de la gruta, començaron a desgajarse con horrible fragor aquellos duros peñascos y a caer con tan *e*spantoso *e*struendo ..." (*C.*, I, ii, 117).

Antimetabole. (Words repeated in successive clauses in reverse grammatical order): "Doctor. —Dicen que, *al buen entendedor, pocas palabras.* / Autor. —Yo diría que, *a pocas palabras, buen entendedor* ..." (*D.*, VIII, 97).

Antithesis. (Juxtaposition of contrasting ideas): "No se venció a sí mismo, sino que se rindió" (*D.*, VI, 94); "No nace de alteza de ánimo, sino de vileza de corazón, pues no aspiran a la verdadera honra, sino a la aparente; no a las verdaderas hazañas, sino a la hazañería" (*D.*, XX, 131); "No fueron triunfos los de Domiciano, sino hazañerías; ... triunfaban tal vez por haber muerto un jabalí, que no era triunfo, sino porquería" (*D.*, XX,

---

* I do not include the examples of metaphor, allegory, or simile which appear in the text of this study, nor the examples of such common devices as *interrogatio, exclamatio,* and parenthesis. (Emphasis added in the quotes is mine.)

132); "Tropiezan todos en el ladrillo que sobresale a los demás, de modo que no es aquélla eminencia, sino tropiezo; así en muchos el querer campear no viene a ser realce, sino tope" (D., XI, 105); "¿Qué aprovecha la fragancia de los ámbares, si la desmiente la hediondez de las costumbres? Bien pueden embalsamar el cuerpo, pero no inmortalizar el alma" (D., XVI, 118-119); "Tiene a medias el mando con el sol: si él haze el día, ella la noche; si el sol cumple los años, ella los meses; calienta el sol y seca de día la tierra, la luna de noche la refresca y humedece; el sol govierna los campos, la luna rige los mares: de suerte que son las dos valanças del tiempo. Pero lo más digno de notarse es que, assí como el sol es claro espejo de Dios y de sus divinos atributos, la luna lo es del hombre y de sus humanas imperfecciones: ya crece, ya mengua; ya nace, ya muere, ya está en su lleno, ya en su nada, nunca permaneciendo en un estado ..." (C., I, ii, 126).

Apostrophe. (Direct address to person or thing): "¡O tú, que hazes mofa del fabulosamente necio, advierte que eres el verdadero, tú eres el mismo de quien te ríes, tanta y tan solemne es tu demencia! Pues, instándote que dexes los riesgos del vicio y te acojas a la vanda de la virtud, respondes que aguardas acabe de passar la corriente de los males" (C., II, ix, 281).

Asyndeton. (Omission of conjuctions between series of clauses): "Precipítase ya la mocedad en un impetuoso torrente, corre, salta, se arroja y se despeña, tropeçando con las guijas, rifando con las flores, va echando espumas, se enturbia y se enfurece" (C., II, i, 18); "De suerte que, si bien se nota, todo quanto ay se burla del miserable hombre: el mundo le engaña, la vida le miente, la fortuna le burla, la salud le falta, la edad se passa, el mal le da priessa, el bien se le ausenta, los años huyen, los contentos no llegan, el tiempo buela, la vida se acaba, la muerte le coge, la sepultura le traga, la tierra le cubre, la pudrición le deshaze, el olvido le aniquila: y el que ayer fué hombre, oy es polvo, y mañana nada" (C., I, vii, 241-242).

Conduplicatio. (Repetition of a word or words in a series of clauses): "... començava abrir el *día, día* claro, *día* grande, *día* felicíssimo, el mejor de toda mi vida" (C., I, ii, 118); "*Mirava* el cielo, *mirava* la tierra *mirava* el mar ..." (C., I, ii, 119); "Lo que yo mucho celebrava era el ver *tanta* multitud de criaturas con *tanta* diferencia entre sí, *tanta* pluralidad con *tan* rara diversidad ..." (C., I, iii, 130).

Ellipsis. (Omission of a word or words implied by the context): "Autor. —No *hay cosa* más fácil que el *conocimiento* ajeno. / Doctor. —Ni más dificultosa que el proprio" (D., VIII, 98); "Autor. —Las motas percibe en los *ojos* del vecino. Doctor. —Y las vigas no divisa en los proprios" (D., VIII, 98); "... que si oy son flores, mañana estiércol, ayer maravillas y oy sombras, que aquí parecen y allí desaparecen" (C., III, vii, 224).

Epiphonema. (Summary comments concluding a discourse): "—Es el sol —ponderó Critilo— la criatura que más ostentosamente retrata la magestuosa grandeza del Criador. ... él es, al fin, criatura de ostentación, el más luciente espejo en quien las divinas grandezas se representan" (C., I, ii, 121-122); "Pero lo más digno de notarse es que, assí como el sol es claro espejo de Dios y de sus divinos atributos, la luna lo es del hombre y de sus humanas imperfecciones; ... de modo que es mudable, defectuosa, manchada, inferior, pobre, triste, y todo se le origina de la vecindad con la tierra" (*C.*, I, ii, 126); "—Esse es otro bien admirable assunto de la divina providencia— dixo Critilo, —pues previno que no todos los frutos se sazonassen juntos, sino que se fuessen dando vez según la variedad de los tiempos y necessidad de los vivientes ... de suerte, que acabado un fruto, entra el otro, para que con comodidad puedan recogerse y guardarse, entreteniendo todo el año con abundancia y con regalo" (*C.*, I, iii, 131).

Erotesis. (Raising questions with moral connotations which imply affirmation or denial): "Pero, ¿qué desigualdad más monstrosa que la de Nerón?" (*D.*, VI, 94); "¿Qué aprovecha la fragancia de los ámbares, si la desmiente la hediondez de las costumbres?" (*D.*, XVI, 118); "Infeliz genio el que se declara por de una sola materia, aunque sea única, aun la más sublime; pues ¿qué si fuera vulgar?" (*D.*, VII, 95).

Hypallage. (An interchange in the syntactic relationship between two terms): "... bramava el *furioso viento* vomitando en tempestades por la boca de la gruta, começaron a desgajarse con *horrible fragor* aquellos duros peñascos y a caer con tan *espantoso estruendo* que parecían quererse venir a la nada toda aquella gran máquina de peñas" (*C.*, I, ii, 117).

Hyperbole. (Use of exaggerated terms for the purpose of emphasis): "Aborrecibles monstros, de quienes huyen todos más que del bruto de Esopo, que cortejaba a coces y lisonjeaba a bocados" (*D.*, IX, 100); "Desta suerte hay algunos que no son soldados, pero lo desean ser, y lo afectan y lo procuran parecer ... y meten más maquina en una antojada aventura que el belicoso y afortunado marqués de Torrecusa en un romper las trincheras de Fuenterrabía, en un socorrer a Perpiñán y desbaratar campalmente tantas veces los bravos y numerosos ejércitos de Francia" (*D.*, XX, 131); "Muéstranse otros muy ministros afectando celo y ocupación, ... de suerte que llevan más máquina que el artificio de Juanelo, de igual ruido y poco provecho" (*D.*, XX, 131-132); "Lo que llegó ya a ser ansia de rebentar y agonía de morir ..." (*C.*, I, i, 114); "... y el deseo de ver y de saber quién era ... me traía a extremos de morir" (*C.*, I, i, 114).

Hypophora. (Raising questions and answering them): "... ¿qué será, sin ser Davo, en una grave conversación estar chanceando? Será hacer farsa con risa de sí mesmo" (*D.*, IX, 100); "Pero, ¿qué remedio habría tan eficaz, que curase a todos estos de figuras, y los volviese al ser de hombres? Pues de verdad que lo hay, y es infalible" (*D.*, XVI, 120).

Hysteron proteron. (Reversal of normal order in a sentence): "Acertadamente discurría quien comparava el vivir del hombre al correr del agua, quando todos morimos y como ella nos vamos deslizando" (*C.*, II, i, 17).

Isocolon. (Phrases symmetrical in length and similar in structure): "Doctor. —Las verdades que más nos importan vienen siempre *a medio decir.* / Autor. —Así es, pero recíbanse del advertido *a todo entender*" (*D.*, VIII, 97); "Impropios nombres la dió la vulgar ignorancia llamándola *fea y desaliñada,* no aviendo cosa más *brillante y serena;* injúrianla de triste, siendo *descanso* del trabajo *y alivio* de nuestras fatigas" (*C.*, I, ii, 123); "... distílense las aguas *saludables y odoríferas,* que *recreen el olfato y conforten el coraçón:* tengan todos los sentidos *su gozo y su empleo*" (*C.*, I, iii, 132); "Las aguas *limpian y fecundan,* los vientos *purifican y vivifican* ..." (*C.*, I, iii, 140); "Quando parece que se acaba todo, entonces comiença de nuevo: *la naturaleza se renueva, el mundo se remoça, la tierra se establece* y el divino govierno es admirado y adorado" (*C.*, I, iii, 139); "... los montes ... en ellos *se recogen* los tesoros de las nieves, *se forjan* los metales, *se detienen* las nubes, *se originan* las fuentes, *anidan* las fieras, *se empinan* los árboles para las naves y edificios, y donde *se guarecen* las gentes de las avenidas de los ríos, *se fortalecen* contra los enemigos y *gozan* de salud y de vida" (*C.*, I, iii, 140).

Onomatopoeia. (Use of words with sounds corresponding to their meaning): "Es la niñez fuente risueña: nace entre menudas arenas, que de los polvos de la nada salen los del cuerpo, *brolla* tan clara como sencilla, *ríe* lo que no murmura, *bulle* entre campanillas de viento, *arrúllase* entre pucheros y cíñese de verduras que le fajan" (*C.*, II, i, 18).

Procatalepsis. (Anticipating an objection and answering it in advance): "Diránme que todo es desigualdades este mundo, y que sigue a lo natural lo moral. ... Pues si el hombre es un otro mundo abreviado, ¿qué mucho que cifre en sí la variedad? ... Pero no hay perfección en variedades del alma que no dicen con el Cielo. De la luna arriba no hay mudanza" (*D.*, VI, 94).

Synonymia. (Repetition by means of the use of words having similar meanings): "Que es de ver uno destos *destemplados de agudeza, siniestros de ingenio,* ..." (*D.*, IX, 101); "... viene a rematar en un vilísimo vaso de su *ignominia* y *descrédito*" (*D.*, XI, 105); "Pero así como a unos los hace *aborrecibles* y aun *intratables,* esta enfadosa afectación ..." (*D.*, XVI, 119); "El remedio de todos éstos es poner la mira en otro semejante *afectado, paradojo, extravagante,* figurero ..." (*D.*, XVI, 120); "De suerte que sola una *omnipotencia divina,* una *eterna providencia,* una *inmensa bondad* pudieran aver dispuesto una tan gran máquina, nunca bastantemente *admirada, contemplada* y *aplaudida*" (*C.*, I, iii, 140).

INDEX OF ABBREVIATIONS

AFA	*Archivo de Filología Aragonesa*
AHSI	*Archivum Historicum Societatis Iesu*
B.A.E.	*Biblioteca de Autores Españoles*
BH	*Bulletin Hispanique*
BHS	*Bulletin of Hispanic Studies*
CA	*Cuadernos Americanos*
CL	*Comparative Literature*
ELH	*Journal of English Literary History*
HR	*Hispanic Review*
JHI	*Journal of the History of Ideas*
MLN	*Modern Language Notes*
MLR	*Modern Language Review*
MP	*Modern Philology*
PMLA	*Publications of the Modern Language Association of America*
RFE	*Revista de Filología Española*
RH	*Revue Hispanique*
RIE	*Revista de Ideas Estéticas*
RJ	*Romanistisches Jahrbuch*
RR	*Romanic Review*
SRen	*Studies in the Renaissance*

BIBLIOGRAPHY

Texts Used

Gracián y Morales, Baltasar. *Agudeza y arte de ingenio.* Edited by E. Correa Calderón. 2 vols. Madrid: Castalia, 1969.

———. *El Criticón.* Edited by Miguel Romera-Navarro. 3 vols. Philadelphia: University of Philadelphia Press, 1938-40.

———. *Obras completas.* Edited by Miguel Batllori and Ceferino Peralta. Vol. I. In *B.A.E.*, Vol. CCXXIX. Madrid: Ediciones Atlas, 1969.

———. *Obras completas.* Edited by Arturo del Hoyo. Madrid: Aguilar, 1960.

———. *Oráculo manual y arte de prudencia.* Edited by Miguel Romera-Navarro. Madrid: Jura, 1954.

Works Consulted on Gracián

Arco y Garay, Ricardo del. "Gracián y su colaborador y mecenas." *Baltasar Gracián, escritor aragonés del siglo XVII. Curso monográfico.* Zaragoza: Hospicio provincial, 1926. Pp. 133-158.

Azorín. "Baltasar Gracián." *Lecturas españolas.* Buenos Aires: Espasa-Calpe, 1943. Pp. 54-58.

Baquero Goyanes, Mariano. "Perspectivismo y sátira en *El Criticón.*" *Homenaje a Gracián.* Zaragoza: Institución "Fernando el Católico," 1958. Pp. 27-56.

Batllori, Miguel. *Gracián y el Barroco.* Roma: Edizioni di Storia e Letteratura, 1958.

———. "Un lustro de estudios gracianos: 1959-1963." *AHSI,* XXXIV (1965), 162-171.

Bethell, S. L. "Gracián, Tesauro, and the Nature of Metaphysical Wit." *The Northern Miscellany of Literary Criticism* (Autum 1953), pp. 19-38.

Blecua, José Manuel. "El estilo de *El Criticón* de Gracián." *AFA,* I (1945), 7-32.

Borges, Jorge Luis. "Baltasar Gracián." *Sur,* No. 252 (1958), pp. 9-10.

Bouillier, Victor. "Notes sur l'*Oráculo manual* de Balthasar Gracián." *BH,* XIII (1911), 316-336.

Correa Calderón, Evaristo. *Baltasar Gracián. Su vida y su obra.* Madrid: Gredos, 1961.

———. "Gracián y la oratoria barroca." *Acta Salmanticensia. Filosofía y Letras,* XVI (1962), 132-138.

Coster, Adolphe. *Baltasar Gracián.* Translated by Ricardo del Arco y Garay. Zaragoza: Institución "Fernando el Católico," 1947. (Originally published in French in 1913.)

Croce, Benedetto. "I trattatisti italiani del 'concettismo' e Baltasar Gracián." *Atti della Academia Pontaniana,* XXIX, Series II, Vol. IV, memoria no. 7. Naples, 1899. Pp. 1-32. Included in *Problemi di estetica.* 4th ed. Bari, 1949. Pp. 313-348.

Foster, Virginia Ramos. "The Status of Gracián Criticism: A Bibliographic Essay." *RJ,* XVIII (1967), 296-307.

Gariano, M. C. "Simbolismo y alegoría en *El Criticón* de Gracián." *Asomante,* XXII, No. 2 (1966), 39-50.

Gili Gaya, Samuel. "Agudeza, modismos y lugares comunes." *Homenaje a Gracián.* Zaragoza: Institución "Fernando el Católico," 1958. Pp. 89-97.

González Casanova, Pablo. "Verdad y agudeza en Gracián." *CA,* XII (1953), 143-160.

Green, Otis H. "Sobre el significado de 'crisi(s)' antes de *El Criticón.* Una nota para la historia del conceptismo." *Homenaje a Gracián.* Zaragoza: Institución "Fernando el Católico," 1958. Pp. 99-102.

Hafter, Monroe. *Gracián and Perfection. Spanish Moralists of the Seventeenth Century.* Harvard Studies in Romance Languages, Vol. XXX. Cambridge: Harvard University Press, 1966.

Hatzfeld, Helmut. "The Baroquism of Gracián's *El Oráculo manual.*" *Homenaje a Gracián.* Zaragoza: Institución "Fernando el Católico," 1958. Pp. 103-117.

Heger, Klaus. *Baltasar Gracián; estilo lingüístico y doctrina de valores. Estudio sobre la actitud literaria del conceptismo.* Zaragoza: Institución "Fernando el Católico," 1960. (Appeared originally in German as dissertation, Heidelburg, 1952.)

Hoyo, Arturo del. "Noticia de *El Discreto.*" *Insula,* XIV, No. 147 (1959), 1 and 9.

Ilie, Paul. "Gracián and the Moral Grotesque." *HR,* XXXIX (1971), 30-48.

Iventosch, Herman. "Moral-Allegorical Names in Gracián's *Criticón.*" *Names,* IX (December 1961), 215-233.

Jansen, Hellmut. *Die Grundbegriffe des Baltasar* Gracián. Genève: E. Droz, 1958.

Krauss, Werner. *La doctrina de la vida según Baltasar Gracián.* Translated by Ricardo Estarriol. Madrid: Rialp, 1962. (Originally published in German in 1947.)

Lacoste, Maurice. "Les sources de l'*Oráculo manual* dans l'œuvre de Gracián et quelques aperçus touchant a l'*Atento.*" *BH,* XXXI (1929), 93-101.

Maldonado de Guevara, Francisco. "La teoría de los géneros literarios y la constitución de la novela moderna." *Estudios dedicados a Menéndez Pidal,* III (1952), 299-320.

May, T. E. "Gracián's Idea of the *Concepto.*" *HR,* XVIII (1950), 15-41.

―――. "An Interpretation of Gracián's *Agudeza y arte de ingenio.*" *HR,* XVI (1948), 275-300.

Montesinos, J. F. "Gracián o la picaresca pura." *Cruz y Raya,* No. 4 (1933), pp. 37-63. Reprinted in *Ensayos y estudios de literatura española.* Edited by J. H. Silverman. México: Andrea, 1959. Pp. 132-145.

Navarro-González, Alberto. "Las dos redacciones de la *Agudeza y arte de ingenio.*" *Cuadernos de Literatura,* IV (1948), 201-213.

Pring-Mill, Robert D. F. "Some Techniques of Representation in the *Sueños* and the *Criticón.*" *BHS*, XLV (1968), 270-284.
Reyes, Alfonso. *Cuatro ingenios.* Buenos Aires: Espasa-Calpe, 1950.
Romera-Navarro, Miguel. *Estudios sobre Gracián.* Hispanic Studies, Vol. II. Austin: University of Texas Press, 1950.
Sánchez Alonso, Benito. "Sobre Baltasar Gracián (Notas linguo-estilísticas)." *RFE*, LXV (1962), 161-225.
Sarmiento, Edward. "Clasificación de algunos pasajes capitales para la estética de Baltasar Gracián." *BH*, XXXVII (1935), 27-56.
―――. "Gracián's *Agudeza y arte de ingenio.*" *MLR*, XXVII (1932), 280-292.
―――. "On Two Criticisms of Gracián's *Agudeza.*" *HR*, III (1935), 23-35.
Schröder, Gerhart. *Baltasar Graciáns "Criticón." Eine Untersuchung zur Beziehung zwischen Manierismus und Moralistik.* München: W. Fink, 1966.
Selig, Karl-Ludwig. "Gracián and Alciato's *Emblemata.*" *CL*, VIII (Winter 1956), 1-11.
―――. *The Library of Vincencio Juan de Lastanosa, Patron of Gracián.* Travaux d'Humanisme et Renaissance, Vol. LXIII. Genève: E. Droz, 1960.
―――. "Some Remarks on Gracián's Literary Taste and Judgments." *Homenaje a Gracián.* Zaragoza: Institución "Fernando el Católico," 1958. Pp. 155-162.
Spitzer, Leo: "'Betlengabor' — Une erreur de Gracián? (Note sur les noms propres chez Gracián)." *RFE*, XVII (1930), 173-180. Article also appears as "Uber die Eigennamen bei Gracián." *Romanische Stil-und Literaturstudien.* Vol. II. Marburg a Lahn: N. G. Elwert'sche Verlagsbuchhandlung, 1931. Pp. 181-188.
Unamuno, Miguel de. "Leyendo a Baltasar Gracián." *Nuevo Mundo*, 23 julio 1920. Reprinted in *Obras completas.* Vol. V. Madrid: Afrodisio Aguado, 1952. Pp. 112-115.
Vossler, Karl. "Introducción a Gracián." *Revista de Occidente*, CXLVII (1935), 330-348.
Walton, L. B. "Two Allegorical Journeys. A Comparison Between Bunyan's *Pilgrim's Progress* and Gracián's *El Criticón.*" *BHS*, XXXVI (1959), 28-36.
Woods, M. J. "Gracián, Peregrini and the Theory of Topics." *MLR*, LXIII (1968), 854-863.
Yndurain, Francisco. "Gracián, un estilo." *Homenaje a Gracián.* Zaragoza: Institución "Fernando el Católico," 1958. Pp. 163-188.

Other Works Consulted

Alarcos, Emilio. "Los sermones de Paravicino." *RFE*, XXIV (1937), 162-197, 249-319.
Alemán, Mateo. *Guzmán de Alfarache.* In *La novela picaresca española.* Edited by Angel Valbuena y Prat. Madrid: Aguilar, 1966.
Arco y Garay, Ricardo del. "Estimación española del Bosco en los siglos XVI y XVII." *RIE*, X (1952), 417-431.
Aristotle. *The "Poetics" or Aristotle.* Translated by S. H. Butcher. London: Macmillan and Co., 1911.

Blanco González, Bernardo. *Del Cortesano al Discreto. Examen de una "decadencia."* Vol. I. Madrid: Gredos, 1962.
Boehlich, Walter. "Heliodorus Christianus. Cervantes ünd der byzantinische Roman." *Freundesgabe für Ernst Robert Curtius.* Bern: Francke, 1956. Pp. 103-124.
Booth, Wayne C. "Distance and Point-of-View. An Essay in Classification." *Essays in Criticism,* XI (1961). Reprinted in *The Novel: Modern Essays in Criticism.* Edited by Robert Murray Davis. Englewood Cliffs, N. J.: Prentice Hall, 1966. Pp. 172-189.
———. *The Rhetoric of Fiction.* Chicago: University of Chicago Press, 1961.
Bronson, Bertrand. "Personification Reconsidered." *ELH,* XIV (September 1947), 163-177.
Browne, Sir Thomas. *Religio Medici.* New York: E. P. Dutton, 1951.
Burke, Kenneth. *The Philosophy of Literary Form. Studies in Symbolic Action.* New York: Vintage Books, 1957.
Bush, Douglas. "The Isolation of the Renaissance Hero." *Reason and Imagination. Studies in the History of Ideas, 1600-1800.* Edited by J. A. Mazzeo. New York: Columbia University Press, 1962. Pp. 57-69.
Caballero, Ramón. *Diccionario de modismos de la lengua castellana.* Buenos Aires: Librería el Ateneo, 1942.
Calderón de la Barca, Pedro. *Autos sacramentales, alegóricos y historiales del Phénix de los poetas.* Edited by Don Juan Fernández de Apontes. 6 vols. Madrid: Viuda de Fernández, 1760.
Castro, Américo. *Hacia Cervantes.* Madrid: Taurus, 1967.
Censorinus. *De die Natale.* Translated by William Maude. New York: Cambridge Encyclopedia Co., 1900.
Cervantes Saavedra, Miguel de. *Obras completas.* Edited by Ángel Valbuena Prat. Madrid: Aguilar, 1965.
Chevalier, Maxime. *L'Arioste en Espagne (1530-1650), recherches sur l'influence du "Roland furieux."* Bordeaux: Institut d'études ibériques et ibéro-americaines de l'Université de Bordeaux, 1966.
Close, J. A. "Art and Nature in Antiquity and the Renaissance." *JHI,* XXX (1969), 467-486.
Contreras, Jerónimo de. *Selva de aventuras.* In *B. A. E.* Edited by D. Buenaventura Carlos Aribau. Vol. III. Madrid: Rivadeneyra, 1846. Pp. 469-505.
Correas, Gonzalo. *Vocabulario de refranes y frases proverbiales y otras fórmulas comunes de la lengua castellana.* Madrid: Revista de Archivos, Bibliotecas y Museos, 1924.
Croll, Morris W. *Style, Rhetoric and Rhythm; Essays.* Edited by J. Max Patrick *et al.* Princeton, N. J.: Princeton University Press, 1966.
Curtius, Ernst Robert. *European Literature and the Latin Middle Ages.* Translated by Willard R. Trask. New York: Harper & Row, 1963. (Originally published in German in 1948.)
Elliott, Robert. *The Power of Satire.* Princeton, N. J.: Princeton University Press, 1960.
Espinel, Vicente. *La vida de Marcos de Obregón.* In *La novela picaresca española.* Edited by Ángel Valbuena y Prat. Madrid: Aguilar, 1966.
Fletcher, Angus. *Allegory. The Theory of a Symbolic Mode.* Ithaca, N. Y.: Cornell University Press, 1964.

Forcione, Alban K. *Cervantes, Aristotle and the "Persiles."* Princeton, N. J.: Princeton University Press, 1970.
Forster, E. M. *Aspects of the Novel,* New York: Harcourt, Brace & World, 1927.
Frank, Robert Worth, Jr. "The Art of Reading Medieval Personification-Allegory." *ELH,* XX (December 1953), 237-250.
Freud, Sigmund. *Wit and Its Relation to the Unconscious.* Translated by A. A. Brill. London: Kegan Paul, Trench, Trubner and Co., 1922.
Friedman, Norman. "Point of View in Fiction: The Development of a Critical Concept." *PMLA,* LXX (1955). Reprinted in *The Novel: Modern Essays in Criticism.* Edited by Robert Murray Davis. Englewood Cliffs, N. J.: Prentice Hall, 1966. Pp. 142-169.
Frye, Northrop. *Anatomy of Criticism: Four Essays.* New York: Atheneum Press, 1969.
Granada, Fray Luis de. *Guía de pecadores.* Edited by M. Martínez Burgos. Madrid: Espasa-Calpe, 1966.
———. *Los siete libros de retórica eclesiástica.* In *B. A. E.* Vol. XI. Madrid: Rivadeneyra, 1849. Pp. 488-642.
Haley, George. *Vicente Espinel and Marcos de Obregón. A Life and Its Literary Representation.* Brown University Studies, Vol. XXV. Providence, R. I.: Brown University Press, 1959.
Hatzfeld, Helmut. *El "Quijote" como obra de arte del lenguaje." RFE,* Anejo LXXXIII. Madrid: Consejo Superior de Investigaciones Científicas, Instituto "Miguel de Cervantes," 1966.
Heniger, S. K. "Some Renaissance Versions of the Pythagorean Tetrad." *SRen,* VIII (1961), 7-33.
Hippocrates. Œuvres complètes d'Hippocrate. Translated by E. Littré. 10 vols. Paris: Baillière, 1839-61.
Honig, Edwin. *Dark Conceit. The Making of Allegory.* Evanston, Ill.: Northwestern University Press, 1959.
Horace, *Carmina.* Edited by James Gow. Cambridge: Cambridge University Press, 1914.
Juan Manuel. *El Conde Lucanor.* Edited by José Manuel Blecua. Madrid: Castalia, 1969.
Kayser, Wolfgang. *Interpretación y análisis de la obra literaria.* Translated by María D. Mouton and V. García Yebra. Madrid: Gredos, 1961. (Originally published in German in 1948.)
———, ed. *Kleines literarisches Lexikon.* Sammlung Dalp, 17. Vol. III. München: Francke, 1966.
Kernan, Alan B. *The Plot of Satire.* New Haven, Conn.: Yale University Press, 1965.
Lanham, Richard A. *A Handlist of Rhetorical Terms.* Berkeley and Los Angeles: University of California Press, 1969.
Lausberg, Heinrich. *Handbuch der literarischen Rhetorik; eine Grundlegung der Literaturwissenschaft.* 2 vols. München: M. Hueber, 1960. Available in Spanish as *Manual de retórica literaria. Fundamentos de una ciencia de la literatura.* Translated by José Pérez Riesco. 3 vols. Madrid: Gredos, 1966.
Levin, Harry. *The Myth of the Golden Age in the Renaissance.* Bloomington: Indiana University Press, 1969.

Levisi, Margarita. "Hieronimus Bosch y los *Sueños* de Francisco de Quevedo." *Filología*, IX (1963), 163-200.
López Pinciano, Alonso. *Philosophía antigua poética*. Edited by Alfredo Carballo Picazo. 3 vols. Madrid: Consejo Superior de Investigaciones Científicas, Instituto "Miguel de Cervantes," 1963.
Lovejoy, Arthur O. and George Boas. *Primitivism and Related Ideas in Antiquity*. New York: Octagon Books, Inc., 1965.
Lukacs, Georges. *La théorie du roman*. Translated by Jean Clairevoye. Switzerland: Gonthier, 1963. (Originally published in German in 1920.)
Martí, Antonio M. "La retórica sacra en el Siglo de Oro." *HR*, XXXVIII (1970), 264-298.
Mazzeo, Joseph Anthony. "A Critique of Some Modern Theories of Metaphysical Poetry." *MP*, L (1952), 88-96.
———. "Metaphysical Poetry and the Poetic of Correspondence." *JHI* XIV (1953), 221-234. Reprinted in *Renaissance and Seventeenth Century Studies*. New York: Columbia University Press, 1964. Pp. 44-59.
———. "A Seventeenth Century Theory of Metaphysical Poetry." *RR*, XLII (1951), 245-255. Reprinted in *Renaissance and Seventeenth Century Studies*. New York: Columbia University Press, 1964. Pp. 29-43.
Mena, Fernando de. *Historia Etiópica de los amores de Teágenas y Cariclea*. Edited by Francisco López Estrada. Madrid: Aldus, 1954.
Menéndez y Pelayo, Marcelino. *Historia de las ideas estéticas en España*. 9 vols. Madrid: Editorial Hernando, 1928-33.
Meyerhoff, Hans. *Time in Literature*. Berkeley: University of California Press, 1955.
Miriam Joseph, Sister. *Rhetoric in Shakespeare's Time: Literary Theory of Renaissance Europe*. New York: Harcourt, Brace & World, 1962. Originally published as part of the author's *Shakespeare's Use of the Arts of Language*. New York: Columbia University Press, 1947.
Morreale, Margherita. "Quevedo y el Bosco. Una apostilla a *Los Sueños*." *Clavileño*, VII (1956), 40-44.
Navarro y Ledesma, Francisco. *El Ingenioso hidalgo Miguel de Cervantes Saavedra*. Madrid: Sucesores de Hernando, 1915.
Nuñez de Reinoso, Alonso. *Historia de los amores de Clareo y Florisea*. In *B. A. E.* Edited by D. Buenaventura Carlos Aribau. Vol. III. Madrid: Rivadeneyra, 1846. Pp. 431-468.
Parker, A. A. *The Allegorical Drama of Calderon*. Oxford: Dolphin Book Co., 1968.
Paulson, Ronald. *The Fictions of Satire*. Baltimore: The Johns Hopkins Press, 1967.
Pfandl, Ludwig. *Historia de la literatura nacional española en la Edad de Oro*. Translated by Jorge Rubió Balaguer. Barcelona: Sucesores de Juan Gili, 1933. (Originally published in German in 1929.)
Plato. *The dialogues of Plato*. Translated by B. Jowett. 3 vols. New York: Scribner, 1887.
Poulet, Georges. *Études sur le Temps Humain*. Edinburgh: Edinburgh University Press, 1949.
Raleigh, John Henry. "The English Novel and Three Kinds of Time." *Sewanee Review*, LXII (July-September 1954). Reprinted in *The Novel: Modern Essays in Criticism*. Edited by Robert Murray Davis. Englewood Cliffs, N. J.: Prentice Hall, 1966. Pp. 242-252.

Riley, E. C. *Cervantes' Theory of the Novel*. Oxford: Clarendon Press, 1962.
———. "Aspectos del concepto de *admiratio* en la teoría literaria del Siglo de Oro." *Studia Philológica (Homenaje a Dámaso Alonso)*, III (1963), 173-183.
Roche, Thomas P., Jr. "The Nature of the Allegory." *The Kindly Flame*. Princeton, N. J.: Princeton University Press, 1964. Pp. 3-31. Reprinted in *Elizabethan Poetry: Modern Essays in Criticism*. Edited by Paul Alpers. New York: Oxford University Press, 1967. Pp. 401-421.
Rodríguez Marín, Francisco. *Los 6.666 refranes de mi última rebu ca*. Madrid: Bermejo, 1934.
Salas, Xavier de. *El Bosco en la literatura española*. Discurso leído en la Real Academia de Buenas Letras de Barcelona y contestación de Carlos Sanllehy. Barcelona: Imprenta J. Sabater, 1943.
Shroder, Maurice Z. "The Novel as a Genre." *The Massachusetts Review* (1963). Reprinted in *The Novel: Modern Essays in Criticism*. Edited by Robert Murray Davis. Englewood Cliffs, N. J.: Prentice Hall, 1966. Pp. 43-57.
Sieber, Harry. "Apostrophe in the *Buscón*: An Approach to Quevedo's Narrative Fiction." *MLN*, LXXXIII (March 1968), 178-211.
Spitzer, Leo. *Linguistics and Literary History. Essays in Stylistics*. Princeton, N. J.: Princeton University Press, 1948.
Switzer, Rebecca. *The Ciceronian Style in Fray Luis de Granada*. Lancaster, Pa.: Lancaster Press, 1927.
Tayler, E. W. *Nature and Art in Renaissance Literature*. New York: Columbia University Press, 1964.
Terry, Arthur. "The Continuity of Renaissance Criticism: Poetic Theory in Spain Between 1535 and 1650." *BHS*, XXXI (1954), 27-36.
———. "A Note on Metaphor and Conceit in the Siglo de Oro." *BHS*, XXXI (1954), 91-97.
———. "Quevedo and the Metaphysical Conceit." *BHS*, XXXV (1958), 211-222.
Tillyard, E. M. W. *The Elizabethan World Picture*. London: Chatto & Windus, 1952.
Togeby, Knud. "La composition du roman *Don Quijote*." *Orbis Litterarum*. Supplementum 1. Munksgaard, 1957.
Tuve, Rosemund. *Allegorical Imagery. Some Medieval Books and Their Posterity*. Princeton, N. J.: Princeton University Press, 1966.
Vossler, Karl. *Introducción a la literatura española del Siglo de Oro*. Madrid: Cruz y Raya, 1934.
Wain, John. "The Conflict of Forms in Contemporary English Literature." *Essays on Literature and Ideas*. New York and London: Macmillan & Co., 1963. Reprinted in *The Novel: Modern Essays in Criticism*. Edited by Robert Murray Davis. Englewood Cliffs, N. J.: Prentice Hall, 1966.
Wardropper, Bruce W. *Historia de la poesía lírica a lo divino en la cristiandad occidental*. Madrid: Revista de Occidente, 1958.
Williams, R. H. *Boccalini in Spain*. Menasha, Wis.: George Banta, 1946.
Worcester, David. *The Art of Satire*. New York: Russell & Russell, 1960.
Ynduraín, Francisco. "Refranes y 'frases hechas' en la estimativa literaria del Siglo xvii." *AFA*, VII (1955), 103-130.

NORTH CAROLINA STUDIES IN THE ROMANCE LANGUAGES AND LITERATURES

I.S.B.N. Prefix 0-88438

Recent Titles

THE OLD PORTUGUESE "VIDA DE SAM BERNARDO," EDITED FROM ALCOBAÇA MANU-SCRIPT ccxci/200, WITH INTRODUCTION, LINGUISTIC STUDY, NOTES, TABLE OF PROPER NAMES, AND GLOSSARY, by Lawrence A. Sharpe. 1971. (No. 103). *-903-0.*

A CRITICAL AND ANNOTATED EDITION OF LOPE DE VEGA'S "LAS ALMENAS DE TORO," by Thomas E. Case. 1971. (No. 104). *-904-9.*

LOPE DE VEGA'S "LO QUE PASA EN UNA TARDE," A CRITICAL, ANNOTATED EDITION OF THE AUTOGRAPH MANUSCRIPT, by Richard Angelo Picerno. 1971. (No. 105). *-905-7.*

OBJECTIVE METHODS FOR TESTING AUTHENTICITY AND THE STUDY OF TEN DOUBTFUL "COMEDIAS" ATTRIBUTED TO LOPE DE VEGA, by Fred M. Clark. 1971. (No. 106). *-906-5.*

THE ITALIAN VERB. A MORPHOLOGICAL STUDY, by Frede Jensen. 1971. (No. 107). *-907-3.*

A CRITICAL EDITION OF THE OLD PROVENÇAL EPIC "DAUREL ET BETON," WITH NOTES AND PROLEGOMENA, by Arthur S. Kimmel. 1971. (No. 108). *-908-1.*

FRANCISCO RODRIGUES LOBO: DIALOGUE AND COURTLY LORE IN RENAISSANCE POR-TUGAL, by Richard A. Preto-Rodas, 1971. (No. 109). *-909-X.*

RAIMON VIDAL: POETRY AND PROSE, edited by W. H. W. Field. 1971. (No. 110). *-910-3.*

RELIGIOUS ELEMENTS IN THE SECULAR LYRICS OF THE TROUBADOURS, by Raymond Gay-Crosier. 1971. (No. 111). *-911-1.*

THE SIGNIFICANCE OF DIDEROT'S "ESSAI SUR LE MERITE ET LA VERTU," by Gordon B. Walters. 1971. (No. 112). *-912-X.*

PROPER NAMES IN THE LYRICS OF THE TROUBADOURS, by Frank M. Chambers. 1971. (No. 113). *-913-8.*

STUDIES IN HONOR OF MARIO A. PEI, edited by John Fisher and Paul A. Gaeng. 1971. (No. 114). *-914-6.*

DON MANUEL CAÑETE, CRONISTA LITERARIO DEL ROMANTICISMO Y DEL POSROMAN-TICISMO EN ESPAÑA, por Donald Allen Randolph. 1972. (No. 115). *-915-4.*

THE TEACHINGS OF SAINT LOUIS. A CRITICAL TEXT, by David O'Connell. 1972. (No. 116). *-916-2.*

HIGHER, HIDDEN ORDER: DESIGN AND MEANING IN THE ODES OF MALHERBE, by David Lee Rubin. 1972. (No. 117). *-917-0.*

JEAN DE LE MOTE "LE PARFAIT DU PAON," édition critique par Richard J. Carey. 1972. (No. 118). *-918-9.*

CAMUS' HELLENIC SOURCES, by Paul Archambault. 1972. (No. 119). *-919-7.*

FROM VULGAR LATIN TO OLD PROVENÇAL, by Frede Jensen. 1972 (No. 120). *-920-0.*

GOLDEN AGE DRAMA IN SPAIN: GENERAL CONSIDERATION AND UNUSUAL FEATURES, by Sturgis E. Leavitt. 1972. (No. 121). *-921-9.*

THE LEGEND OF THE "SIETE INFANTES DE LARA" (*Refundición toledana de la crónica de 1344* versión), study and edition by Thomas A. Lathrop. 1972. (No. 122). *-922-7.*

STRUCTURE AND IDEOLOGY IN BOIARDO'S "ORLANDO INNAMORATO", by Andrea di Tommaso. 1972. (No. 123). *-923-5.*

STUDIES IN HONOR OF ALFRED G. ENGSTROM, edited by Robert T. Cargo and Emanuel J. Mickel, Jr. 1972. (No. 124). *-924-3.*

NORTH CAROLINA STUDIES IN THE ROMANCE LANGUAGES AND LITERATURES

I.S.B.N. Prefix 0-88438

Recent Titles

A CRITICAL EDITION WITH INTRODUCTION AND NOTES OF GIL VICENTE'S "FLORESTA DE ENGAÑOS", by Constantine Christopher Stathatos. 1972. (No. 125). -925-1.

LI ROMANS DE WITASSE LE MOINE. Roman du treizième siècle. Édité d'après le manuscrit, fonds français 1553, de la Bibliothèque Nationale, Paris, par Denis Joseph Conlon. 1972. (No. 126). -926-X.

EL CRONISTA PEDRO DE ESCAVIAS. UNA VIDA DEL SIGLO XV, by Juan Bautista Avalle-Arce. 1972. (No. 127). -927-8.

AN EDITION OF THE FIRST ITALIAN TRANSLATION OF THE CELESTINA, by Kathleen Kish. 1973. (No. 128). -928-6.

MOLIERE MOCKED: THREE CONTEMPORARY HOSTILE COMEDIES, by Frederick W. Vogler. 1973. (No. 129). -929-4.

INDEX ANALYTIQUE DE "CHATEAUBRIAND ET SON GROUPE LITTERAIRE SOUS L'EMPIRE" DE SAINTE-BEUVE, by Lorin A. Uffenbeck. 1973. (No. 130). -930-8.

THE ORIGINS OF THE BAROQUE CONCEPT OF PEREGRINATIO, by Juergen S. Hahn. 1973. (No. 131). -931-6.

THE "AUTO SACRAMENTAL" AND THE PARABLE IN THE SIXTEENTH AND SEVENTEENTH CENTURIES, by Donald T. Dietz. 1973. (No. 132). -932-4.

FRANCISCO DE OSUNA AND THE SPIRIT OF THE LETTER, by Laura Calvert. 1973. (No. 133). -933-2.

ITINERARIO DI AMORE: DIALETTICA DI AMORE E MORTE NELLA VITA NUOVA, by Margherita de Bonfils Templer. 1973. (No. 134). -934-0.

L'IMAGINATION POETIQUE CHEZ DU BARTAS, ELEMENTS DE SENSIBILITE BAROQUE DANS LA "CREATION DU MONDE," by Bruno Braunrot. 1973. (No. 135). -935-9.

ARTUS DÉSIRÉ, PRIEST AND PAMPHLETEER OF THE SIXTEENTH CENTURY, by Frank Giese 1973. (No. 136). -936-7.

JARDIN DE NOBLES DONZELLAS BY FRAY MARTÍN DE CÓRDOBA, by Harriet Goldberg. 1974. (No. 137). -937-5.

MOLIERE: TRADITIONS IN CRITICISM, by Laurence Romero. 1974 (Essays, No. 1). -001-7.

STUDIES IN TIRSO, I, by Ruth Lee Kennedy. 1974. (Essays, No. 3). -003-3.

LAS MEMORIAS DE GONZALO FERNÁNDEZ DE OVIEDO, Vols. I and II, by Juan Bautista Avalle-Arce. 1974. (Texts, Textual Studies, and Translations, Nos. 1 and 2). -401-2; 402-0.

ESTUDIOS DE LITERATURA HISPANOAMERICANA EN HONOR A JOSÉ J. ARROM, edited by Andrew P. Debicki and Enrique Pupo-Walker. 1975. (Symposia, No. 2). 952-9.

When ordering please cite the *ISBN Prefix* plus the last four digits for each title.

Send orders to:

    University of North Carolina Press
    Chapel Hill
    North Carolina 27514
    U. S. A.

The Department of Romance Studies Digital Arts and Collaboration Lab at the University of North Carolina at Chapel Hill is proud to support the digitization of the North Carolina Studies in the Romance Languages and Literatures series.

DEPARTMENT OF
Romance Studies
Digital Arts and Collaboration Lab

www.ingramcontent.com/pod-product-compliance
Lightning Source LLC
Chambersburg PA
CBHW022019220426
43663CB00007B/1146